CREATING ON PURPOSE

Other Works by Anodea Judith, PhD

Wheels of Life: A User's Guide to the Chakra System

The Sevenfold Journey: Reclaiming Mind, Body, and Spirit through the Chakras (with Selene Vega)

Eastern Body, Western Mind: Psychology and the Chakra System as a Path to the Self

Waking the Global Heart: Humanity's Rite of Passage from the Love of Power to the Power of Love

Contact: The Yoga of Relationship (with Tara Guber)

The Chakra System: A Complete Course in Self-Diagnosis and Healing (audio)

The Beginner's Guide to the Chakras (audio)

Wheels of Life (audio)

Chakra Balancing: A Guide to Healing and Awakening Your Energy Body (multimedia kit)

The Illuminated Chakras: A Visionary Voyage into Your Inner World (video)

Other Works by Lion Goodman

Transform Your Beliefs: Unleash Your Magnificence & Change Your World

Menlightenment: A Book for Awakening Men

The Heart of Healing: Inspired Ideas, Wisdom, and Comfort (with Deepak Chopra, Anodea Judith, Andrew Weil, and others)

ANODEA JUDITH and
LION GOODMAN

CREATING ON PURPOSE

THE SPIRITUAL TECHNOLOGY
OF MANIFESTING THROUGH THE CHAKRAS

SOUNDS TRUE
Boulder, Colorado

Sounds True, Inc.
Boulder, CO 80306

Cover design by Rachael Murray
Book design by Lisa Kerans
Cover image © argus, shutterstock.com

Printed in Canada

Library of Congress Cataloging-in-Publication Data

Judith, Anodea, 1952–

Creating on purpose : the spiritual technology of manifesting through the chakras / Anodea Judith and Lion Goodman.

   p. cm.

ISBN 978-1-60407-852-7

1. Chakras. I. Goodman, Lion. II. Title.

BF1442.C53J78 2012

131—dc23

2012012375

Ebook ISBN 978-1-60407-915-9

10 9 8 7 6 5 4 3 2

Anodea Judith

To my granddaughter, Seraphine, and all future generations,
who will reap the benefits of those who co-create heaven on earth

Lion Goodman

To my parents, Jerry and Joanne,
and to my daughter, Sara, the Next Generation

Contents

The Invitation

The greater danger for most of us lies
not in setting our aim too high and falling short;
but in setting our aim too low,
and achieving our mark.

—Michelangelo Buonarroti

———————————

Joseph was unhappy in his job as a middle manager in an investment firm. His salary was sufficient to cover his bills, but he felt like he was running on a hamster wheel. Something deeper kept calling to him. He felt the pain of all the people out of work—millions of good folks whose jobs had simply vanished. He wanted to do something—anything—to improve the situation, but he didn't know how. He wondered, "Even if I figured out how to do that, how would I find the time to pursue it with two kids about to enter college?"

Mary finally felt ready for her dream relationship. Divorced a few years earlier, she had taken time to clear away the past, learn from her mistakes, and get crystal clear on what she wanted. She longed for a partner who shared her passion (she worked as an environmental attorney); but as a single mother with two children, she could barely find time to date, let alone find the man of her dreams.

Jonathan had lots of ideas, but money was a constant stumbling block. Forever in debt, he felt like he was always behind, running to catch up. He was a dedicated social justice activist, but every time he started a new project that was in line with his passions, the bills would pile up, and he'd have to change gears to earn money in a job he didn't like. Then his projects would grind to a halt. He couldn't figure out how to combine his passion for social justice with a reasonable income; the nonprofits he approached only paid minimum wage.

Patricia was a superb healer. She had great results with her clients, but she didn't know how to get paid at the level she deserved. She was afraid that if she raised her prices, she'd lose her clients. Jerome wanted to get his art into a gallery, but he couldn't handle all the rejection that gallery owners could dish out. Martina wanted to buy a house, but she didn't have a down payment, and her credit score had deteriorated during the economic downturn. Thomas, an adoptee, wanted to make adoption easier for racial minorities, but he didn't know where to start.

What did all of these people have in common?

They could hear their heart's desire. They had an urge toward something more. Yet they weren't able to bring their dreams into reality. They faced obstacles they didn't know how to overcome. They each wanted to give something back, to make the world a better place. But they had difficulty bringing the gifts of their hearts into the reality of needing to earn a living. They longed to fulfill their life's purpose but couldn't bring it to fruition. They could feel their higher calling but didn't know how to answer it. They wanted to work with others, to be part of a team, working for the greater good. They wanted to help create heaven on earth.

These descriptions depict just a small sampling of the people who have attended our workshops around the world, representing the millions of people who have a dream but don't know how to create it on purpose, step by step.

Some people don't know what their dreams are, and they feel the frustration of not living up to their own potential. Many people know that their lives have a purpose, but they have no idea what that purpose is or how to find it. Some suffer from having too many dreams; they spin their wheels, confused about how to narrow down their options and focus their energy. Most people have been plagued by negative inner voices, doubts, and fears, all of which stop them in their tracks. And everyone has faced obstacles that seem overwhelming.

Have you come to a place in your life where the frustration is simply untenable? If your answer is "yes," we have good news. This book can help you find your way to a life of vision, inspiration, and action—to creating on purpose. Together, humankind can create a world that reflects its highest aspirations, a world we refer to as *heaven on earth*.

This book is an invitation for you to step up to who you really are and to manifest your magnificence in the world. Our intention is to help you co-create a better world by bringing your purpose, your vision, and your true gifts to the world—a world that sorely needs you. This book is an urgent call to everyone to step up and take responsibility for our precious world. Every individual has the potential of becoming an agent of change, a *conscious evolutionary*.

A Call to Awakening

The trajectory of evolution is entering its next great awakening, a time when we are being asked to claim our divine nature and take responsibility for creating our future. Never before have the stakes been so high, the challenges so perilous, or the possibilities so glorious. We live at the cusp of the greatest awakening humanity has ever experienced.

We also have access to more information than any civilization has ever had before. The world's greatest spiritual traditions, many of them once hidden and esoteric, are now available through every media source. Political, economic, and scientific information comes in overwhelming flows, along with trivia, celebrities' status, advertising, news, and entertainment. Yet, at the same time, we are being called to grow up, stand up, and speak up. It is time for us to take power into our own hands and use that power in service to something greater.

Our friend and political humorist Steve Bhaerman (a.k.a., Swami Beyondananda) has often said, "It's time to stop being children of God and start being adults of God." Children have little say about where they live or the rules they live by. They do as they're told and adjust to their surroundings, one way or the other. They either perish or prosper, depending on their choices and their circumstances. People carry this childhood passivity into their adult years, believing that Big Daddy (now in the guise of the Company or the Government or God) will take care of everything, and that Big Mama (now in the guise of the earth or the economic machine) will provide sustenance forever. This concept extends to politics, in which many people believe that if we elect the right president or empower the right leaders, then everything will be OK. We would be able to go peacefully back to "normal" life, where everything is taken care of by someone else.

But these times call for more than that. The dangers we face call for us to awaken as adults and become *active participants* in the creation of our reality. According to Stewart Brand, futurist and founder of *The Whole Earth Catalog*, "We are as Gods. So we might as well get good at it." In democratic countries, the tools of power, which at one time were only in the hands of the elite, are now in the hands of common people. Anyone can write and broadcast their ideas publically on the Web. Every printer is equivalent to a printing press. Video cameras and videophones allow anyone to make a film with impact. We are able to travel and see the world. The entirety of human knowledge is available to anyone through the Internet.

You are not a passive bystander, helplessly watching the world self-destruct. You are an active agent in the creation of reality. When everything is rapidly changing, you can't be certain what life will look like in ten or twenty years, but you can become an expert at manifestation to fulfill your life purpose and your destiny. Now is the time.

It *is* possible to create heaven on earth, but it won't happen by itself. It will take millions of people learning how to co-create with the Divine and with each other, through inspiration and vision, potent truth, open hearts, strong wills, passionate involvement, and the tools of manifestation. It's time to create a magnificent world worthy of the planet we've been given. It is time for you to create the world you want. It is time to create on purpose.

Co-creation and Evolution

*Of all the creatures on earth, only human beings can change
the pattern of their behavior. Man alone is the architect of his
destiny . . . Human beings, by changing the inner attitudes of
their minds, can change the outer aspects of their lives.*

—William James

All creation is actually *co-creation*. We co-create with what is already
here. We co-create with each other. And we co-create with the source
of creation, which we call the Divine or Source. The good news is that
you don't have to do it alone (and none of us can). You don't have
to create out of nothing. Since you are part of evolution, you are co-
creating with the evolutionary impulse. Nothing is actually separate
from the Divine, so you are *always* co-creating with the Divine. This is
the natural state of things. You can create something new, but it's likely
you will use some of what already exists.

When we look backward and trace millions of years of human
evolution, we see that it moved very slowly for the first two million
years. It then picked up speed during the Neolithic era, when plants
and animals were first domesticated, around 10,000 years ago. When
humans gathered into towns and cities a few thousand years later, life
became much more complex. Humans became more dependent on
their culture rather than on the natural world around them. When the
Industrial Revolution took off, life began to accelerate like crazy, and
these past hundred years have turned everything traditional into everything modern. Tom Atlee, founder of the Co-Intelligence Institute,
said, "The world is getting better and better and worse and worse faster
and faster, simultaneously."[1]

The evolution of life is often seen as an arrow that began with single-
celled creatures and moved its way, over billions of years, to multicellular
life, sea creatures, land creatures, mammals, apes, and finally human
beings—as if we were the end of the evolutionary impulse. Imagine
for a moment that it is not an arrow shot from some ancient bow;
instead, imagine that some extraordinary force in the future is pulling

life forward. Our potential is drawing us inexorably forward toward a more integrated, healthier, and more evolved reality. The philosophical term for this idea is *teleology*, a theory that explains the universe in terms of its end, or its final cause. It's the proposition that the universe has design and purpose, and it is unrolling toward that purpose, pulling us along with it.

Jean Houston, one of the founders of the human potential movement, called this process *entelechy* —the pull of the future toward its manifestation.[2] The French Jesuit Pierre Teilhard de Chardin (1881–1955) coined the term *Omega Point* to describe this idea—a point in the future toward which we are drawn by a supreme point of complexity and consciousness. Our evolution toward higher levels of material complexity and higher consciousness is the inevitable result of this pull. Imagine that the Divine is pulling us toward itself, toward an Omega Point of heaven on earth. Evolution, then, is God's way of making more gods. You are part of this plan, and your destination is clear: to become a god or goddess in your own universe, a master co-creator doing your part in a larger system that evolves us all.

Two powerful evolutionary forces are at work simultaneously— one from the top down, and the other from the bottom up. Spirit, or the light of consciousness, is evolving *downward* into embodiment, infusing matter with Spirit. At the same time, matter is evolving *upward* into Spirit, into conscious awareness. You are a rainbow bridge that ties these two forces together. You stand between heaven and earth as both a co-creation *of* these two forces and a co-creator *with* these two forces. You are being trained to become a more capable co-creator with the Universe. You have the ability to draw down your own vision of what you want to create in your life and to manifest it here in the physical world. Your soul has a purpose for being here. (You wouldn't be reading this book otherwise.)

When you align your heavenly wisdom with the love in your heart and combine your future vision with your unique skills and abilities, you can begin to drive your vehicle toward your destiny, giving the gifts you have to offer for the benefit of all beings. The Divine plan wants to be birthed into reality on earth—through *you*. You can do your part by being who you are and doing what you came here to do. This journey toward wholeness and fulfillment is a long and winding road, with many twists and turns along the way. It is similar to a great expedition, such as mountain climbing in the Himalayas. You wouldn't start your journey until you had everything prepared: food, water, oxygen, climbing companions and guides, sherpas, equipment of all kinds, and a map of the territory, with a route well laid out. When you are completely prepared, you take the first step. There will be obstacles, barriers, and difficulties, but in your heart, nothing can stop you. You are ready. The mountain is here. Adventure awaits.

This guidebook maps out the manifestation process, the journey toward your fulfillment. It describes the territory—as well as the hazards and challenges—that awaits. We are your guides, for we have climbed this mountain before, and we know the way. We want you to succeed, so your success can be shared by many others. We will guide you from where you are now to where you want to be.

We offer many exercises and practices throughout the book to help you move your dreams into reality. Some exercises will be more meaningful and powerful than others. Try each practice at least once to test the value it may have for you. If an exercise has a positive result, either internally or externally, it's a good bet that repeating it will create even better results. If you don't feel much impact, you can safely discard it. Do give one hundred percent effort when you try an exercise for the first time. In any activity, if you don't make a full commitment, you miss out on the great results you would have gotten had you given your all.

To make the exercises easier, we've recorded and posted them on our website, creatingonpurpose.net. On this page, you'll find free access to the audio and video recordings, as well as free membership in our Creating on Purpose community. On the community forum you can request help and support from others on the path, and serve others with your own wisdom.

To begin, you need an accurate map. Our map for this journey of manifestation is based on the ancient system of human energy called the chakra system.

The Path of
Manifestation

If you have built castles in the air,
your work need not be lost;
that is where they should be.
Now put the foundations under them.

—Henry David Thoreau

The Chakra System as a Map for Manifestation

Chakras are organizational centers for the reception,
assimilation, and transmission of life-force energy. They are the
stepping-stones between heaven and earth.

—Anodea Judith

The chakra system describes the architecture of the human soul. It is a profound formula for wholeness, a template for transformation, and a map for manifestation. Its seven major energy centers correspond to nerve ganglia along the body's core. As a whole, the system forms a bridge that connects universal polarities: spirit to matter, heaven to earth, and mind to body. The chakras are stepping-stones along that bridge, bringing those polarities into union. "Union" is the meaning of the word *yoga,* the system from which the chakras originated. Used as a map, the chakras show us a path to follow. They function as doorways, or portals, that lead to the journey's next level. By following this map, you can ensure your success along the path.

Everything alive has a core: every blade of grass, every animal, and every tree. The trunk of a tree has a core, as does every branch and every leaf. Even planets and stars have cores. You have a core running through the middle of you, from your crown to your base, from heaven down to earth. Creation proceeds from the core. We grow outward from our core, and our core is our sacred center.

The seven chakras are embedded into our nervous system. When aligned, they form a vertical channel along our core. Within this channel, two major currents of energy move upward and downward: the currents of liberation and manifestation. This guidebook focuses specifically on the *current of manifestation*, the downward current from crown to base. This current moves step-by-step from ideas to reality. As a map, it can guide you in creating the life of your dreams—*on purpose.*

The chakras can be thought of as jewels along a necklace. When you hold the necklace in your hands and pull the two ends vertically, upward and downward, the jewels line up, one on top of another. When you align your chakras vertically, they enhance the flow of universal energy and move this flow through your body in the most efficient and direct way possible. With this opening, you have the most direct access to Source, the universal creative energy (you may call it God, Goddess, Higher Self, Holy Spirit, and so on). The chakras act as portals between the inner world of your experience and the outer world of your environment. When your chakras are aligned and open, your mind and body work in harmony, making your actions more effective in the world.

Like any gateway or channel, chakras can become blocked, crimped, or closed. When you take the time to remove blockages from within the chakras, your life-force energy flows in and out in a more harmonious and productive manner. It becomes easier to relate to your environment and achieve your dreams. In this guidebook, we share methods for clearing the blocks that prevent you from moving forward in the manifestation process.

The chakra system is a map of the broad vertical terrain between heaven and earth. It shows the way up to the heights of pure awareness and the way down to the realities of the material world. Most treatises on the chakras emphasize the journey upward. This journey begins with the body and the material world, entering subtler and higher planes with each step upward. The ancient texts called this upward journey *mukti*, or freedom; we call it the *current of liberation*. This current allows you to liberate yourself from fixed forms and attachments. It enables you to break free from limitations that hold you back from spiritual realization. This is the path most closely associated with the chakras and is described in great detail in my (Anodea's) other books.

Less understood is the downward path, which the ancient masters called *bhukti* (meaning "enjoyment"). In this path, the flow of creation begins in the vast plane of pure awareness. It enters our individual consciousness as a thought or idea. The chakras act as condensers, giving thoughts shape and form, moving them into words and then into actions, until they are dense enough to manifest on the material plane. We call this energetic path the *current of manifestation*. It is by this path that we enjoy the play of life, the myriad ways the Divine can manifest into the world.

Most living things grow upward, expanding toward the light. A tree reaches for the sky; a child grows continually taller until he or she becomes a "grown-up." Buildings are constructed from the ground up. The liberating current moves us toward greater consciousness.

Meanwhile, the earth's gravity pulls everything downward. Leaves fall to earth in autumn. The tree pushes its roots downward in order to grow tall. A building must have a solid foundation, connected to solid rock beneath the ground, to support many floors.

As upright creatures, we walk with our feet on the earth and our heads in the sky. We are led by ideals and intentions, but our feet carry us along our path. We sit up, stand up, grow up, and wake up as we move through life. But we also let down, get down, and fall down many times as we go. These two polarities of *up and down* make us vertical beings, standing on our hind legs, with our consciousness organized along the spine. Branching out from the spinal column are seven major nerve ganglia, or bundles of nerve fibers, that process energy on different planes of manifestation. These nerve bundles correspond to the seven chakras (see Figure 1).

As you travel the upward path of liberation, you move from dense matter to pure consciousness. Your focus on each chakra is to clear away the *granthis,* or knots, that create blockages. These knots restrict the flow of energy in the same way that old beliefs can limit our possibilities.

Blocks in the chakras can take many forms. A chakra may be deficient in its functioning, meaning there is constriction that results in too little energy flowing in and out of that chakra, or it may be excessive, meaning there is too much energy flowing. The goal of chakra healing is to balance the energy flow through each chakra and, subsequently, through your whole mind-body-energy system. Blocks

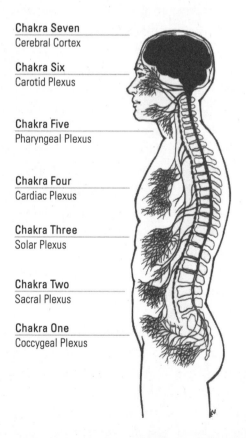

Chakra Seven
Cerebral Cortex

Chakra Six
Carotid Plexus

Chakra Five
Pharyngeal Plexus

Chakra Four
Cardiac Plexus

Chakra Three
Solar Plexus

Chakra Two
Sacral Plexus

Chakra One
Coccygeal Plexus

Figure 1 The major nerve ganglia corresponding with the chakras

in the chakras impede your ability to manifest, because they impede the flow of energy. To manifest anything, you need all of your energies available and flowing. Trying to bring a dream to reality with a blocked chakra is like trying to paint a masterpiece without having one of the major colors of paint.

The chakra system is a master map and an elegantly profound system for understanding the links between the Self and the world. The chakras have been used to identify states and stages of consciousness, developmental periods of human growth and maturity, and eras of human history. I (Anodea) have written extensively about the philosophy, psychology, and collective sociology of the chakra system in my books: *Wheels of Life* describes the basic philosophy of the chakra system, *Eastern Body, Western Mind* charts the system's inner psychology, and *Waking the Global Heart* looks at the history of human civilization through the chakra lens.

Each chakra has been associated with particular colors, sounds, deities, mantras, yoga postures, and psychological complexes. We've created a chart of correspondences (Table 1) to show you various ways of understanding the chakras. If you are unfamiliar with the chakra system, we suggest you check out my (Anodea's) other books while working through this book.

Transcendence and Immanence: The Liberating and Manifesting Currents

We didn't rise up from mud. We fell from the stars.

—Neal Rogin

Most people believe that being spiritual means transcending the realms of the body and the material plane and rising up into the higher planes of existence, ultimately to the infinite emptiness of pure consciousness. This idea can be traced from Patañjali's *Yoga Sutras* (written around 200 BCE), through Saint Augustine's writings in the fourth century CE, and to René Descartes's philosophy in the 1600s. This movement up toward mind or spirit and away from the physical realm has

Table 1 Chakra system correspondences

Chakra	Location	Central Issue	Goals	Rights	Developmental Stage
7	Top of head, cerebral cortex	Awareness	Wisdom, knowledge, consciousness, spiritual connection	To know	Throughout life
6	Brow	Intuition, Imagination	Psychic perception, accurate interpretation, imagination, seeing	To see	Adolescence
5	Throat	Communication	Clear communication, creativity, resonance	To speak and be heard	7–12 years
4	Heart	Love, Relationships	Balance, compassion, self-acceptance, good relationships	To love and be loved	4–7 years
3	Solar Plexus	Power, Will	Vitality, spontaneity, strength of will, purpose, self-esteem	To act	18 months to 4 years
2	Abdomen, genitals, low back, hips	Sexuality, Emotions	Fluidity, pleasure, healthy sexuality, feeling function	To feel, to want	6 months to 2 years
1	Base of spine, coccygeal plexus	Survival	Stability, grounding, physical health, prosperity, trust	To be here, to have	Womb to 12 months

been a thrust of major spiritual and philosophical traditions. Integral philosopher Ken Wilber said, "In the West, from the time roughly of Augustine to Copernicus, we have a purely Ascending ideal, otherworldly to the core. Final salvation and liberation could not be found in this body, on this Earth, in this lifetime."[3]

Science and industry took a parallel path, denying spirituality and consciousness because there was no proof that they existed in the world of physical reality. Anything not provable was discounted as merely "subjective experience." Denying the validity of consciousness and

Table 1 continued

Identity	Demon	Excessive Characteristics	Deficient Characteristics	Element
Universal Identity (Self-Knowledge)	Attachment	Over-intellectualism, spiritual addiction, confusion, dissociated body	Learning difficulties, spiritual skepticism, limited beliefs, materialism, apathy	Thought
Archetypal Identity (Self-Reflection)	Illusion	Headaches, nightmares, hallucinations, delusions, difficulty concentrating	Poor memory, poor vision, inability to see problems, denial	Light
Creative Identity (Self-Expression)	Lies	Excessive talking, inability to listen, over-extendedness, stuttering	Fear of speaking, poor rhythm, aphasia	Sound
Social Identity (Self-Acceptance)	Grief	Codependency, poor boundaries, possessiveness, jealousy, narcissisism	Shyness, loneliness, isolation, lack of empathy, bitterness, criticalness	Air
Ego Identity (Self-Definition)	Shame	Domination, blaming, aggression, scatteredness, constant activity	Weak will, poor self-esteem, passivity, sluggishness, fearfulness	Fire
Emotional Identity (Self-Gratification)	Guilt	Over-emotionalism, poor boundaries, sex addiction, obsessive attachments	Frigidity, impotence, rigidity, emotional numbness, fear of pleasure	Water
Physical Identity (Self-Preservation)	Fear	Heaviness, sluggishness, monotony, obesity, hoarding, materialism	Frequent fear, lack of discipline, restlessness, emaciation, spaciness	Earth

interior experience has spawned a materialistic view of the universe. The central idea of materialism is to get as much as you can, using any means necessary. Materialism is disconnected from the upper chakras, treating them as if they were of no importance. This philosophy leads people to exploit the earth and its inhabitants, with dire consequences.

In this book, we promote a philosophy and way of life that leaves nothing out; instead, it integrates mind and body, above and below, and heaven and earth in a tapestry of wholeness. When we use practices such as yoga and meditation, we expand our consciousness to include everything, creating the highest possibilities by integrating spirit and matter, transcendence and immanence (or embodiment of the Divine). Wilber continued, "And in that radiant awareness, every I becomes a God, and every We becomes God's sincerest worship, and every It becomes God's most gracious temple."[4]

The Tantric philosophy of yoga, from which the chakra system originated, is based on a similar integration of polarities. Following the yoga philosopher Patañjali, the Tantric period (roughly 500 to 1000 CE) produced most of the texts that we have on the chakras. The word *Tantra* means "to stretch" and can also mean "loom." Tantric teachings *weave* together many different philosophies and principles. The purpose of Tantra is liberation and higher consciousness, but it achieves this goal through weaving together both the upward and downward currents—both liberation (the ascending path) and embodiment (the descending, or manifesting, path).

Consider the craft of a weaver. On her loom, she creates a fabric by pulling thread in a back-and-forth pattern, from front to back; she then weaves a complementary thread, over and under, from one side to another. We create the fabric of our existence by weaving archetypal polarities together, giving life texture and strength. When the warp and weft are uneven, or when a thread doesn't make it to the other side of the loom, the fabric is no longer strong and whole, and it can fray. Likewise, when we give unequal value to abstract spirit or pure materialism, we lack wholeness and integrity. The web of life gets fragile and frayed, and it ultimately unravels.

What is needed most at this time is a philosophy of wholeness. When you follow only the upward current, denying your body and the material world, you may become spiritually strong but physically weak or ineffective. Temporary withdrawal from the material world is important from time to time, as it offers the ability to gain wider perspectives. But eventually, you must come back down to earth to apply what you've learned to the real world and deal with the situation around you.

The chakras are the stepping-stones between the poles of heaven and earth. In yoga philosophy, the two poles are called *purusha* and *prakriti*. *Purusha* is the upper realm of pure consciousness—your true and eternal

Self. It is the force of creation, the intelligence that shapes reality, and the limitless mind that is at one with Source. *Purusha* is associated with the god Shiva, the destroyer of illusion and the master of meditation; it is the masculine pole of the chakra system. *Prakriti* is the feminine field of creation. In alchemical terms, *prakriti* is the *prima materia*, the primordial substance from which all things are created, including matter, form, and energy. These primordial forces are given form by the masculine force of *purusha*. The currents of liberation and manifestation integrate these two poles into union through each act of creation.

When you bake a cake, the idea of the cake and the knowledge of how to bake it are the domain of *purusha*, and the raw ingredients are *prakriti*. The finished cake is the result of combining the raw ingredients according to the information in a recipe. Without consciousness and will, flour and sugar remain as they are, unchanged. But without the raw ingredients, the most sophisticated wisdom can't bake a cake.

For some people, spirituality is something to think about only on Sundays in church. For others, it is limited to the yoga mat or meditation cushion, or perhaps to backpacking in the wilderness. The rest of the time, spirituality is placed on a back burner, separated from daily life. Some people feel lucky if they have a few minutes to consider spirituality *after* dealing with the mundane matters in life—going to work, cooking meals, and putting the kids to bed. There are important requirements in life to take care of!

Our philosophy is that spirituality cannot be separated from the mundane world. Manifestation is the process of bringing the spiritual and material together to create a good life for yourself, your family, and your community. It begins with your best ideas for your life—your true desires and dreams, how you want life to be. All ideas are conceived in the infinite pregnant void, which we call Source, just as babies are conceived inside a mother's womb.

If you could create anything, what would you create? Open your mind, free yourself of limitations, and open your heart to your own truth. The path of manifestation begins here, in the realm of pure possibilities. If there were no restrictions, and you could manifest the life of your dreams, what would you choose? When you allow your thoughts to expand in this wide-open direction, you have already begun the journey. What powers would you harness? What tools would you need to bring your ideas down into reality, to create the kind of world we all deserve? When you create from this open space, from Source, you're creating in alignment with your life purpose.

Working from the Top Down

This book will guide you step-by-step through the top-down process of manifestation. It takes you from the realm of pure idea and your connection with Source, down to the bottom, or your day-to-day reality, your connection to the real-world physical reality. This is how to manifest a dream: Move it downward through the chakras, one step at a time, leaving nothing out, integrating mind, body, and spirit along the way.

The manifestation path begins in the sea of infinite awareness (chakra seven). An idea arises, and it moves down into consciousness—*your* consciousness. You receive it as guidance, a good idea, a dream, or a vision. This is the *conception* of an idea. Next, you check to see whether it's aligned with your life purpose. If it is, you set an intention to bring it to fruition so it can be shared with the world.

You examine your beliefs to see whether any of them would interfere with the fulfillment of your intention, eliminating internal conflicts. You flesh out your dream in detail, using your imagination (chakra six) to visualize the fulfillment of your dream at a specific point in the future.

Then you step it down to the realm of communication (chakra five), where you tell others your dream and inspire them to join you or to have them provide you with feedback, information, and support. This step then brings you into the realm of relationship (chakra four), where you find others to work with, to serve, and to supply what you need along the way.

Using your will (chakra three), you begin to move yourself and others toward your desired objectives. You have broken down your dream into specific goals and objectives, projects and tasks; when obstacles appear, you have ways of dealing with each one.

At this point, your dream takes on a life of its own. You begin to see results, which further fuels your passion (chakra two). Naming and asking for what you want, you attract what you need. You make your daily actions fun and emotionally fulfilling, so your passion can sustain you to the end. You are heading, step-by-step, toward your destination.

Finally, through *completion* of all these steps (chakra one), you have brought your dream into reality. You have a fully functioning new business, an ideal relationship, a community project, a finished book, a movie ready for distribution, or a new home. Your thriving vision brings value to others and makes a contribution to the world around you.

This process of manifestation isn't a secret, and there's nothing mysterious about it. It simply follows the downward path through the chakras—the path of manifestation—through which you become a master manifestor, a creator of miracles. This is sometimes called the Path of the Avatar. In Sanskrit, an *avatar* is a god who can create a world (or universe) and then incarnate inside of it. When you consciously create the world you prefer, you are acting as a god or goddess in your universe.

Each chakra points to specific actions and activities along the path of bringing your dream into reality. Manifestation isn't just about thinking the right thoughts or becoming attractive to what you want; this simplistic idea is why so much manifestation advice today is ineffective. To move the world, you must *engage* with the world. To bring something into reality, you must work with the reality in which you want it to land. Here are the essential *core manifestation principles:*

Chakra Seven: **Consciousness Creates**
Chakra Six: **Vision Vitalizes**
Chakra Five: **Conversation Catalyzes**
Chakra Four: **Love Enlivens**
Chakra Three: **Power Produces**
Chakra Two: **Pleasure Pleases**
Chakra One: **Matter Matters**

Table 2 Stepping down through the chakras

Kosmos	7	6	5	4
Be One with Universe and Consciousness	Know Your Life Purpose	Visualize Your Dreams	Choose Specific Goals and Communicate With Others	Find and Create Relationships
Om	Why	What	How	Who
Awaken to who you are as Source, Spirit, God.	Awaken to who you are as a unique embodied being.	Awaken your power to dream.	Awaken your ability to choose and express.	Awaken your connections with others.
It is.	I am.	I envision.	I intend. I share.	I love.
Be	Know/Choose	See/Plan	Discover/Share	Love/Relate
Kosmos	Personal Universe/ Kosmos	Personal Universe	Personal Universe/ Social Universe	Social Universe
Meditate. Explore and change your beliefs. Discover how your beliefs create your reality.	Know thyself. Remember your life purpose. See the possibilities for manifesting your purpose.	Define your dreams in each arena of life: health, love, community, family, leisure, work, career, finance, money, relationships, learning, spirituality.	Refine the dreams into specific goals and project plans within each dream. Communicate your goals to others. Find aligned teammates.	Bring your passion to others through enrollment, promotion, and alignment. Use Communication for Action.
Who am I? What is God? What is Universe? What do I believe?	What is my life purpose? How do I want to live? Who shall I serve?	How do I align with my life purpose? What kind of world do I want to live in?	How do I communicate my dream? What are my SMART goals?	How do I want to be in relationship and with whom? To whom shall I bring my love and gifts?

In the ensuing chapters, we detail each principle and its corresponding activities. We also provide exercises and practices so you can strengthen your ability to handle whatever comes up along the way. Remember that this is an expedition, requiring great awareness and a healthy body, mind, and spirit. The principles in this book are the keys that will unlock the portals between your inner world and the world you want to create—the world of your dreams.

Table 2 continued

3	2	1	0	Earth
Create an Action Plan Move from Ego to Possibilities	Move with Passion	Complete Steps	Have, Enjoy and Celebrate Rest and Open	
When	With	W.O.W.	Ahhh . . .	
Awaken your will through actions.	Awaken your passion.	Awaken your power to complete.	Awaken your willingness to have, receive, celebrate, and rest.	
I shall.	I am with you.	I complete.	I have.	
Will/Do	Connect/Move	Complete Parts Handle Counter-Intentions	Receive and Feel Gratitude	
Personal Universe/ Social Universe	Social Universe	Physical Universe	Personal Universe/ Kosmos	
Remember your way back from the future. Use project planning with timelines and resource requirements.	Make commitments to the plan and calendarize the actions. Identify ego motivations and love possibilities.	What will you do within one week? Take action each day, moving forward step by step. Acknowledge each small move forward.	Celebrate each victory. Rest and enjoy the process of creation. Feel the joy of your connections and accomplishments.	
What shall I and others do to accomplish my goal? What are my commitments?	How do I continue to move things forward? What other resources do I need?	What counter intentions are coming up? How shall I handle them? What needs to be completed?	How do I feel now that it is complete? How shall we celebrate? What shall I create next?	

The upward current of liberation is different from the downward current of manifestation in one significant way: When you are liberating yourself, moving from chakra one to chakra seven, your work is to clear blocks within each chakra, opening the chakras so that the energy of consciousness can more easily free you from limitations. In the downward current, blocks tend to prevent manifestation energy from moving from one chakra to the next chakra down. For example, one person may have a clear vision of a dream (chakra six) but may not be able to articulate it clearly and inspire others (chakra five). Another person may be very articulate and inspiring but not able to establish lasting relationships that result in partnership and support (chakra four).

In Table 2, we have identified multiple elements involved in the manifestation process, especially focused on the movement *between* chakras. A careful study of this table will illuminate the complex relationships between the chakras and the movement of energies from heaven to earth and from idea to reality.

This book will act as your guide as you move your creation downward from idea to reality, from chakra seven to chakra one. Our goal is to break down the process into bite-sized steps so you can study your own process in detail and find effective ways to move your project forward. The following example demonstrates more concretely how this process works in the real world.

Imagine that you're ready to build your dream house. You began in the seventh chakra with a thought or idea, and you set your *intention:* "I'm going to build my house." It begins as an abstract dream of something you'd like to do, but the more you think about it, the more you find yourself imagining what the house should look like. You've now moved down into the sixth chakra stage of *visualization.* You envision a great view, a sunken living room, and a big, modern stainless-steel kitchen. Detailed pictures fill in your vision. You've painted a picture of this dream house in your mind.

After you've spent time dreaming up the design, you *communicate* your vision to others. This brings you into the realm of the fifth chakra. You talk to an architect about your idea, and she asks you specific questions: Where will the house be located? What style of house do you want? How many windows do you want, and how big will they be? How many bedrooms and bathrooms do you need? What size will the sunken living room be? What kind of cabinets do you want in the kitchen? How much money can you spend? What materials do you want to use? This process of communication and feedback turns vague ideas into clear pictures. Communication begins to crystallize your vision.

The architect then brings your ideas into the physical world through drawings and architectural renderings, visual representations of your vision. These plans exist to *inform others* about what the house is to look like and what they are to do when the construction starts. The architect helps you apply for a permit, communicating with the county's planning department, contractors, and others with whom you'll have ongoing *relationships*. You've moved down into the fourth chakra—the social realm of people, organizations, and institutions. Your architect will also compute how much money you'll need (a social convention) and how much time it will take to get through the bureaucratic process. You have to establish relationships with a banker, a real estate agent, building inspectors, contractors, decorators, landscapers, and neighbors. It's all about relationships at this point. The house must fit with or relate to the surrounding land and community. In addition, parts of the house must relate well to each other. Even the cement, wood, nails, and glass enter into very specific relationships. They aren't placed just anywhere; they follow a detailed *plan*—a description of the entire set of physical relationships.

Still, planning and preparation are not enough to get the house completed. There are things that have to get *done* (chakra three). The will of many people must be exercised. Someone has to show up at the building site and use *energy* to move and cut lumber, hammer nails, pour the foundation, and conduct the many tasks that actually construct the house.

You can't do things randomly; each step requires expertise, even mastery. The pieces have to fit together in *harmony* (chakra two). The windows have to fit the openings designed for them. *Aesthetics* also comes into play. You want the colors and interior design to look attractive, to feel good sensuously. As the house goes up, you'll *feel* your way into the details, choosing paints, materials, and decor. If you don't like what you're building—or even more important, if you don't have a certain amount of passion for your project—you won't enjoy the process, and this lack of enthusiasm will create resistance and frustration. At this point you may change small details, such as colors of paint or carpet, but you can't change the big details anymore.

The size of the foundation is set. You've brought your idea down to a particular piece of the earth (chakra one). The land you chose to build upon cannot be moved.

You also need *deadlines*—dates on a calendar when each phase of the house must be completed. You count backward from that date to schedule other steps along the way. You know by what date materials need to be on the jobsite, and you make your plans accordingly. Based on the flow of events in time, your workers must be paid, the inspectors must be satisfied, and your painters must have the right colors. You work around the inevitable slips, errors, and problems that occur along the way. And you set a date to move in, letting go of your other house. Being *specific* makes things happen in a timely fashion.

Finally, the house is *completed,* and you get to have it. You can move in, have a party, kick back, and celebrate. Congratulations! You applied all the steps and brought an idea into completion. You brought your dream into reality.

If these steps are diligently applied, a result will *always* occur. The goal of the manifestation game is to get the result you want. Then, your manifestation matches your intention and exceeds your expectations. The result: your happiness and the happiness of those around you.

Being, Doing, and Having

Being, doing, and *having* represent three basic modes of relating to the world. Everything we do employs all three modes, yet we can choose the most appropriate one to start with, depending on what we want to create. How we work with these three modes has a profound impact on our outlook on life and what we can create.

Most people begin with what they want to *have.* They say, "If I could *have* the money I want, I could *do* everything I want to do, and then I'd *be* happy (fulfilled, successful, satisfied)." Or they might start with *doing,* by saying, "If I could *do* the thing I want to do (drive race cars), then I would *have* an exciting career, and I would *be* fulfilled."

A more powerful way of creating is to begin with *being* and ask the question, "Who or how would I have to *be* in order to create what I want to *have* and *do?*" The answer results in a state of empowerment: "I need to *be* disciplined and organized in order to *do* the writing I need to do, so I can *have* my book published by the end of the year."

Being, doing, and having relate to three different realms of existence. Being relates to the realm of your *personal world*. It represents what goes on inside you as a person: your experiences, beliefs, sensations, feelings, thoughts, dreams, and states of consciousness. Inside yourself, you can create any state you prefer. You can create happiness or sadness, peace or excitement. You create within your personal world by deciding, choosing, declaring, and creating. (For example, declare "I am happy" to create the feeling of happiness.) Because this realm is personal, it does not depend on what anyone else says or does. The only obstacles to creating a state of being are the ones within—your personal blocks, habits, and beliefs. Therefore, a being state is the easiest and most direct state to achieve.

When you go about doing, however, you usually enter the *social world*. (We say "usually" because some activities, such as meditating, are still largely personal experiences.) The social world involves other people who may have their own agendas. If my dream of doing involves going on a date with you or driving your car, you'll have a say in the matter. If my doing involves practicing vocal exercises in the middle of the night, you might have objections if you live in the same house. In the social world, we create through communication, negotiation, agreements, contracts, exchanges, requests, and promises—or at worst, through dominating, bullying, coercing, or pleading. We have power over these actions, but we don't have ultimate power over other people's realities.

The state of having usually involves the *physical world*. "I want to have apple pie for dessert." "I want to have a nicer home." "I want to have a new dress for the party." The physical world, which is even bigger than the social universe, operates by physical laws. We have to work with gravity and limitation, timing and cycles. Sometimes this state also involves the social world; for example, you buy an apple pie in a store or ask a waitress to bring one from the restaurant kitchen. We create in the physical world by moving and shaping, cutting and joining, planting and harvesting, decorating and transforming, or otherwise acting upon something that already exists. The wood already exists, but you can cut it and join it to create a table.

Since being is the easiest realm in which to create, it's wise to start the manifestation process there. If you want to have a thriving business, then you must create within yourself the kind of being state required to build it. You have to *be* focused, disciplined, centered, grounded, and organized. When you create the appropriate being state, you are more likely to *do* the work of organizing others and creating a business plan in order to *have* the thriving business.

Manifestation Tip: Be first.

By "be first," we don't mean that you push others out of the way to get your own way. We mean that you should begin with the being state you want to create. If you want to *be* happy and you begin by creating that state of happiness, you may not need to *do* and *have* the things that you believed would make you happy. The right being state will allow you to do things more effectively. Later in this chapter, we'll show you a technique for creating a being state.

Dealing with Resistance

Whether you think you can or you can't, you are usually right.

—Henry Ford

As we have said, in the downward path, chakras operate as condensers, making things more solid and more real at every stage. The elements associated with each chakra become denser and denser, from ethereal thought to solid matter:

Chakra Seven: **Pure awareness or thought**
Chakra Six: **Light**
Chakra Five: **Sound**

Chakra Four:	Air
Chakra Three:	Fire
Chakra Two:	Water
Chakra One:	Earth

With increased density, there is more *resistance* at each stage. Consider a meteor flying through outer space. In the vacuum of space, there is no resistance. When the meteor hits the earth's atmosphere, it encounters air, which provides some resistance, and this resistance slows the meteor's speed and heats it up until it burns. Water is even denser than air, providing more resistance; when the meteor hits the ocean, it slows even more. But the meteor continues its descent. At the bottom of the ocean, the earth is completely dense, creating so much resistance that the meteor stops moving. In the same way, each chakra provides more density than the one above it. More resistance occurs at each level of manifestation, from crown to ground.

It's easy to dream big dreams and fantasize about their fulfillment. It's more difficult to bring those dreams into manifestation. Imagination is easy compared with doing the hard work of writing a book or advertising copy, and those tasks may seem easy compared with organizing a team and managing a meeting. When someone asks you to be more specific about your goals or plans, you may feel resistance coming up. When you see a long list of to-do items, you may feel resistance to doing them all. Resistance comes in many forms. The most common is the inner voice: "Why should I have to do that?" "I don't wanna!" "Isn't there some other way to make that happen? Like saying the right affirmation?" Or you might hear resistance coming from another person: "You're going to do *what?*"

One difference between people who are successful and those who are not successful is that the former—the manifestors—have learned ways to deal with their resistance, while others let their resistance stop them somewhere along the path. You can be sure that every mountain climber hits resistance at some level of the climb. There's nothing wrong with failure—not everyone reaches the peak. But stopping and turning around because you're experiencing some resistance is tragic.

Whatever you choose to be, do, or have, you will meet resistance. If you decide to go on a diet, you will immediately hear voices in your head that counter your intention: "You never stick to your diet," one voice says. "It's going to be really hard to diet right now—the holidays are coming up," says another. The chocolate cake in the refrigerator calls out to you, "Eat me!" Your inner child gets pouty and says, sniffling, "I want some cake!" This chorus of counterintentions can get very loud, until a diet really does sound like a bad idea, and you find yourself thinking, "Where's that chocolate?"

Resistance is defined as "a force that tends to oppose or retard motion." "Resistance happens" is as sure a law as "gravity exists." Nothing new can be created without encountering resistance along the way. Here's a little known fact: Creation actually *creates* its own resistance. If you allow resistance to stop you, you're stuck with how things already are. If you resist resistance when it comes up, you're really stuck! You might as well give up and go eat some cake.

There are two major resistance forces to contend with: internal resistance, which occurs inside yourself, and external resistance, which occurs in the world around you. We usually call these forces *obstacles*. Let's begin by examining the internal force, since it's the one that stops too many good people and good ideas from manifesting. If you want to master the art of manifestation, master the art of dealing with resistance. In this section, we start by providing some important background about resistance and how it operates. Then, we offer some practical ways to deal with it in your life.

It can be said that every creation has a beginning, a middle, and an end. Each creature has a birth, life, and death; a civilization gets organized, rises to a peak, and then collapses; a star is born, burns brightly, and explodes in a supernova; a feeling of sadness arises, is felt, and disappears. We call this sequence the *creation spiral*.

You've probably heard the aphorism "What you resist, persists." When you resist something and push against it, it gets stronger. Think of lifting weights in the gym. The weight provides resistance to your muscle, pushing or pulling against it. Your muscle builds in response to the challenge. Matter itself provides the strongest resistance. Try pushing against a big tree and see what happens. The tree provides more resistance than any force you can muster (until you bring out a chainsaw—a tool for dealing with the tree's resistance to being moved).

Internal experiences also go through a creation spiral. Although we live in a stream of multiple simultaneous experiences, you can identify a particular experience, such as a feeling of sadness, and identify its cause for arising (for example, upon hearing news of a friend's illness), the feeling itself (a heaviness in the heart and chest, tears behind the eyes), and its ultimate disappearance at some point in time.

You could say that experiences *want* to be experienced. If you resist an experience, it persists inside your mind-body system, waiting to complete its cycle. It gets stuck—usually just beneath the surface of awareness. If you push hard against it, it will push back even harder in return. Resisted experiences accumulate in the body like plaque in your arteries, limiting the flow of joy and happiness through your system.

Most of us welcome pleasurable experiences and resist unpleasant ones, but the mind tends to resist any feeling that's overwhelming or threatening. There are dozens of excellent strategies for not experiencing an unwanted experience or not feeling an unpleasant feeling, such as the following:

- **Suppressing:** Not feeling the feeling—pushing it down, ignoring it, or withdrawing from it

- **Thinking:** Moving from body sensations to mental calculations—figuring it out, analyzing it, building a case against it, or comparing one experience to another

- **Dissociating:** Separating yourself, or a part of yourself, mentally, emotionally, or spiritually from the experience, so it doesn't seem to be happening to you

- **Substituting:** Feeling something else (such as fatigue, hunger, or anger) in place of the emotions of the experience

- **Distracting:** Finding something else to put your attention on (such as emails, kids, TV, housework, shopping, or exercising)

- **Controlling:** Attempting to manipulate, manage, or change the situation that is causing the feeling in order to take control of the situation

- **Verbalizing:** Talking about the situation (often endlessly) to someone else, especially to find validation or empathy for your point of view

- **Somaticizing:** Shifting the problem into the body, where it produces symptoms such as headache, stomachache, rashes, fever, or pain

- **Fantasizing:** Daydreaming or coming up with pleasant (or unpleasant) scenarios other than what is actually taking place

- **Remembering:** Focusing on previous similar incidents and stories from the past

- **Role playing:** Responding to a situation by taking on a role, such as teacher, parent, or police officer, rather than just being present with the feelings

- **Playing victim:** Feeling like a victim of the circumstances and identifying a perpetrator who caused the experience, rather than taking responsibility and feeling what's true

- **Perpetrating:** Attacking another person physically, emotionally, or intellectually as a way to override unpleasant feelings, such as vulnerability, confusion, or shame

Do any of these strategies feel familiar to you? What other methods do you use to avoid feeling what you're feeling or experiencing what you're experiencing?

Embracing Your Experience: A Key Element in Healing

If you allow yourself to experience something fully, it will move through you, complete its purpose, and disappear back into nonexistence. Here's a set of little-known rules that can transform your life by eliminating the feeling of being stuck:

1. If you're experiencing or feeling something you don't want to feel, embrace it instead and feel it fully, just as it is. Within sixty seconds, it will either disappear completely or change in some way.

2. If the experience disappears, allow it to be gone. If you want it to come back, you can always re-create it later.

3. If it changes in some way, feel the new experience fully. Within sixty seconds, it will either disappear completely or change in some way.

4. If you want an experience to go away completely, repeat Step 3 until the experience is completely gone.

Here's a practical example of this principle at work: Remember a moment when you banged your shin on a piece of furniture. If you're like most people, you immediately started cursing: "Damn! I'm so stupid! Who the hell put that there? Oh—I did. What a stupid place for a table!" You may have hopped around and rubbed your shin, but most of your energy was focused on your own (or someone else's) stupidity.

The next time something like this happens, do an experiment: Feel the pain fully, with all of your attention. Press the part of your body (your shin, in this case) back onto whatever object it contacted (the table, in this case, wherever it made contact). Allow the excruciating pain to move all the way through your body. (Screaming is encouraged.) You may find, strangely, that it will bruise less or not at all. When all of your attention is offered to a sensation, without resistance, a bad experience will move through you and out of you. The attitude that works best is embracing the experience and welcoming the pain as a testament to your aliveness. When *fully experienced*, a sensation or feeling lasts only thirty to sixty seconds. Then it subsides and disappears. (There are exceptions to the sixty-second rule, such as deep grief over the loss of someone close. The feeling of grief can last for weeks or months, even when fully experienced. But even grief will move faster when welcomed.) A resisted experience, on the other hand, can last hours, days, or years. Experiences *want* to be experienced, and they will be—one way or the other. You have a choice: Either you can experience something unpleasant very intensely for a short period of time, or you can experience it as a subtle, annoying feeling for a very long time. Remember that whatever you resist, persists.

The word *emotion* comes from the same root as *motion,* which means "movement." An emotion is like a weather system moving across a landscape. When you were young, powerful emotions overwhelmed you. You were little; they were big. They felt dangerous, and you figured out ways to not feel them. The good news is that you're no longer a child. You're now bigger than any feelings. But you must be willing to experience those feelings *fully.*

Resisted experiences create a variety of symptoms: circumstances that keep repeating in one's life, persistent pain, recurring nightmares, fixed or intractable attitudes. When repressed emotions get stacked up and stored in the body, the body reacts to them as if they were foreign objects. Hardened resistance can turn into heart disease, immune disorders, or cancer.

Some people have avoided so many experiences that their ability to feel becomes compromised or deadened. They become numb to the world and depressed about life. They feel separated and isolated from others. Their resistance to past experiences is so strong that they live behind impenetrable walls, hoping one day to be rescued.

Healing begins with *willingness*—willingness to confront the past, willingness to feel old hurts, traumas, and injuries. Become willing to explore your shadow places, the dark and scary places where dangerous creatures may lurk. Be willing to dredge up the buried past: old experiences that you couldn't handle at the time or repressed emotions that got hidden in the basement. When you tell the truth about the past, you free your soul for the future. Allow every experience, sensation, pain, and problem to complete its creation cycle. Take off the resistance and dive in. Wallow in it, if you must, until it is complete. Enjoy even uncomfortable feelings and sensations. They are the proof that you are alive! You will survive them. We promise.

You don't have to face all those old experiences all at once. Relax. Take a gradual approach. Only do a little at a time, as you are ready. Life itself will bring up old wounds and hurts that are still waiting in the background to be handled. As they come up, face them with full-frontal acceptance and the willingness to experience them as they emerge, in the present moment, just as they are right now. The more willing you are to dig down and clean up the stuff stored in the basement, the more rapid your progress will be.

Your willingness to experience resisted experiences is the key to clearing up what's in your way. It's the way out of pain and the way back to freedom, health, and happiness.

Dealing with Obstacles

An obstacle is anything that gets in your way, slows you down, delays or distracts you, or causes you to stop or give up. Here's an important secret that can transform your ability to manifest:

> Obstacles are natural, normal, and predictable. They are the world's natural response to your creation.

Obstacles do not appear in your way in order to stop you. Rather, they appear in order to strengthen and hone you and your plans. They are not your enemy. They are your secret ally, but only if you treat them as friendly forces of nature.

In physics, Isaac Newton's First Law of Motion states, "An object that is at rest will stay at rest unless an unbalanced force acts upon it *[inertia]*. An object that is in motion will not change its velocity unless an unbalanced force acts upon it *[momentum]*." In other words, objects (and processes) tend to keep on doing what they're doing unless something forces them to change their state of motion. Whenever you create something new, you become the unbalanced force that acts on the world's inertia and momentum: "Things have been going along just fine, thank you. And now you want to change them? Hold on a minute." There's a similar law of inertia inside the human psyche: You tend to keep doing what you've been doing unless some other force (such as pain, intention, or conscious choice) motivates you to change your direction or your habitual behavior. Thus, the saying, "If you keep going the direction you're going, you'll end up where you're headed."

The bigger your dream, vision, or project, the more obstacles you'll encounter. Again, the biggest difference between successful people and everyone else is that successful people have ways of handling obstacles so that those obstacles don't stop forward progress. Master manifestors learn how to deal with obstacles effectively, moving them out of the way, one by one. Those who ignore obstacles will later trip over them; likewise, those who focus too much attention on their obstacles will get mired in them, and their dreams will sink into a sea of problems.

The most powerful success strategies we teach are the specific techniques that deal with resistance and obstacles when they come up (as they inevitably will). We don't meditate them away or cover them with positive affirmations; rather, we apply specific, effective tools that are matched to the actions required at each chakra level.

If you had absolutely no resistance, then all of your intentions would manifest effortlessly. This is illustrated in the biblical quotation, "God said, 'Let there be light,' and there was light." This is what happens when a powerful being declares an intention into the clear open space of possibility: The intention manifests effortlessly.

Why don't your intentions manifest all the time? Because of resistance. As we said earlier, resistance can come from deep within your own psyche (your old programming and beliefs) or from the world (external obstacles). At some level, you actually do manifest every one of your intentions, beliefs, thoughts, and desires. The problem is, you keep changing your mind about what you want, think, and intend. At any one moment, you want, think, and intend many different things at once. The Universe does its best to grant your wishes, but you're sending mixed messages, so you get mixed results.

If every one of your thoughts and desires manifested instantly, what would your life look like? You may have opposing intentions that work directly against each other. For example, "I want to lose weight, but I don't want to stop eating desserts," or "I want that job, but I don't want to work for that boss." One part of you is saying, "Yes, yes!" and another part is saying, "No, no!"

Whenever two opposing or competing intentions are trying to manifest at the same time, it creates tension. One of your desires is to lose weight; another real desire is to eat that delicious chocolate cake in the refrigerator. The tension creates experiences of conflict, discomfort, guilt, shame, upset, uncertainty, or frustration. Some people live inside *constant* conflict and discomfort. In a high-tension, high-stakes situation, you may have three, five, or even ten competing intentions, commitments, and desires! You are probably aware of some of them at the conscious level, but most of them lurk in your subconscious.

Here's a little-known, but very important, law of manifestation: Whenever you decide to create something new in your life, whenever you declare a new intention or belief into existence, this act *automatically stimulates all previous conflicting intentions and beliefs to reassert themselves.* You've no doubt experienced this in your own life. You make a commitment, such as, "I'm going to lose ten pounds by the end of the year," and that simple intention unleashes a torrent of responses from within. They appear most often as internal thoughts or voices, loud protests or criticisms: "That's going to be hard." "You've tried that before, and it's never worked." "The holidays are coming, and it's impossible to lose weight during the holidays." "You have to exercise to lose weight, and you don't exercise!"

We call these responses *crosscurrents.* They're also referred to as *counterintentions, doubts, fears,* or *second thoughts.* Your intention is to move yourself toward your new goal. But as soon as you state your intention, your old beliefs are stimulated to respond. They cross your path, interfere with your forward movement, or knock you off course.

Crosscurrents are nothing more than intentions or beliefs that existed before you made up your new intention. They exist in the physical world, too. If you intend to build a road, the boulders or trees that are already there could be called crosscurrents. You could say that the rocks and trees have a previous intention to continue existing where they already are. You have to handle them and get them out of the way in order to build your road. You expect them to be there, and you have your bulldozer ready to deal with them.

One of your intentions may be to become well known in your field. This is in conflict with another intention from the past, which is to avoid attention by withdrawing and hiding. This was a successful strategy that you developed in the past to stay safe, but it's now in conflict with your current intention. Your successful strategy of hiding is now your crosscurrent.

Your mind holds thousands of previously created intentions. When you declare a new intention, those older intentions rise up and reassert themselves: "Hey! What about me! You created me first!"

Crosscurrents can appear in many different forms, including the following:

- Internal voices
- Body sensations
- Doubts or second thoughts
- Habitual or addictive behaviors
- Physical movements (tics)
- Urges
- Feelings such as fear, anxiety, or confusion
- Reactions to someone or something
- Thoughts
- Judgments or criticism
- Dissociation (going blank or spacing out)
- Desire for validation or approval
- Attempts to assert control over or change something

Crosscurrents can appear as anything that shows up in response to your declaration—anything other than what you intended, that is.

Crosscurrents are natural, and you can expect them to show up. They are simply obstacles to handle—nothing more and nothing less. Think of them as pebbles in your shoe rather than barriers that stop your forward movement. Simply stop, take off your shoe, remove the pebble, put your shoe back on, and take the next step. Learning to deal with crosscurrents is essential to success. If you know that crosscurrents are certain to show up and you expect them, they won't waylay you. If you have tools for navigating through them, they become interesting features on the grand journey toward your goal.

Most people get stopped by their crosscurrents. If they start a diet and get a sudden urge to eat a pint of ice cream, they say, "Oh well, I guess I can't lose weight. Might as well not even start." How many projects have you begun and given up somewhere along the way because of your crosscurrents? Don't allow your crosscurrents to stop you from reaching your goal. If you ignore them, minimize them, deny them, push them away, or attempt to outrun them, they will find other ways to express themselves. Instead, find ways to move through them. There are many choices: You can push hard and move them out of the way, walk along their edges until you find a way around them, rise above them and get over them, dig down and tunnel beneath them, use dynamite to blow them up, learn to move through their solid walls, get help to figure out alternatives, make friends with them, or offer them new jobs. Or, you can do the "Declare Your Intentions" exercise (below).

If you want to manifest more in your life, find the sources of resistance inside you and remove them. This guidance sounds simplistic, but it's actually the easiest path to getting what you want. It requires some work, but it's the most effective way to move your life toward your dreams.

Exercise: Declare Your Intentions

First say to yourself what you would be;
and then do what you have to do.

—Epictetus

When you declare an intention and put the full weight of your commitment behind it, you initiate a magical process that works invisibly in the background of your life. But when you have conflicting intentions or beliefs, the process gets muddled. The universe doesn't know what you want, so it gives you a little of this and a little of that. When you clear away the conflicts and hold only one clear intention with no resistance, that invisible force can work in the background to help you create what you intend. This exercise will enable you to sweep the conflicts out of the way and clear the path so your intention can manifest.

Step 1: Identify Competing Commitments and Desires

Write down the major goals you have for your life and what prevents you from achieving them. Instead of using *but* ("I want to lose weight, but I love eating sweets."), use *and.* For example:

- "I want to lose weight, and I want to eat sweets."
- "I want to earn more money, and I want to have more time off."
- "I want to travel, and I want to pay off all of my debts."

Writing down your goals is a good way to acknowledge the truth—you have many competing commitments, needs, desires, and beliefs. That's okay. We all do. The first step is allowing them all to be true, without resisting any of them.

Step 2: Identify Competing Beliefs

Pick one of the following subjects, and spend five minutes writing down every belief you've ever had about it:

- Money
- Sex
- Power
- Religion
- Your body

For example, "I believe money is the root of all evil. Money is good. Money gives me freedom. Money is dirty. Money is the key measurement of success." You may find that you can list thirty or more beliefs.

Next, notice how many of those beliefs compete directly with each other. The key is to expose unconscious competing beliefs to your conscious awareness. In "The Belief Process" exercise later in the book (page 70), we'll show you how to eliminate beliefs you don't want anymore.

Step 3: Release Crosscurrents

To complete and clear a crosscurrent, you have to be willing to *experience it fully* and *express it fully*. One of our favorite ways to do this—and certainly the most fun—is to exaggerate it. This technique has evolved out of theater games and drama therapy, where it's used to help people fully express a particular character or emotion. It works equally well when applied to crosscurrents (which behave like character actors) that operate below the conscious level.

To *exaggerate* means "to make bigger than it is." You see exaggeration in character actors, stand-up comedians, and cartoon characters. What makes them funny is how they express normal human characteristics in a way that's over the top, outside the norm, beyond what you usually see. Many shows and movies use exaggeration for comic effect. One of our favorites is the animated film *Who Shot Roger Rabbit?* Both the cartoon characters and the real people act in over-the-top ways. That's the spirit we're talking about.

Thoughts and voices inside your head sound just like you, so you mistakenly believe they *are* you. But they're not. They're crosscurrents reasserting themselves. How can you tell? If they repeat the same messages over and over, they're not you. They're part of the mind's automatic machinery, but they are trying to get your attention. In fact, when they're active, they're competing for your attention. Until you give it to them, they will continue to assert themselves. They act like a messenger who's been hired to personally deliver a message to you. He raps on your door to let you know he's there. If you don't answer, but he knows you're there, he knocks louder. If you continue to ignore him, he rings your bell, then shouts—louder and louder—until you finally open the door, and say, "What?!" He hands you the message, and when you say, "Thank you," he turns around and disappears, having completed his duty.

When you exaggerate a crosscurrent, you allow the message to come through—fully and completely. Then, both the messenger and the message can complete the cycle of their creation, and they can go away. You'll prove this to yourself when you do this exercise. We've taught this method to hundreds of people, and every one of them has been surprised at how easy it is to eliminate thoughts and feelings that have been present in their consciousness for years—even decades.

You can do this exercise by yourself or with a partner. Be ready and willing to look and act silly. The more fun you have, the better the technique works.

To begin, choose an intention that you want to manifest. Start with a *being* intention—one that starts with "I am." The simpler it can be said, the better. Here are examples:

- "I am happy."
- "I am peaceful."
- "I am healthy."
- "I am worthy."
- "I am organized."

Write down your intention as simply and as clearly as possible. Put your intention in present time and as a statement of the positive. If your intention is to be without pain, say, "I am vibrantly healthy." If your intention is to be debt free, say, "I am living in abundance." Take time to craft a powerful intention—one that stirs you up and produces immediate reactions. As you clear the crosscurrents, one by one, you will get closer and closer to the state you desire.

If you're working with a partner, sit facing each other. If you're working on your own, it helps to face a mirror. In the example below, we'll use the intention, "I am happy."

1. State your intention out loud as a declaration: "I am happy." Say it as if you are declaring a new reality into the Universe. Making a declaration is a creative act. Bring your full energy and intention to your declaration. Faith can move mountains; say it as if it were already 100 percent true. At this moment, you are the creator of your life.

2. Notice whatever response comes up first. It might be an internal voice, a doubt, a feeling, a sensation—anything at all

that you notice in your space. Name it; then describe it briefly. For example, "I noticed that I heard a voice saying, 'You are not happy! You're miserable!'"

3. If you're working with a friend, he or she listens with interest from a neutral place, without reacting, and says, "Okay, exaggerate that." If you're working on your own, give yourself the same instruction.

4. In an exaggerated manner, act out the voice you heard. Exaggeration removes resistance to what came up and gives it freedom to exist. It allows the crosscurrent to fully express itself. Exaggeration can be done in many different ways, but imagine how a very bad actor on stage might express himself or a cartoon character might speak with her own particular voice. Or simply make the voice louder than it sounded in your head: "You're not happy! You're miserable! You are a sorry excuse for a human being!" Exaggeration means that you *increase* the amount of energy that already exists. If your voice or body movements are at the same energy level as what you heard or felt inside you, amp it up! This exercise should get loud and funny. If you and your partner laugh at your exaggerated expression, you're going in the right direction.

5. Return to your intention and state it again, as you did before, from a place of declaring it to be true: "I am happy."

6. Check to see whether the crosscurrent is still there. Do you still see, feel, or hear it? Look for the same energy, voice, sensation, urge—however the crosscurrent originally appeared. Look to wherever the crosscurrent came from. It will either be (a) gone (meaning you no longer feel it), (b) still there but with less intensity, or (c) still there with the same intensity.

7. If it's no longer detectable, don't spend time looking for it. It's gone. Don't re-create it. It really disappeared! That's the point of the exercise: to make crosscurrents disappear. Acknowledge whatever is true by stating the condition:

a. "It's gone."

b. "It's still there, but it's lighter/smaller/less intense."

c. "It's still there."

8. If it's still there (b or c), exaggerate it some more. Amp up the energy of your exaggeration. You have to get bigger than the crosscurrent in order to make it disappear. If it's a voice, stand up and take on the character behind the voice (such as a critical mother, wagging her finger, speaking to your empty chair as if you were still sitting there). Silly imitations (even of Mother) are welcomed! Act it out and have fun.

9. Continue to exaggerate until the crosscurrent is gone completely.

10. When you feel complete, return to your chair and restate your intention: "I am happy."

Repeat the process, working with the next crosscurrent that comes up when you say your intention. If many crosscurrents come up all at once (a common occurrence), work only with the *first* one that appeared. Tell the others, "Stand in line and wait your turn."

At the end of each cycle and in between each step, state your intention again clearly. Doing so transfers the energy from your crosscurrent to your intention. We say it "harvests the charge" of the crosscurrent. It's like righting your sailboat after the wind pushes it over. You'll learn that your intention is more powerful than your crosscurrents.

Every crosscurrent has a particular energetic signature. It has some form and location inside your body or mind; at times it can appear outside of your body. It may have a direction and movement, or it might be still. Some crosscurrents come with sounds, urges, or movements. Let them come; exaggerate them. When you're looking and listening for crosscurrents, look for anything that comes up *other than* what you stated as an intention.

When a *sensation* appears, find a way to make fun of it. If you have a slight headache, you might pound your head with your fist, saying, "Oh, my aching head! A thousand-pound sledgehammer is whacking me!" If you feel sad, make it like cartoon crying, like Betty Boop wiping her eyes, saying, "Oh, boo-hoo-hoo!"

There are many ways to exaggerate any particular crosscurrent, so have fun! You'll know it worked when that particular crosscurrent has disappeared. If the crosscurrent doesn't disappear in one or two tries, try a different way of exaggerating it. Continue with the process as long as you like—or until you feel clear, present, and powerful.

This is an amazing technology that works to remove any internal resistance that comes up and gets in your way. You may be surprised to find out how easy it is to make a thought, emotion, voice, or sensation disappear—especially those that have been annoying you your whole life.

Chakra Seven:
Consciousness Creates

*Some men see things as they are and ask, why? I dream things
that never were and ask, why not?*

—George Bernard Shaw

———————————

Yosemite Falls is a majestic sight to behold. The highest waterfall in
America and the sixth largest in the world, it plunges nearly half a
mile (2,425 feet) from top to bottom in two gigantic plumes. When
the snow melts in spring, its awesome gush thunders throughout the
valley, drawing millions of visitors each year to stand in amazement of
its mighty power.

As I (Anodea) stood before the falls in May of 2011, surrounded by
huge granite walls carved out by glaciers over millions of years, I was
awed by the presence of the Divine. I realized that one aspect of the
Divine is sheer scale; a natural phenomenon this large creates an expan-
sion of perspective. We see ourselves anew, and our sense of self expands
far beyond what we previously believed we were.

Of course, the Divine is all around us at any scale, but something special occurs when we confront the majesty of something so
expansive—an ocean, a hurricane, a sunset, a galaxy, the joy of a
child, the love of a mother. Just as the waterfall contains rain and
melted snow that fell from the heavens, the manifestation process
begins with the highest we can reach for and flows all the way down
through the chakras to the earth plane.

To make your creation majestic, to really bring heaven down to earth, you need to start with the highest. What are the highest principles that you aspire to? What are the highest qualities or virtues you want to embody? What is the greatest service you can perform? What is the most profound sense of wisdom, order, or inspiration you can align with? What aspect of divinity most inspires you to do your best?

What is your life purpose? And which of your dreams will you bring down to reality? "Consciousness Creates" is a core principle of the manifestation process. Whatever you can conceive and believe, you can achieve. Everything human-made began in awareness first—with an *idea,* a *vision,* a *dream,* or an *intention.* All of these words describe the world of consciousness—the inner, subjective world that has no physical "reality."

In this chapter, we examine four basic processes that relate to the seventh chakra:

- Opening to the power of emptiness
- Receiving guidance and grace
- Clarifying ideas into intention
- Clearing limiting beliefs

Chakra Seven

The seventh chakra is the highest chakra in the human energy system. It relates to the uppermost part of the body, the crown of the head. Symbolically, a crown signifies someone of high stature, such as a king or queen. In monarchies of the past, the *heads* of state made the decisions, called the shots, formed the game plan, and told everyone else what to do. In the same way, the Crown chakra is the beginning of your quest. It is the entry point of universal spirit into your individual body-mind. Just as a solar panel receives the sun's shining energy and brings it into a house as electricity, your Crown chakra is the receiver of Source consciousness.

The seventh chakra is the thousand-petaled lotus that is infinitely blooming, called *Sahasrara,* meaning "thousandfold" or "infinite" in

Sanskrit. Your awareness is the *dimensionless point* at the very center of this lotus. As the lotus blooms all around you, through activities, projects, conversations, people, noises, urges, and thoughts, there are thousands of things competing for your attention. Yet the lotus reminds you to remain centered in pure awareness, connected to your central channel or core, even as chaos and complexity unfold around you. Staying centered helps you keep connected with Source in the most direct way, without getting pulled off track by all the events blossoming around you.

Like a prism that breaks white light into its rainbow frequencies, the body breaks down the universe's raw energy into its seven levels of manifestation through the chakras. The seventh chakra, your first "transducer," turns the raw energy of the cosmos into personal *consciousness,* which is a lofty and infinite realm. In the individual, consciousness occurs as thoughts, awareness, intelligence, ideas, beliefs, interpretations, information, understanding, intention, and attention.

The seventh chakra is the gateway to universal or divine consciousness. In this sense, we begin by "downloading the Divine." John Friend, the founder of Anusara yoga, described it this way:

> There is one Supreme Consciousness, aware of itself, with the capacity to know itself. It is the ground of the entire universe. It is blissful, infinitely joyful, and free to express itself creatively. Out of its freedom, it creates limitations, cloaking itself in myriad shapes and forms. This gives the impression of differences, which deepens its own self-knowing and its expression as beauty. This is the joy of the dance—concealing, then revealing—drawing in as contraction and then blooming forth as expansion. In this way, it expresses its joyful nature.
>
> When we are in alignment with this deep order, beauty, and goodness of the universe, we are part of something grand. When we align with the Divine—the source of joy, happiness, and love—and when we share this heart freedom, we experience its revelation as joy, insight, and knowledge of our interconnectedness. The inherent bliss of that great force is revealed to us.

When we're misaligned, veils appear. We notice differences instead of sameness, and we judge one part as better and another part as worse. We lose our compassion. We create more divisions, more cloaking, more pain and suffering.

Everyone wants to be happy and free from suffering. When we align in our hearts and in our yoga, we align our intention with the Divine in order to manifest more of the Divine. We experience moments of revelation and opening, and they begin to happen more often. When we support and nurture each other to align with this bliss nature, we become part of life's grand pulsation. Even the galaxies are breathing. It's a grand symphony, and you are one instrument—play your music in tune with it![5]

How do you call this higher force down into your being? The first step of the manifestation process is to open yourself to the Divine.

Opening to the Power of Emptiness

If you want to bake a cake, you start with a clean bowl, because you don't want the remnants of last night's spaghetti dinner included in your recipe. If you want to build a house, you clear the ground of trees, rocks, and debris before you bring your materials to the site. Before you go on a date, you take a shower to clear the day's accumulation of stress.

Beginning in emptiness cleans your slate and gives you the widest access to creative Source. In the vast realm of openness, anything is possible. Once something comes into form (in*form*ation), its future becomes partially defined. When this occurs, some possibilities come into being, and others are eliminated. But in the infinite emptiness of the pregnant void, the entire field is open. There are no predefinitions or preconceived notions, no "already is," "always has been," or "certainly ought to be." There is great power in nothing, because it gives rise to something. Human awareness and creativity arise in the gap between *nothing is* and *everything is.*

Matter has something in common with the kosmos[6]—they are both mostly empty space. Matter is composed of atoms, but if a hydrogen atom's nucleus were enlarged to the size of a baseball, the orbit of its electrons would be about two-and-a-half miles away. If you enlarged the entire atom to be a mile in diameter, its nucleus would be the size of a marble. What we perceive as solid is primarily emptiness.

Though the night sky might seem equally empty, we now know how full it is. Many of those pinpoints of light are galaxies millions of light years away, each one containing billions of stars. The fact that our little planet is a mere speck of dust in this starry local universe, yet is so vast and complex itself, represents an unfathomable depth of creative potential. There's plenty of room to think outside the box in which we normally live.

The manifestation process works by first condensing possibilities into probabilities, then molding them into likely outcomes, and finally making them into solid certainties. At each step along the way, it gets more condensed. If you start small, you end up even smaller. So at this top level, where we begin, start big—in *infinite possibility.*

Most people keep their eyes downward and live in the limitations of what already exists. They see the big accomplishments of noteworthy celebrities—the ones we read about in the news—as something that "other people" do. Who are those other people? They're people just like you. The only difference is they dared to dream big and then followed a step-by-step procedure for getting there. The founder of Matsushita, the $38 billion consumer electronics giant, wrote a 250-year business plan for his company. That's dreaming big!

Most people simply don't dream big enough. And by the time their dream gets whittled down by the condensation process, it's too small to be inspiring—even to them. Big dreams require a lot more chutzpah, but they also attract more notice and have more gravitational force. Your big dream will evolve over time, but dreaming big now will open possibilities and will call you to your best, so you can become more than you already are.

Emptiness can also mean clearing out something that was created earlier but that now is in the way: an unfinished project that is taking up room in the closet or garage, old papers lying on your desk, or an unfinished conversation with a loved one. Emptiness sets the stage for beginning. In Western magical traditions, most rituals start with a banishing—getting rid of what you don't want. Sometimes those things need a moment's attention: "Thank you, but I no longer need you. Goodbye." This act of completion frees up energy to begin something new. It allows us to conceive. All manifestation begins with conception—the birth of something from nothing.

When your father's sperm and mother's egg came together in fertilization, they were composed of very little matter. However, they were full of information—a pattern (from *pater,* "father") that had all the data necessary to make you into you. Your gender, eye color, height, and hair color were all specified by the sperm's and egg's combined DNA. You were made to order. Your mother (*mater,* which is derived from *materia* or "matter") created your flesh according to that information. She took raw substance—in the form of molecules, atoms, and breath—and organized it into the pattern of your DNA. It began with conception; in fact, the Latin root of the word *conceive* means "to take in."

We have to conceive of something in order to create it. An idea comes in from . . . somewhere. To us, the word *idea* can be seen as a combination of *I,* representing the central channel or core of the Self, and the feminine form of the word for God: *dea.* Conception is a pattern or thought that comes into the flesh of our brains and bodies for the purpose of manifestation. It is made of concepts, which form the substance of our beliefs. (We'll deal with beliefs in depth later in this chapter.)

Receiving Guidance and Grace

Arjuna Ardagh, author of *The Translucent Revolution,* interviewed hundreds of the most successful people from all arenas of life. One thing they all had in common was their ability to tap into the depth of silence or Source. Some of them waited a long time until the impulse struck them to do something. This is different from the typical success-oriented manifestation training, which is to decide and then go out and make it happen.

When your chakras are aligned, you have the most direct access to Source, however you may define Source (within yourself, outside yourself, or both simultaneously). Just as you hold a glass under the tap so it can be filled, we align with Source by facing into it, turning our attention toward it, and opening our "vessel" in the most direct way possible to receive whatever we are seeking (or whatever Source has in mind). Aligning with Source should be a regular part of your practice whenever you're focused on manifestation.

To open yourself to receive guidance and grace, you may have to clear some space in your life. It could mean setting aside time for just being alone, away from work, family, and friends. It could mean taking a break from email, television, cell phones, texting, and news. It might be going on a vision quest for a week, fasting for a few days, or even taking deep journeys in a sensory-isolation tank. For me (Anodea), it is sometimes paddling alone in a kayak while the early morning mist is still on the water. All of these are viable methods, and some will work better for you than others. However, there's nothing like the tried-and-true practice of meditation for entering into stillness and emptiness. Meditation is a practice of emptying the mind so that it becomes clear and still. In this stillness, the mind can receive messages that come from outside the mind.

When I (Anodea) meditate, I find that sets of instructions are often waiting to be downloaded into my consciousness. I keep a pad and pencil by my cushion to record the things that just pop into my mind. But first I have to be quiet long enough to hear these whispers.

Meditation is essential—not just for the start of a project, but also for the start of any part of your project and for the start of your day. It allows you to get beyond your ego needs and connect directly with Source. *Grace* could be defined as the creative flow of the Universe coming into manifestation through you. Emptiness leaves room for grace to enter. Meditation quiets the mind, calms the nerves, slows the breath, and opens us to the deeper underlying reality—the unified field of ever-present consciousness. Meditation serves many purposes, but it is also an end in itself.

Just as a woman needs to be fertile in order to conceive a child, our minds need to be fertile to conceive of new ideas. Meditation is like clearing the weeds of the mind so new things can take root. But the soil also needs nutrients. Nutrients of the body include food, water, air, and exercise. Nutrients of the mind include knowledge and inspiration.

To fertilize the mind, study something or someone in depth. Participating in other people's projects stimulates imagination and ideas. Julia Cameron, in her book *The Artist's Way,* recommends taking yourself on an artist's date at least once a week. That date could mean going to an art museum, seeing a play or concert, reading a book, watching a good movie, eating at a fine restaurant, or going to a fashion show. The important thing is that it feeds your mind and fertilizes the ground so new ideas can sprout.

Exercise: Spend Time in Silence

Whether or not you meditate, spend some time in silence, either alone or with a companion. It is a powerful way of entering emptiness and opening your inner listening. Just as we need time after a busy day to putter and put things away, our minds need time to process information and integrate our experiences. *Doing nothing is actually very productive!* One of our favorite recommendations comes from a Portuguese saying: "How good it is to do nothing all day, and to rest afterward."

Exercise: Step into the Sacred

At least once this week, go to a place or do an activity that you consider holy or sacred. A sacred place could be a church or a synagogue, or it could just as easily be a forest, meadow, or special place on the beach. A holy activity could be very conscious lovemaking with your partner (complete with candles, music, and other elements to make it sacred) or a ceremony you make up with your kids. It could be spending time in deep meditation, a yoga class, or a visit with a spiritual teacher. It could even be reading a sacred text—the Bible, the Bhagavad Gita, or the poetry of Rumi. What's important is that you get in touch with a sense of the sacred or Divine, however you experience it. Separate yourself for a few moments from your mundane life. If you can't find time for this act out of seven full days, you may have to examine your priorities. What does it mean to live a whole week without touching into the sacred?

In addition, imagine that as you open the front door to your home, step into your office, or get on your yoga mat, *you are stepping into a temple.* Just pause for a moment before stepping across the threshold. Align your energies and set your intention, just as you might do when entering a really special temple somewhere in a foreign land. Begin to court a sense of the sacred in your everyday life.

Exercise: Ponder One Question Each Day

Deepak Chopra says that the Universe forms itself around your questions. It's as if your question is a tagline typed into a cosmic search engine that then calls up all the appropriate sites where your question might be answered. It draws information toward you.

Consider and craft your question during meditation or while you take a shower, make your coffee, go to the gym, or drive to work. When your question is well crafted, send it out to the Universe, to Source, or to God. Then let it go. Empty your mind to receive the answer. It may come immediately, or it may take some time. Simply prepare yourself to receive it whenever and however it comes. You can even ask to have it come in a form that is clear and obviously the answer. You will find that Source is always answering your questions; you just may not be paying attention when the answers arrive.

In addition, explore the question by asking friends, loved ones, and strangers. Other people may be the vehicle through which your answers come to you. Record the results in your journal at the end of the day. We suggest that your first question be related to the seventh chakra, such as "What is consciousness?" "What is grace?" or "What is thought?" Or it could be more practical, such as, "What is important for me to do (notice, feel, share, see, say) today?" or "How do I solve the problem of . . . ?" Notice what shows up in your thoughts, your conversations, your chance encounters with others or the world.

Sometimes I (Anodea) spend many months with a particular question. When I was working on the book *Waking the Global Heart,* my question was "What's the next organizing principle for humanity?" That question drew me to books that seemed to practically fall off the shelves of book-stores and friends' libraries, and it led to fascinating conversations with interesting people.

Clarifying Ideas into Intentions

*Intention appears to be something akin to a tuning fork,
causing the tuning forks of other things in the universe
to resonate at the same frequency.*

—Lynne McTaggart

Once you get an idea that really sings, one that grabs your attention, you can choose to bring it into manifestation. It becomes an intention, the starting point of a long trajectory. The word *intention* shares a root with the word *attention: tendere,* which is Latin for "to stretch." *Attention* comes from *ad tendere,* "to stretch toward." When you place your attention on something, you stretch toward it. *Intention* comes from *in tendere,* "to stretch inward." Your intention is something that comes from deep within you. It takes you out of emptiness and into creation. Intention focuses your consciousness and puts your attention on a particular direction in which you want to go. It also informs the rest of you that the tide has turned. When the lead bird in a flock changes direction, the entire flock moves in that direction. If your intention is to build a house, you'll begin to notice the architecture of other houses. If your intention is to start a family, you'll notice children and pregnant women.

Ideas are like arrows in a quiver. Setting your intention is like pulling out a single arrow, nocking it on the bowstring, and pointing it in a particular direction. Pulling back on the string creates the power that will send your idea flying toward your target. Once released, the arrow will move in that direction until it hits something solid—your target, an obstacle, or the ground. Like the wind blowing the arrow sideways, your beliefs are forces that act on your intention as it moves toward its destination. If your beliefs conflict with your intention, your arrow won't fly straight. You will miss your target if you don't compensate in some way for the wind.

Your intention directs the random bits of the world *(prakriti)* toward a particular form. When you set an intention, your world begins to bend around it. You do this all the time—if you know have an appointment at 8 a.m., you use an alarm clock to make sure you get out of bed, get breakfast, get prepared, and leave your house early enough to travel to your destination. You have made your future reality conform to your intention to be in a certain place at a certain time. You already shape your reality with your intention; it's just that you may not have considered how you are doing it.

Stretching Toward Your Goal

Setting an intention is like putting a stake in the ground at a future place and time and saying, "I want to be there, then."

Think of intention as a rubber band stretching from your current reality to the reality you intend. If you want to lose twenty pounds by June 1, then your rubber band stretches between your current weight now to your intended weight on June 1.

Tension always seeks resolution. The word *tension* has the same root as *attention* and *intention*. As soon as you let go of a stretched rubber band, it snaps back to its original shape. When you release the bowstring, the tension of the bow snaps the string back into place, pushing the arrow toward its target.

"Putting a stake in the ground" means that you make a firm, uncompromising commitment to the future state. You tie your rubber band to that point in the future. The tension must resolve, and since the stake can't move, it draws the other side of the rubber band—where you are—to the stake. The commitment you make to the future pulls you toward it. If, on the other hand, you let the rubber band go at the stake end, then the future snaps back to the present. You've let go of your commitment, and what you have left is the same reality you started with.

If you keep your *attention* on your *intention*, then your current reality will be pulled toward your intention. Your current situation will change in accordance with the vision you have of the future. Your intention, when held firmly in place, shapes your reality.

Reflect upon the following questions and statements to examine your intentions:

- What is your intention for how you want to live your life?
- What do you intend to create, accomplish, or change in the coming year? In the coming decade?
- Name three things outside yourself that support your intention. (Example: "I've received great support from my friends and family. I have the education I need and the motivation to succeed.")
- What is your intention in reading this book?
- What is your intention for the upcoming conversation you're going to have with someone who is important to you?
- What is your intention in your choice of food you eat? In your planned activities?

Exercise: Set a Daily Intention

Set an intention at the beginning of each day. Write it down and tape it to your computer, refrigerator, or wall—wherever you will be certain to see it. At the end of each day, note whether you fulfilled your intention and, if so, how it occurred.

Manifestation Tip: Never let your reality define your reality.

By this we mean never let what you can accomplish be defined or limited by your current reality. Let your reality be defined by your dream.

You may say to yourself: "I don't have the time it will take." "I don't have enough money." "I don't have the necessary skills." "I don't have the right partners." "I don't have the right location." "I'm not worthy." "I'm too old/young/fat/thin/weak/stupid." These are simply limiting beliefs, a set of conditions—they are not unchanging truths. Don't let them define you. Instead, let your *intention* define how you create your reality: "I can make time for this." "I can borrow the money." "I can learn the skills I need." "I can hire people to help me." These beliefs are empowering; they put you in charge of your reality.

Your intentions and your beliefs mutually shape each other. Henry Ford has been attributed with saying, "Whether you think you can or can't, you are usually right." Carefully examine your intentions and your beliefs; they're intimately linked to each other, as well as to your values, priorities, attitudes, and behaviors. All of these together create your experience of life and your ability to manifest your dreams. The more you put them under the microscope, the more you will become the master of your reality.

Further Reflections

There are many ways to open to the Divine coming through you. Circle the ones you intend to work with in the coming three months:

- Invoking—calling in the Divine and asking for guidance or support
- Praying—communicating with the Divine
- Meditating—spending time in emptiness
- Creating rituals and engaging in forms of worship
- Aligning with your highest virtues, values, morals, and ethics
- Discovering your life's purpose
- Asking big questions—"Who am I? What is life? Where am I going?"
- Setting clear intentions
- Studying and reflecting
- Asking others for support, guidance, or coaching
- Reading or listening to the words of great teachers and saints
- Getting involved in a faith-based or spiritual community

How can you tell if you're opening to the Divine? Use this list to gauge your progress:

- "I feel the presence of grace."
- "I hear guidance from someone or something outside of me."
- "I experienced a miracle, coincidence, or synchronicity."
- "I notice new ideas popping into my head."
- "I received sudden insights into long-standing problems or issues."
- "I connected with the right information at the right time."
- "I feel an increased sense of joy and lightness."
- "I have the sense of being on purpose."

Following is a list of ways you can increase the fertility of your mind so it's better prepared to receive and conceive of ideas. Circle ones you intend to use in the coming three months:

- Study a new subject.
- Expose yourself to things that are new and different.
- Use something you're familiar with in a new way.
- Open yourself to new people and find out what they know.
- Engage in some kind of artistic expression.
- Do something out of character.
- Observe your thoughts.
- Question everything.
- Ask, "Who am I?"

Clearing Limiting Beliefs

Once you have stated an intention, you set in motion a set of organizing principles in your world. Your attention starts to focus, and the universe begins to seek ways to support you in your creation. You have already seen that an intention or new creation will stimulate previous intentions to reassert themselves, creating natural resistance and obstacles, or crosscurrents. In Step 3 of the "Declare Your Intentions" exercise (page 39), we demonstrated that exaggeration of crosscurrents is one method of clearing them. It is a great exercise to use whenever you're confronted by an internal voice of doubt, fear, or criticism. But if you want to permanently rid yourself of the *cause* of those old voices, habits, and conditioning, you have to deal with your beliefs.

Beliefs lurk beneath the radar of your conscious mind and can sabotage even the best of intentions, motivations, and plans. No matter how hard you work on financial success, you may find that hidden costs pop up as soon as you earn more money. No matter how diligent you are at the dating game, you may find that you keep attracting the wrong kind of partner. Regardless of your commitment to lose weight, you may find yourself digging into a pint of ice cream as a way of comforting yourself after a bad day.

Beliefs are primary structures of consciousness, and they underlie all of our automatic behaviors. If some feeling, situation, or condition keeps appearing in your life, you can bet that there are limiting beliefs at work, undermining your best intentions.

What Are Beliefs? Where Do They Come From?

Most people think of beliefs as convictions, ideas, or propositions they hold as true about the world: "I believe in women's right to choose." "I believe taxes on the poor should be lowered." "I believe in God." In the manifestation process, however, we see beliefs as something much deeper. When we use the term *belief,* we're describing a deep and fundamental structure of consciousness—as fundamental as your bones are to the structure of your body. Beliefs are the building blocks of human experience, the Lego-blocks that construct your perceptions, emotions, thoughts, and experience. They are akin to your computer's operating system, the core programs that enable the rest of your applications to run—in this case, your thinking, emotions, and behavior.

It is commonly said, "Your beliefs create your experiences." In our research and exploration, we have found this to be literally true. The experiences you have in life are aligned with your beliefs about yourself, others, and the world. When you change your beliefs, your experiences change. You can prove this to yourself right now: Take a moment now and feel what it feels like to hold the belief, "There's something wrong with me." Take this belief on as if it were 100 percent true. Say it to yourself and feel what it feels like to believe it. If you're like most people, you'll feel something very unpleasant inside yourself. Now throw that belief away and take on a different belief: "I appreciate the good person I am." Again, feel what it feels like to believe that statement with 100 percent conviction. You probably noticed that the feelings are much more pleasant than those you felt with the first belief. You were able to consciously shift your beliefs—and your experience—in a matter of seconds.

Why don't we manage our beliefs all the time? For two reasons: First, most of your beliefs and old programs lie at the core of your psyche, deep in the subconscious mind. They operate below your conscious awareness. You have tens of thousands of beliefs programmed into you by the time you finish school. The second reason that most people don't manage their beliefs is because their parents and teachers didn't understand their own belief structures, nor did their parents' and teachers' parents and teachers. Since the beginning of human consciousness, people have lived inside their own belief structure. It has only been in the past few decades that we've learned enough to teach people how to consciously change their beliefs. This is the cutting edge of human psychological and spiritual development.

A particular belief can have a negative, positive, or neutral affect on your experience. A negatively charged belief (e.g., "I'm stupid. I'll never succeed.") limits your possibilities and creates uncomfortable feelings. A positively charged belief (e.g., "I can accomplish anything I set my mind to.") opens possibilities and empowers possibilities. Neutral beliefs (e.g., "That is a cat." "It's raining outside.") are simply statements of fact; they have no particular effect on your experience. When you can identify negative and limiting beliefs and replace them with positive, empowering beliefs, the past will no longer limit your future. You will have an open space in which to create your dream.

Let's start by examining where your beliefs come from and how they operate. On that foundation, we'll then teach you a powerful method for shifting the beliefs that no longer serve you.

Indoctrination and Socialization

As an infant, you had no choice but to adopt the beliefs of your parents, caretakers, and elders. This built-in evolutionary mechanism helped you survive in a dangerous, uncertain world. Humans are social creatures, and your survival as a child depended on you being cared for by your family, your group, and your community. The more you adapted to those around you, the better your chances for survival. In the ancient past, if individuals were too different from the group, they were banished—pushed out of the community—which was the equivalent of a death sentence. Thus, at the deepest psychological level, belonging to the group and believing what your elders believe is a matter of life or death.

You got your first sense of life and began to accumulate beliefs while you were in the womb. Your body grew inside your mother's electrochemical field. You felt and sensed her emotional state. If she lived in fear and produced stress hormones, you were bathed in those chemicals. Because you didn't have words or language yet, your "beliefs" were body-based sensations, reactions, and feelings: "I am safe," or "I am not safe." "I am wanted," or "I am not wanted."

After you were pushed out of the relative safety of the womb and into the bright and dangerous world, your number one job was to survive. Infants are like tiny scientists trying to figure out a new world. They observe their parents to determine what will please them. The limbic system—the brain's emotional center—relaxes and signals, "All is well," when it feels safety, harmony, and connection with caretakers. When it feels the opposite—danger, disharmony, or disconnection—it fires off an alarm that feels like anxiety, fear, panic, or terror. These feelings depend on two things: what's actually happening and what the psyche *believes* is happening. Beliefs are at the core of our emotional responses.

At birth, your brain contains millions of *mirror neurons,* which enable you to observe, sense, and reproduce what you see around you. Mommy smiled down at you, and you mirrored the smile back. This ability is a significant factor in learning, but it also functions to program our belief structure. We see Mommy afraid of lightning and thunder, so we feel her feelings as our own and reproduce her fear as our own.

You observed your parents' accumulated experiences and came to conclusions: "When I cry, someone comes to care for me. When I laugh, I get positive attention." These early experiences formed more beliefs. They were nonverbal, somatic experiences that organized your behavior. They were the way you figured out the world, step-by-step. Your internal structures of consciousness were formed one belief at a time.

As your brain and nervous system grew and matured, your parents and caretakers loaded you with even more beliefs: "What a darling little girl." "Her name is Sandra." "She is so cute!" Your subconscious mind acted like a recording device in this early stage of development, receiving input, layer upon layer, as you learned about the world. The programs met no resistance, because you had nothing to compare them to: "I am a darling little girl. My name is Sandra. I am cute."

Historically, babies were seen as empty containers to be filled rather than as complete, whole, growing human beings. It was your parents' job to teach you what you needed to learn. They wanted you to survive, so they taught you what they believed was right and wrong: "Don't put that in your mouth—it's dirty!" "What a mess you've made!" "Good girl!" "Bad boy!" "Stop that!" "What's the matter with you?" As you grew, you were taught, via rewards and punishments, how to perform according to your parents' expectations: "Here's how to do it." "No, that's wrong." "Don't ever do that again!" "What a good boy you are."

Other beliefs streamed in from every direction. Your siblings taught you how to behave by controlling or manipulating you. Images and messages from radio and TV (the beliefs of our culture) were fed to you while you sat in your high chair. You learned to imitate speech and to name objects. (Language was a skill you eagerly wanted to master so you could communicate with those creatures upon whom you were dependent.) Every word, name, and label was another belief added to the pile. What we call *learning* is more like *programming*—a constant, relentless pressure to shape you into the mold of your culture. Everyone wanted to help you look, talk, and be like them. They generously helped you fit in by programming you with their beliefs.

Then you went to school. Another structured set of beliefs got laid in: "The doggie says bow-wow." "If you don't sit still, you'll get in trouble." "It's better to be smart than dumb." "Girls should be nice." "If you want to speak, raise your hand." "Some animals are dangerous." "Pilgrims were good. Indians were bad."

If your parents brought you to their church, mosque, or synagogue, you were told what to believe about God, the world, and life: "This is what God is." "Bad people go to hell." "This is what's true." You were told to accept religious beliefs on faith and to never question them. In the not-too-distant past (and in some countries to this day), you could be tortured or killed if you questioned religious or political authorities. If you don't align with a group's beliefs, you get pushed out of the group, or ostracized. To the ego, this is a fate equivalent to death. It takes great courage—at any age—to question religious and cultural programming.

You were indoctrinated by people who loved you. *Indoctrinated* means that doctrines (beliefs) are installed into you, like applications on a computer. On top of all this early programming, you grew up inside an information-based culture. Advertisers programmed you with beliefs about products they wanted you to buy. Television, radio, magazines, billboards, and computer screens have fed you new beliefs during almost every waking moment:

- "Crime is rampant. Life is dangerous."
- "It's Good versus Evil out there, and Good always overcomes Evil."
- "Conflicts are best solved with fists or guns."
- "Buy this—and you'll be happy!"
- "If you use this product, you'll be sexy."
- "If you own one of these, others will see you as successful."
- "This pill will stop your pain and make everything wonderful."

It takes great courage and awareness to remain an independent thinker in the face of this torrent of indoctrination. To whatever extent you have been successful, congratulations!

Self-Created Beliefs

Not all beliefs are indoctrinated. Whenever you figure things out on your own and draw your own conclusions, you become your own source of indoctrination. You program your conclusions into your psyche as new beliefs. These beliefs are particularly strong because they're *your own.* They get planted deeply in the rich soil of your unconscious mind.

Self-installed beliefs can form in a variety of ways as we're growing up. When a child is traumatized, he or she needs to figure out what happened and prevent it from happening again. The conclusions that the child comes up with get deeply anchored. For example, a child might come to believe, "If I stay quiet and hidden, I won't get beaten." If you experienced any of the following extreme physical or emotional experiences as a child, you probably formed deep-set beliefs that are still affecting you:

- Loss of a beloved family member, friend, relative, or pet
- Physical or emotional invasion
- Excruciating or repeated pain
- Not getting the love or care needed to thrive
- Injury or illness
- Being abandoned, ignored, or left alone at times
- Physical, emotional, or sexual domination or abuse

Young children do not yet have the sophistication required to see their parents as flawed—after all, their parents are the gods who gave birth to them. Consequently, when their parents are the source of the traumatic experiences, most children conclude, "There's something wrong with me," and in addition, "I am not lovable" or "I'm not safe."

Children come up with explanations and beliefs to explain what is happening to them. Do any of these beliefs feel familiar?

- "Nobody likes me."
- "I don't belong."
- "If they really knew who I was, they wouldn't like me."

- "I'm all alone."
- "It's better to be pretty than smart."
- "If I do something wrong, they'll reject me."
- "If I look and act like them, I'll be accepted."

If you admired someone, you might have taken on their beliefs to be like them. If you didn't like someone, you might have taken on opposite beliefs to ensure that you were not like them, forming beliefs out of rebellion against them.

- "I want to look just like her when I grow up."
- "I'll never get angry and hurt people like he does."
- "If I'm smart, teachers will like me."
- "Being good at sports is important."
- "Needy people feel yucky, and nobody likes them."

As you grew from childhood to a young adult, depending on how you were raised, you found that you had your own will and could let go of some of your programming, replacing it with your own preferred beliefs, such as the following:

- "I don't believe in that God who looks like an old man with a beard."
- "Being a responsible adult sucks. I'm going to focus on having fun."
- "If I do well in school, I can go to a good college and have the kind of life I see on TV."
- "I don't care what my parents want me to do. I'm going to do it my way."

How Beliefs Accumulate

Every belief, whether indoctrinated by other people, by your culture, or by your own choice, settles into your open, impressionable mind, creating a structure that affects your experience. Beliefs clump together with other similar beliefs, forming masses that affect your perceptions. Beliefs act like colored lenses in front of your eyes. They filter out certain realities and let others in. Beliefs are always self-reinforcing. You see through them and find evidence for your beliefs all around you, regardless of what the belief is. This is what makes it difficult for humans to understand each other: "How could you even say that? Don't you see this evidence?" "No, the evidence you're offering is completely ridiculous. It was created by people with an agenda." If you've ever tried changing people who hold strong, fixed beliefs, you know that it's almost impossible. Your arguments only serve to harden their position.

As you grow and learn, your earlier beliefs get pushed down into your subconscious mind. With tens of thousands of beliefs accumulated over your lifetime, this collection has weight and density. You can feel it as limitation and lack, loneliness, or depression. It restricts your life and limits your possibilities. It can even affect your body—becoming slumped shoulders, bad posture, a permanently furrowed brow, or extra fat in all the wrong places.

When you look at the world, everything looks consistent, and most of it makes sense. Since you're not conscious of most of your beliefs, you can't question them. They are transparent to you. They sound like this: "That's just the way life is." "That's just how I am." "There's nothing I can do about it." Your accumulated beliefs interfere with the flow of your attention, until you are literally blinded by your own belief structures. When people's view of the world is so fixed that they see only what they believe and are closed to other points of view, we call them *fundamentalists*. They exist in every sector of society—social, political, economic, religious, and scientific. They all sound alike at one level: "Don't confuse me with facts. My mind is made up."

Your beliefs not only filter what you see and how you see the world; they also attract specific experiences to you. (This idea has been made popular as the Law of Attraction.) People who believe "I am a victim" easily attract victimizers—both by how they act and by the vibration they put out in the world. Perpetrators of crime seek out people who appear to be weak and afraid. Victims and perpetrators are thus naturally attracted to each other. This is not meant to blame victims, nor does it excuse or justify perpetrators. It is important, however, to understand what happens in the victim-victimizer dynamic that causes the pattern to reoccur: What you believe will be perceived as a reality, and it will become a reality in your life.

The more convinced you are about a particular belief, the more likely circumstances reinforcing that belief will appear in your life. If you strongly believe in angels, it is more likely that they will appear to you. If you believe in the power of a pill to heal you, you will more likely be healed by swallowing it. This connection, called the *placebo effect,* is well documented in medicine.

On the other hand, when you learn that beliefs are tools for creating particular experiences, and you find that you can switch them on or off depending on your circumstances, you won't experience the world in the same way over and over. People who stay open to possibilities have a wider range of experience than those who don't. Holding the point of view "Maybe it's true, and maybe it isn't" is a great way to stay flexible and responsive to the Universe's infinite flow.

The greatest leverage for moving yourself and your life forward is to examine and change your beliefs, as this is, we believe, one of the most significant opportunities to speed your personal development and your ability to manifest what you want. When you change the lens you're looking through, your world changes. New opportunities appear, and you attract a different set of experiences. If these changes alter your view of yourself, you may say, "I feel like a different person." And so you are.

If you don't manage your own beliefs, you automatically allow others to manage them for you—and there are plenty of people who are very happy to do so. They will tell you what to believe, what to do, what will make you happy, and what to buy to relieve your pain.

People who let go of old beliefs look and feel lighter, younger, and more open. They laugh more easily and enjoy more of life's abundant possibilities. The word *enlightenment* actually means "to lighten up."

Would you like to change a few beliefs?

Exercise: Belief Self-Diagnosis

This exercise will help you expose your subconscious beliefs to your conscious mind. At the end of the exercise, you'll choose a few limiting beliefs that you want to change.

Step 1: Uncover Your Beliefs

Contemplate each category that follows. Using a journal or a pad of paper, write down every belief you can think of within that category. Begin with the first category: "Myself." Say to yourself, "Something I believe about myself is . . . ," and write down the first things that come to mind. For example, "I am a good person," or "I'm a hard worker." Let your thoughts flow onto the paper as a stream of consciousness. When the next thought comes to mind—"I'm not a good person,"—write it down. Don't judge your beliefs, argue with them, or censor them. Just allow whatever comes up to be written down, even if it sounds absurd or strange. When your subconscious talks, it's a good time to listen. Give yourself many minutes to write freely on each question.

What I believe about . . . is:

- Myself
- My body
- My health
- My work
- My financial situation
- My sexuality
- My abilities
- My limitations
- My attitudes
- My soul, spirit, or spiritual self
- My circumstances
- God/Spirit/Source
- Money
- Handicaps/injuries/illnesses
- My family
- My relationships
- My government
- The world
- Good and evil
- Truth
- Life
- The past
- The future
- My beliefs

Repeat the process with as many of the categories as you can in one sitting. Then come back and explore the remaining categories as soon as possible, so you don't lose momentum.

Step 2: Understand Your Beliefs

Review the beliefs you've written on your list. Circle five to ten that have the most *negative* charge for you—that is, the beliefs that most interfere with your life. For each circled belief, write down answers to the following questions:

- How has this belief interfered with your life or limited you?
- Was this belief *indoctrinated* into you? If so, by whom? Did you ever consciously *choose* to believe it? If so, when? And why?
- What has been the *advantage* of having this belief? How has it served you? What did you get or gain by having this belief? What did you avoid by having this belief?
- What would be different in your life if you held a different belief about this subject?
- Are you willing to change this belief and replace it with a different belief?
- Who would you be if you didn't have this belief?

After you've answered these questions about the beliefs you circled, pick the *three* beliefs you would most like to change. Write them down on a separate piece of paper; you'll use this page in both the next step and the next exercise, "The Belief Process" (page 70).

Step 3: Create New Beliefs

When you delete an old belief, you create space—a sense of openness, a new possibility. You then have an opportunity to install a new, more empowering belief in its place. If you don't fill the space with something new, the old belief may creep back in.

Look at the first of the three beliefs on your list. On the same piece of paper, write some potential replacement beliefs. What would be a more beneficial belief? What would you like to believe instead?

A good place to start is the opposite of your current belief, but don't stop there. You can enhance your new belief so that it feels very supportive and positive in your body, mind, and spirit. For example, if your old belief is "There's something wrong with me," you could replace it with "There's something right with me." That belief is better, but it's not really empowering. If you push it all the way up the scale of good feelings, you might come to "I am amazing!" or "I shine with my unique and perfect light." Can you feel the difference? Go for that "wow" feeling.

Here's another example: If you hold the old belief "I am not loved," you could replace it with "I am loved," which is a good belief to have. But try "I am a beacon of love" and see how it feels to hold that belief. Since you now have the ability to choose the beliefs you want, you might as well find the most empowering beliefs that you can create.

Every belief produces a specific feeling and experience. Ask yourself what feeling you would like to have about this topic. Imagine having that feeling right now. Now ask yourself, "What belief would create that feeling?" This is another way of getting to the belief that's right for you.

You'll soon have an opportunity to try on your new beliefs. You can always make improvements later, tailoring your beliefs to fit your new life perfectly. Do the best you can right now. You've been living with those old beliefs for decades; creating new beliefs is a skill that improves with practice.

Exercise: The Belief Process

Deleting old beliefs and planting new ones is similar to planting a garden. Before you plant seeds, you clear the ground to remove weeds, stones, and dead plants. You clear space for something new. If you've ever used affirmations, then you have experienced the effect of trying to plant new beliefs on top of old ones. Saying affirmations makes you feel better for a while, but it doesn't seem to have any permanent impact. As we showed earlier, declaring something new will automatically cause what is already there to reassert itself, and this is especially true of former beliefs. That's why it's important to eliminate your old beliefs first. When you plant your new belief in cleared ground, it can flourish and grow without resistance or interference.

This exercise provides a small taste of Lion's BeliefCloset Process, which was developed to transform beliefs at the psyche's deepest layer. It is an in-depth process conducted by a trained BeliefCloset facilitator, and it's been proven effective in permanently clearing old beliefs. Find out more at TransformYourBeliefs.com.

The following process uses the power of your imagination to eliminate old beliefs. Read each step, then close your eyes and visualize what you just read. Then slowly open your eyes and read the next paragraph, following this pattern through all the steps. Have the page with your three old beliefs and three replacement beliefs nearby. You'll use the first pair in this exercise. You'll use the next two when you repeat the exercise later.

Step 1: Journey to the Center

Close your eyes and enter a deep state of awareness, deepening your breath. Imagine yourself walking through the woods and coming to a beautiful, open meadow. In the center of the meadow, you see a circle of stones marking a sacred ceremonial site. Inside the stone circle, you see a fire burning and, next to the fire, a full-length mirror in an ornate frame. With reverence, you approach the circle. You see an entrance, and you notice a wooden plaque with lettering carved deeply into the wood. The sign says, "Welcome. Here, Beliefs Are Made Visible."

Step 2: Feel the Limitation of the Old Belief

Recognize that this outfit represents one of your beliefs about yourself. Take note of how it feels. How does it fit? Is it comfortable? You know that you could spend time with this belief outfit, but you have come for a different purpose: to rid yourself of some old beliefs. So take off the outfit and set it aside.

Remember the first belief you wanted to get rid of. (At this point, if you don't remember the belief, open your eyes and read it aloud to yourself, then close your eyes and continue.) Say the belief out loud as if it were true, and feel what it feels like to hold that belief. Check the sensations and feelings in your body and recognize how this belief has limited you. Is this feeling familiar?

When you're ready, look into the mirror. Notice that another outfit of clothing has appeared—one that represents this belief. It could look like anything—from normal clothes to rags to a costume from a play to a physical object. Accept whatever shows up. This is the way your subconscious mind has chosen to represent your belief. Note to yourself what this belief outfit looks like, how it fits, and how it feels on your body.

Step 3: Release the Old Belief

It's now time to make a conscious decision about this belief. Is this a belief you want to have in your life, even though it's not beneficial? Or are you truly ready to let go of this belief?

If you're ready to let it go, take off the outfit—making sure that it comes off completely—and let it fall to the ground. Take a step away from it, and notice what it feels like to no longer have it on your body. You may experience a feeling of relief, lightness, or freedom, but feelings of insecurity or fear can also arise.

When you're ready, pick up the belief outfit in your hands and say the following words out loud, slowly, and with honor, to the belief: "Thank you for having served me in my life. [Pause.] I've outgrown you, and I don't need you anymore. [Pause.] Your job is done. [Pause.] I'm now sending you back to the nothingness from which you came." These ritual words are an important declaration that lets your subconscious know that you are formally letting go of this belief. Add any other statements you wish to make to this belief outfit.

When you're ready, walk over to the fire and place the belief outfit into the fire. Watch it burn until it's completely gone, until nothing is left, not even ashes or smoke. Feel what it feels like to have this belief completely gone from your life. Breathe deeply into the space you've just created.

Step 4: Feel the Possibility of the New Belief

You now have space in which to create a new belief. What would you like to replace the old belief with? Begin with the replacement belief you wrote down. Say it to yourself and see if it feels right for you. Can you make it even more empowering, more comprehensive, or more glorious? It should also be concise—as few words as possible—so that it conveys the idea with power and certainty. Continue to hone it, trying out each version, until you find the belief that really sings and makes you feel wonderful.

State this new belief out loud and feel what it feels like to hold this belief. When you can really feel it inside you and its impact on your life, walk back to the mirror and look at yourself. Your subconscious will have created a new outfit to represent this new belief. Accept whatever shows up. Note the details of the outfit and how it feels on your body. Soak your cells in this feeling and recognize how it will affect your life.

Step 5: Return from the Journey

It's time to make another conscious decision: Do you want to keep this new belief? If so, take a moment to really own it and make it yours. Walk or dance around in it, feeling how good it feels. How will this new belief and this new feeling change your life? Whenever you're in a situation in which this belief or feeling would be useful, remember this outfit and imagine yourself wearing it—the feeling will come back instantly. If you don't want to keep this new belief, decide what belief you would prefer to have regarding this topic. You may have to work with the wording. Keep crafting it until you feel that the belief is just right for you and for your life.

Get ready to leave this ceremonial circle and return home. Look around the circle and recognize that this is a holy place. You can return any time to eliminate beliefs you no longer need and to create new empowering beliefs for your life.

When you're ready, walk toward the entrance of the circle. Before leaving, express your gratitude to the powers that created this magical circle. Then make your way out of the circle, recognizing that you are still wearing your new belief outfit. Enjoy the journey back to where your body is located. Feel yourself wearing your new belief outfit. Before you open your eyes, feel what it feels like to have this new belief in your life. Open your eyes and take a walk, still feeling your new belief outfit around you.

Repeat the exercise later with the other two beliefs you identified. You can use this process as often as you like. We suggest using it every day, replacing one old belief with one new one. One of our workshop students replaced two hundred beliefs in a month, and he reported that he felt like a new person. The blocks and barriers that used to stop his forward progress had simply disappeared. He hardly recognized himself. He continued to enjoy success and happiness from that point forward. Enjoy the process and the impact your new belief wardrobe will have on your life.

———————————————

Chakra Six:
Vision Vitalizes

The only thing worse than being blind
is having sight but no vision.

—Helen Keller

Black Rock City is as close to the middle of nowhere as you can get and still drive a vehicle. Springing to life for only a week each year, this mind-blowing city of more than fifty thousand people is a defiance of all probability and a testament to human possibility. For many days, a parade of trucks, cars, and RVs winds up the Nevada desert highway, each one loaded with carpets, sofas, generators, bicycles, costumes, and enough food and water for each passenger to survive for a week in extreme heat, cold, and dust—all to take part in a collective social experiment in mass creativity. It is arguably the richest concentration of human imagination held anywhere on the planet. And it's as ephemeral as the shifting sand.

For eleven months a year, this flat playa, an ancient lake bed, is a desert without trees, water, electricity, cell phone reception, roads, or stores. But once a year, this rural outland births an urban city with daily newspapers and radio stations, a functioning postal system, public transportation, and more art and entertainment than you could possibly see in a week, even if you gave up sleep entirely.

The city functions on a "gift economy." Although people spend a fair amount of money on their costumes and art projects, once inside the gate, no money changes hands. Nothing is bought or sold between participants, with the exception of one specific location that provides coffee and ice. Instead, the goal is to offer as much as you can to make the city wonderful for everyone else. As a result, it is a land of teeming abundance, rich with color, creativity, and constant amazement.

Vehicles disguised as moving sculptures are the only motorized means of transportation; these "art cars" offer rides to anyone who wants one—although their destination is freely determined in the moment by the driver. Bike-repair stations, nightclubs with food and booze, yoga classes, massage sessions, movies, dance halls, interactive art exhibits, and much, much more can be enjoyed free of charge. To get around this semicircular city, which is nearly four miles across, you walk, ride a bike, or jump on an art car and go wherever it happens to be going.

Every aspect of this city runs rampant with *imagination*. Most attendees dress in outrageous costumes of color and whimsy. Gaily decorated or disguised tents, RVs, trucks, vans, and cars make up the neighborhoods. Residents must transport everything they need to and from the site, even water and garbage. Attendees gather and share resources, forming "camps." Some bring enough water and fuel for a hot tub or even a swimming pool, which are made available to anyone who desires to get wet. Other camps create elaborate buildings, yurts, teepees, or pyramids. Some contain elaborate high-tech lighting, amplified music, and interactive experiences. Others have full-sized sofas, carpets, and pillows for lounging or taking a break from the chaotic and stimulating environment outside.

The focal point of the city's weeklong existence occurs Saturday night, when a wooden sculpture in the shape of a man, standing nearly eighty feet tall and loaded with fireworks, is ceremonially burned. Watching this dramatic inferno are the fifty thousand attendees in various states of attire, drumming, dancing, singing, praying, meditating, or gazing rapturously at the spectacle. Named for this conflagration, the festival is called Burning Man.

The express purpose of this event is Art, with a capital A. People come to offer, experience, and create art together. Many artists work all year long on their Burning Man art installations, even though those pieces may be burned to ashes at the end of the week, never to be seen again. Art installations can be enormous, such as the elaborate, several-story-high main temple, built anew each year. There are performances, light sculptures, sound experiences, 100-foot moving dragons, fire-breathing machines, political statements, and unusual doorways that lead to other worlds.

Burning Man is a playground of imagination. The creativity demonstrated everywhere in the city is beyond belief in terms of scale, originality, humor, and sheer volume. Virtually everywhere you look, at any moment of day or night, you see something unusual and creative that wouldn't happen in the "real" world. It is well worth enduring a week of dust and sweat just to recognize what is possible when all limits are removed. Burning Man is a life-changing experience for most who attend. It makes a mockery of the statement, "It can't be done."

Imagination is a necessary ingredient for creating on purpose. It is an important element of the sixth chakra and a crucial element of the manifestation process. Albert Einstein said, "Imagination is more important than knowledge." If that's true, then our culture is sorely out of balance, focused as it is on knowledge and information. The Industrial Revolution brought material prosperity to the masses by mass-producing objects that were exactly alike. This efficient production lowered the cost and sped the making of things, which, in turn, reduced prices. But at the same time, it reduced originality and craftsmanship. We have gained in convenience while losing our sense of magic and wonder. We have a plethora of information but little meaning. We have plenty of things but little purpose. We seem to have lost the ability to imagine a new and better world.

But all is not lost. Inside every human being, *including you,* lies an unlimited resource: the imagination. As we take the next step on our journey downward, we move from chakra seven to chakra six—the realm of imagination, visualization, dreams, and your vision for the future. Here, you *look* for your life purpose, *envision* your dreams in several areas of life, and *imagine* what life will be like when you fulfill your dreams.

Chakra Six

The core principle of manifestation at this level is that *vision vitalizes.* Your thoughts and beliefs are the starting points for the reality you want to create. The process of visioning gives shape and vitality to your conception. Through the active use of your imagination, you add color and form to your idea, bringing details to life. Just as an artist brings a portrait to life when he touches color to the canvas, your ideas will be embellished by each step you take forward on your path to fulfillment. When you act from your vision, rather than from what the world tells you is possible, your life becomes energized, and your vision becomes contagious to others. But to inspire others (which you'll do in the fifth chakra), you need to start with a clear vision.

Following are the steps for vitalizing your vision in the sixth chakra:

- Imagining possibilities
- Discovering your life purpose
- Dreaming *big* for your life
- Designing your vision vehicle
- Visualizing your path to fulfillment

Here in the sixth chakra, and all along the path, you'll notice that barriers, blocks, and obstacles come up. You will learn to see them for what they are and discover techniques to handle them, one by one. If you don't pay close attention to them and deal with them when they come up, you will surely trip over them later.

Have you ever put your hand to your forehead in the middle of a situation and asked, "What was I thinking?" At times like these, you should actually ask, "What was I *not seeing*?" When you're on the lookout for obstacles, you can take appropriate steps to clear them as they occur. When you have a set of tools for handling obstacles, creation becomes ecstasy.

Imagining Possibilities

Thinking and *imagining* are so closely knit together that it's sometimes difficult to distinguish between them. You drive down the highway and daydream. Your thoughts wander idly through images of your last vacation, and you think how badly you need another one. You remember an intimate encounter you had last night (or wish you had had), along with other secret longings. You begin with the skeleton of a thought and flesh out the details with your imagination—often without even knowing you're doing it. Creating on purpose uses this natural ability in a conscious way to embellish your intention through imaginative visualization.

Chakra six pertains to the element *light,* which is what enables you to see with your physical eyes. What you see becomes part of your memory. From the elements of your memory, you're able to fantasize about the future and imagine something new. Before you set out to design your own house, you look at many other houses. You take note of features you especially like in order to integrate them later into your design. You have memories of pleasant experiences, and you cobble those memories together to fantasize about future possibilities. This faculty operates largely below the conscious level, but in the manifestation process, we make it conscious. We pay attention to our fantasies and form them into specific dreams. We then use visualization to flesh out the details. It's easier to create what you want if you can see it clearly!

Chakra six is called the *Ajna*—or "command center"—chakra. This name may seem odd for such a receptive faculty as seeing and intuition, yet it's appropriate because the pictures you hold in your mind do command your reality.

Your inner imagination is like a stained glass window through which the light of consciousness shines on its way to manifestation. Visualize the sun shining its powerful light through that colored window. An image from the window will land on whatever surface lies in the sunlight's path. If the room is empty, the image that lands on the wall or floor will match the image on the window. If people, chairs, or other objects are in the way, the image on the wall or floor will be distorted. When we don't get what we imagine, it's for a similar reason—our vision, like the light coming through the window, hits obstacles on the way down.

Obstacles, blocks, and barriers can be *internal,* such as limiting beliefs or doubts, or they can be *external,* such as someone's negative response to your ideas or a lack of money required to launch your dream in the real-world economy. Likewise, having conflicting visions or competing commitments is like stacking stained glass windows on top of each other. The image that results is jumbled. If you don't concentrate on manifesting one thing at a time, your energy and attention will get diffused and ineffective.

In a perfect universe, you could probably create anything you wanted simply by imagining it. In the *Star Trek* series, the captain speaks into his computer to order tea, "English Breakfast, hot," and the tea suddenly appears, as if by magic. The Bible describes this type of creation: "And God said, 'Let there by light!' and there was light." When you're asleep and dreaming, the subconscious "imagines" something, and that something immediately appears, because the logical mind doesn't interfere with its creation. Flying through the air is effortless. Things and places change from one to another. There are no limitations when you're dreaming.

In real life, it doesn't quite happen that way, but the principle is similar. First, form a clear vision. Next, eliminate the obstacles that appear. Then, take one step forward at a time until your vision is manifested. Easy! Well, it sounds easy from here, but human life is complex. You have to look outside yourself to see where you're going, while also looking inside yourself to examine your thoughts and beliefs. Pictures in your mind's eye lure you toward your destination. Are those pictures real? Imagined? Purposeful? Intuitive? Are they illusory magnets—power, fame, fortune, or glory—that attract the ego? Or are they the whisperings of your soul, speaking of your life purpose fulfilled?

Ideas and thoughts are subtle, fleeting forms that appear in the realm of consciousness. Although thoughts are things, they are not very concrete things. You can't touch them, smell them, or hand them to another person. They can be realistic or fantastic, pleasant or nasty. They are quite private—and blessedly so. We should be grateful that our thoughts are not broadcast to others!

Manifestation begins as an idea and intention, guided by belief. To become real, it has to move from that lofty realm and begin its descent, down through the chakras. You can *think* of doing almost anything—flying to a distant planet, traveling through time, or hitting the lottery—but that doesn't mean it will (or can) happen. When you begin to bring your thoughts down toward reality, you discover challenges and obstacles that must be overcome. You have to become more specific with each step downward. Impossibilities get trimmed away, and infinite possibilities get reduced in number to more realistic probabilities. At the same time, details get fleshed out and embellished as a vision takes shape.

At the root of *imagination* is the word *image.* Imagination is thought of as the images or pictures we see inside our head. But other senses can be featured as well: sound, feelings, smell, touch, and taste. The bulk of our imagination is a visual movie playing on the screen of our mind. Carl Jung believed that image and soul were one and the same. If "information" is the beginning of creating *form inside,* then image is where that form starts to be shaped with specificity.

Henry Corbin, a French scholar of Islamic studies, coined the term *imaginal realm* in the mid-1900s. Corbin saw the imaginal realm as being distinct from the imaginary realm. What is imaginary is made up, but what is imaginal has a reality in another dimension. Just as thoughts and beliefs are things (ephemeral as they might be), that which descends into our heads through dreams, fantasies, and idle meanderings comes from a realm that exists between spirit and manifestation; they are thoughts gaining density and urges to be realized. There is a sense that something, somewhere, wants to come into being. Our intuition and imagination are like eyes that can perceive that something. We start by opening ourselves to receive the images, then we choose which ones we'll bring into the world. Giving birth to an idea is similar to bringing a child into the world. Children begin as an urge that leads to conception; then, after a long period of gestation, the birth happens, and thus begins the ecstatic joy of—and maddening responsibility for—that new life you've created.

The word *magi* originally referred to members of the Persian priest class. It came into use among the Greeks at the time of Herodotus, the Greek historian, in the mid-fifth century BCE. Magi were mediators between the spirit world and the world of manifestation. They were the magicians, the makers. At the birth of Jesus, three magi came from the east and brought the newborn king gifts of gold, frankincense, and myrrh. Despite this important role, however, magic itself was given a bad rap by later Christianity, because magicians are people who take creation into their own hands. To the early Christian authorities, all of creation was God's responsibility, and humans should never compete with God.

We see creation, or manifestation, as being *complementary* to the Divine's creation, not competing with it. It is an act of the highest worship, a co-creative process with the spiritual realm whereby we bring heaven to earth. Jesus himself was a master magician, and he demonstrated this process through his many miracles. He created sufficient loaves and fish out of scarcity in order to feed everyone who had gathered together. He was able to cause the instantaneous healing of wounds and diseases.

If an *idea* is the feminine form of the word for the Divine *(dea)* entering the core of the Self *(I)*, then *imagination* is where the *I* becomes a *mage,* or *magician*—one who creates a new world from the raw materials of the old. In the Tarot deck, the magician stands with four objects on his altar, representing the tools of earth, water, fire, and air. With these elements and the help of spirit, he creates a new reality. To implement our ideas, we make magic happen. The conception that occurred in chakra seven descends and begins to get flesh on its bones. We embellish our ideas through the use of our imagination.

Imagination is a very spacious realm. The constrictions and considerations of the social and physical worlds don't have much of an impact yet. But as we flesh out the details and our idea gains weight, the force of gravity starts to pull our thoughts down toward earth. But let's not go there too quickly, for the imaginal realm has its own special magic in the art of creation. Here, while we still have our freedom, the mind can play in ultimate creativity and expanded possibilities.

Magic is the art of manifestation. Or you could say it in reverse: The art of manifestation is a magical act. Magic occurs in the space *between* the worlds and has always been closely linked with mystery. In-between places are thresholds and edges, a bridge between what is in form and what is unformed. Like the mysterious realms of dawn and dusk, they are transitional places between light and dark; they are still undetermined and fluid. True creativity happens at the edges, in the realms of the unknown. It is no wonder that the magi attended Jesus's birth. His birth heralded a new era. New things come into being from in-between places.

In physics, *strange attractor* is a term from chaos theory that describes a hidden force that influences the creation of reality by forming a pattern in a chaotic system, much like a magnet beneath a piece of paper influences the shape of iron filings on top of the paper. You can't see the magnet directly, but you can see its effects. Strange attractors create patterns that are somewhat predictable and somewhat unpredictable. You don't know exactly where the magnetic force is going next, but over time you can see the general pattern.

The images you hold in your mind are like these strange attractors. They are invisible influences on the formation of your reality. They serve as a magnetic force, acting upon what is not yet determined, calling it into form in a particular configuration. The more you visualize your dream, the stronger that force becomes, pulling things, people, and events into shape and form.

The root of the word *make* is the Old English *macian,* which means "to fit or match." Making your dreams into reality is equivalent to fitting what *already is* to *what might be.* Your imagination and vision are the makers of reality at the sixth chakra, just as your beliefs created reality at the seventh chakra. The Crown chakra advised you to take control over your attention. The sixth chakra advises you to take control over the pictures you hold in your mind and to become a more conscious creator of those pictures. When you hold the picture that your body is overweight, the image helps create that reality. Holding an image of your debt creates more debt. Focusing repeatedly on your illness, pain, or problems invites more of the same.

Is it possible to avoid focusing on negative pictures without being in denial about the obstacles you really need to handle? Yes—by naming the obstacles, honoring their purpose, and clearing them in service to your vision. Don't deny that the obstacles exist, but give your dreams and vision more energy than you give to your obstacles. (Later in this chapter, we'll say more about sixth chakra obstacles and how to overcome them.) Don't let your reality define your reality. Let your possibilities define it!

If you set an intention to sail your boat to a specific beach on the other side of a large lake, you first look at a map to pinpoint the beach's location in relation to where you are now. Then you look around and compare the map with the territory, looking for that big rock outcropping, the white sand dunes, or other landmarks along the way. If the distance is too far for you to see to the other side, you may rely on navigation equipment, but you first have to be looking at *something*.

As you sail across the lake, you make many turns, depending on how the wind is blowing. Each turn is determined by your destination. You keep a line of sight on where you're going. You don't have to stare at it every minute; you're free to enjoy the scenery, look down at your fishing rod, or talk to your fellow passengers. But you must look at your goal often enough to keep yourself on track. If your boat springs a leak, you have to deal with it, but then you refocus on your destination. You need to be conscious of your obstacles and problems, while keeping your *intention* and *attention* fixed on the vision of what you want to create—in its fullest glory—in order to stay on the path toward its manifestation.

Discovering Your Life Purpose

Your vision will become clear only when you can look into your own heart. Who looks outside, dreams; who looks inside, awakens.

—Carl Jung

When you were born, a new, unique, and precious spark of light was brought into the world. Your light had its own special qualities, and it had a particular purpose for entering this human realm. Your life purpose was a birthday present from the Universe—a unique gift to you. What is the purpose you came here for?

If you knew the purpose of your life, you would be happy fulfilling it. You would live and act in alignment with your highest Self, with your soul. We use the term *soul* as a name for the part of you that evolves—perhaps over many lifetimes. You don't have to believe in the existence of souls or in reincarnation to consider these ideas. There is some part of you—beyond your conscious awareness—that knows who you are and knows your purpose. We refer to that aspect of you as your soul.

Your soul values progress and learning, and it gently guides you forward toward manifesting the purpose you were born to fulfill. Your ego, or personality, is the part of you that gives your soul form. It has an equally important job, enabling you to survive by making distinctions, putting things into categories, and judging things as good or bad, right or wrong, safe or dangerous. It values anything that enhances your survival, including belonging, status, pleasure, and safety. Even though many spiritual traditions instruct us to transcend our ego, the ego plays an important role as the reflection of our worldly Self.

Your soul doesn't make distinctions or judge experiences as good or bad. It is concerned primarily with your progress, and it knows that seemingly bad or unpleasant experiences can be great sources of learning and progress.

There are many good reasons for getting to know your life purpose. The most obvious becomes apparent at the end of your life. Imagine yourself lying on your deathbed, having lived to a ripe old age. As you look back, can you say that you fulfilled your purpose for being here? If you can, you'll feel satisfied and whole. If you can't, you may feel regret or remorse.

Another good reason for discovering your purpose is that when you are living in alignment with your purpose, the wind is at your back. When your actions are purposeful, grace happens. You feel passionate and whole, heartful and happy. Coincidences occur that encourage your progress, and there's magic in the air. You can accomplish anything with intention and determination, but when you're moving in a purposeful direction, your forward momentum is easier, and your progress requires less uphill struggle.

Exercise: Discover Your Life Purpose

Your life purpose has always been with you as your soul's intention. But for most people, this purpose remains hidden, foggy, and difficult to see. A lucky few know their purpose from a young age, but such people are rare. Most of us have to develop ourselves before our purpose emerges. It usually reveals itself when we're in our late forties or fifties, after the ego has gotten a chance to get most of what it needs. But regardless of your current age, you can get a glimpse of your purpose, which will help guide you on your path.

Step 1: Track Your Purpose

Tracking your purpose is similar to tracking an animal in the wild. Imagine you are a photographer, trying to take the perfect photo of a black panther. You know that it is shy and rarely seen. It hides, nearly invisible; so you need the skills of stealth, heightened awareness, and great patience to find it. You look for clues as you walk through its jungle habitat. You find a tuft of fur here and a bit of scat there. In moist soil, you find a few paw prints, so you know you're on the right track. You put the clues together and carefully follow them. And then you catch a glimpse. There's a movement in the brush, like a ghost. You are close to your treasured goal—the perfect photograph.

Here's how to track your life purpose: First, walk through your memories, searching for clues that your soul has left along the way. Your first clue may have been given by Joseph Campbell when he said, "Follow your bliss." Whenever you're "on purpose," you feel wonderfully alive, full of spark and spirit. You feel turned on, passionate about life, centered, and inspired.

Remember back to your childhood, when your connection to Source was strong. Think of times when you felt most alive, most happy, most satisfied, and most excited. Write a brief summary of each incident you can remember. Here's an example: "At age five, I was playing with three friends from my neighborhood. I played the role of captain of a ship and started giving orders. 'Raise that sail! Tote that barge!' They did as I said, and I felt exhilaration rush through my whole body."

Take time to write down five or more incidents. Then move forward into your teenage years. Again, describe five or more times when you felt that perfect flow state. Do the same with your early adulthood and later adulthood. Certain experiences are universal highs, including falling in love, being in nature, experiencing sexual pleasure, and having a child. Although precious, these are not unique to you. Enjoy your memories of these experiences, but don't include them in this exercise.

You should end up with ten or more incidents in which you felt alive, happy, satisfied, and excited. What were you doing? Who were you with? What were the circumstances?

Step 2: Find the Patterns

The next step is to seek patterns and commonalities among the incidents. Pattern detection is difficult when you're standing inside the pattern; it's easier to detect patterns from an objective viewpoint. Therefore, it's easiest to do this step with a partner. Enroll a friend and do the exercise together. If you're doing this step alone, look at your collection of memories as if they belonged to someone else.

Answer these questions as you look at your collection:

- What activities were common across some (or most) of the incidents?
- How were you serving others in these situations?

- How did the condition of people or the environment change as a result?
- What was it about these particular experiences that made you so happy?

We call this step "divining" your life purpose, because it's inexact. A diviner walks the land with a Y-shaped stick to find underground water. Divining is an approximate and indirect method of locating water, but it often results in a good place to drill a well. Here, you're sniffing out your purpose by looking at the results of being in alignment with your purpose, rather than looking at your purpose directly. Other methods of purpose divination include journaling, imagination exercises, guided imagery, and asking for purpose information through your dreams. All of these methods allow your subconscious to speak.

David Fabricius, founder of the Agoge Training and Men of the Code (menofthecode.com), teaches that you can uncover your life purpose when you look for the confluence of five forces:

- Your birth gifts and genetic blessings
- Your enduring passions
- Your frustrations, life wounds, and regrets
- The wants, needs, and desires of others
- Source, Great Mystery, and Spirit

You were born with specific gifts—qualities such as physical prowess, intellectual curiosity, emotional range, sensitivity to others, spiritual insight, musical genius, mathematical understanding, creativity, or artistic expression. These gifts are linked to your purpose or the manifestation of your purpose.

You've also had enduring passions that have been with you since childhood. You may be extraordinarily passionate about sports, fashion, learning, helping the poor, rescuing animals, being in nature, collecting, leading others, or starting enterprises. These early and consistent passions are another clue to your life purpose. They are likely linked to your purpose if they first appeared in childhood and you never outgrew them.

Your frustrations and regrets are also clues that point to your unfulfilled purpose. What would you regret *not doing* if your life ended a year from now? What problem have you always wanted to solve but haven't been able to? Your life wounds have also prepared you in some way for serving others. Your responses to those wounds have given you abilities and skills you will need in order to fulfill your life purpose. All of these are clues that when put together, can lead you to uncover your life purpose.

We all need to earn a living in the world. If you can turn your life purpose into a way to make a living, you'll be fulfilled doing it. Look carefully at the wants and needs of others; almost all businesses are based on providing a product or service that answers the wants or needs of a group of people. Determine how your purpose fits with other people's needs, and you can earn an income by serving those people.

The fifth, and perhaps most important, element is Source, or Great Spirit, the force of the Divine that moves through us all. To discover your life purpose, you have to go beyond your ego, which wants you to be safe and secure. Your ego tends to turn you away from your purpose, which might be dangerous to your reputation or look ridiculous in the eyes of others. A big life purpose would threaten the part of you that needs to stay small. At some point in the process of purpose hunting, you must connect with the larger force of Spirit, which has its own designs for your life. When you open to grace, magic can happen.

Make a list, using all five categories, and look for crossover areas where all five are aligned. There's a good chance that your purpose is lurking there, ready to be uncovered.

Step 3: Identify Your Life Purpose Category

As unique as a life purpose is to each individual, we have noticed that life purposes fit into general categories. Using the tracking you've already done, compare the patterns you've discovered to the categories that follow. Circle words that excite you, that make you feel fully alive, that entice you, and that you do naturally, regardless of what else is happening. You may also notice that some categories appear often in your life as opportunities to serve others or the world.

- Teaching / Learning / Knowledge / Inspiring others
- Creativity / Art / Craft / Making beauty
- Healing / Medicine / Mending the body or mind / Therapy
- Awakening / Spiritual growth / Personal growth / Evolution
- Supporting others / Helping / Assisting / Social work
- Loving / Nurturing / Feeding / Family care
- Giving birth / Mothering / Nurturing
- Fixing / Repairing things, people, or organizations / Cleaning / Restoring
- Building / Developing / Designing / Architecture / Engineering
- Nature / Environment / Earth-based traditions
- Entertaining / Fun / Performing / Play / Enjoyment / Theater
- Discovery / Exploration / Research / Experimenting
- Scouting / Exploring new territory / Journalism / Astronautics / Anthropology
- Defending / Protecting / Military / Warrior
- Control / Mastery / Management / Influence
- Leading / Business / Politics / Military / Public Service
- Variety / Exploring / Changing / Tasting

As you can see, your life purpose is what you do most naturally when you are operating from your highest virtues, values, and aspirations—your True Self. It reflects your innate gifts, develops them, and lets them shine. Life purposes can usually be stated simply. For example, "I open people to new possibilities." "I connect friends through nature." "I build structures for success." "I teach what I know so others can discover what they know." Life purpose is pointed toward *what,* rather than to *how.*

There are many different ways to fulfill your purpose. After you've identified your life purpose, you're ready to move into the realm of your dreams. We make an important distinction among *dreams, visions,* and *goals*—terms that are sometimes used interchangeably. Your dreams are an answer to the question, "How do I want my life to be?" If your dreams are in alignment with your purpose, then you will fulfill your purpose by bringing your dreams into reality. If your life purpose is, "I bring laughter into the world," you might dream of being a stand-up comedian, a producer of comedy films, a joke writer, or a circus clown. If your life purpose is, "I create beauty," you might dream of being a successful painter, pianist, hairdresser, or interior designer.

When your dreams are in alignment with your life purpose, the universe will support you through miracles, coincidences, offerings, lessons, and meeting the right people. As you will learn in the "Dream Up Your Ideal Life" exercise (page 92), you have a vocational dream, a financial dream, a relationship and family dream, a health and fitness dream. In each area, you can define how you want life to be.

Furthering one dream usually furthers others as well. Your dream relationship might be one in which you work together with a partner in your dream career, serving your community. Your financial dream might be the way you fund your philanthropic activities and support your family. Your personal growth dream will support your relationship and family life, and it will certainly further your career.

We define your *vision* as the means to achieve your dream. It's the vehicle through which your dream comes to life. If your life purpose is making people laugh and your dream is to be a comedian, your vision might be to open a nightclub, join an improvisation group, or create a television show. Any of these could become the vehicle that brings your dream into manifestation. If your life purpose is to restore children to wholeness, your vision might be to manage an orphanage in India, become a pediatrician, be a foster parent, or become a child therapist. Your vision has a specific form more than your life purpose. It's the the vehicle that can take you where you want to go.

Dreaming Big for Your Life

Amazingly, most people spend more time planning their next vacation than they do planning the rest of their lives.

—Dave Ellis, *Creating Your Future*

As you take these steps through the sixth chakra, you will visualize your dream in alignment with your life purpose and manifested through the vehicle of your vision. Your vision may be big—or huge. It may take a long time to achieve. How can you possibly get there from here? Where do you start? It's important to dream big and then simply take one step at a time. As you move down through each chakra, you'll refine and condense your dreams into doable goals and action steps. We'll deal with goals and action steps extensively in the next chakra. But first, you need to dream. Allow yourself the room to envision a life that's ideal for you.

Exercise: Dream Up Your Ideal Life

A dream is not just something you can imagine; rather, it is something you would *love* to have in your life. A dream date. A dream relationship. A dream career. We dare you to dream big. The manifestation process will automatically whittle down your dream, so don't start small! Allow yourself the privilege of dreaming up a glorious life that fulfills all your fantasies.

Step 1: Contemplate Your Dream Life

Think about what dreams you have for your life in each of the following areas and write them down. Writing your thoughts on paper brings your ideas, visions, and dreams from the nonphysical realm of the mind to the physical realm of paper and pen. This is one of the most important steps in the manifestation process.

Contemplate your life in each of the following areas; then write down *how you want your life to be*. Take the time—right now—to envision and to dream. Write as much detail as possible about each area. The clearer your vision, the easier it is to manifest.

"I want my life to look and feel this way in the realm of my . . ."

- Primary relationship
- Family and children
- Money and finances

- Career and work
- Leisure, fun, recreation, play, and relaxation
- Body, health, and vitality
- Intellectual stimulation, learning, and growth
- Psychological growth and maturity
- Spiritual and religious life
- Social, political, and community involvement
- Artistic and creative expression
- Home, surroundings, and time in nature
- Service to others and making a difference

Step 2: Identify the Obstacles

List the obstacles and barriers that you believe are in the way of achieving each of your dreams. This list should include the reasons you haven't already accomplished those dreams (for example, not enough money, not enough knowledge, not enough time, someone prevented it, not smart enough) or the potential obstacles that you see ahead (such as: "I'll never get over my low self-esteem." "My old beliefs keep haunting me." "The circumstances will never be right." "It will be difficult."). Next to each dream, identify which specific obstacles are in the way of achieving it. Don't shortcut this part of the exercise; the more time you give to this part of the process, the easier it will be later to handle each obstacle and move it out of your way.

Step 3: Choose One Dream to Work On

Pick one dream from among all your dreams that you want to focus on manifesting as you work your way through this book. Choosing only one dream will enable you to learn and apply each technique and strategy with a singular focus. When you've accomplished that dream, you can go back and apply what you've learned to each of your other dreams, one by one.

Write the dream you have chosen at the end of the dream list you created in Step 1: *The dream I will manifest as I work through this book is . . .*

More About Obstacles and Barriers

The bigger your dream, the more obstacles you will encounter. Naming them is the first step in handling them. Obstacles come in two forms: internal and external. We've already talked about internal obstacles, which we called *resistance* or *crosscurrents*. These include limiting beliefs, self-doubts, self-criticism, judgments, and distractions. There are also social obstacles that go beyond your own internal world. These include limitations in your ability or knowledge, communication or relationship problems, or difficulties keeping commitments to yourself and others. We deal with social obstacles in subsequent chapters.

External obstacles include issues or conditions in the world that you didn't put in place; they are someone else's creation. For example, civic-minded bureaucrats and lawyers created building regulations to limit unbridled growth and to ensure the safety of residents. These regulations may certainly appear to be barriers, especially if you want to use a new, creative, and unregulated building technology, but they're just conditions you need to meet and deal with as you create your dream house. If you are hiking up a mountain and find bushes blocking your path, you wouldn't allow them to stop you. You would look for a way around or through them. The bushes are previous creations that happen to be in the way of your goal.

Every barrier or block has a way around or through it. You may have real limitations, such as a strict budget or a physical disability that prevents you from doing some activities. If you allow these "realities" to kill your dream, however, you haven't given yourself credit for the ability to come up with creative solutions.

Real-world conditions require work-arounds, negotiation, compromise, creative solutions, salesmanship, and, at times, some force applied in just the right way. You may need to raise money from investors or hire people to help you accomplish your goal, or you may need to enlist the help of friends to carry you over the finish line. This is where your positive attitude, ferocity, perseverance, and creativity come in handy.

In the upper chakras, the obstacles that appear are primarily internal. They take place in the realms of intention, beliefs, dreams, and vision.

Clear your intention by using Step 3 of the "Declare Your Intentions" exercise (page 39) to exaggerate your internal obstacles. When limiting beliefs come up, use "The Belief Process" exercise (page 70) to eliminate them. As we move down the chakras, we will provide you with additional techniques to handle obstacles at each level.

Designing Your Vision Vehicle

Vision without action is a daydream.
Action without vision is a nightmare.

—Anonymous

Now that you've dreamed big dreams for your life and opened yourself to the way you want life to be, it's time to bring those huge possibilities into a true *vision*. Your vision is the vehicle you use to fulfill your dream. You can dream of a vacation in Paris, with plenty of money so you can really live it up, but you need a set of vehicles to get you there. For your vacation, it will be a combination of planes, trains, and automobiles, as well as comfortable shoes! You picked a dream in the previous exercise. Now pick a vision that will fulfill that dream.

The final two exercises in this chapter will help you envision your vision. The first is a warm-up to get your imagination going. The second is a process of visualizing the end point of your dream—after you've accomplished it—and then remembering your way backward from the future to the present.

———————

Exercise: Six Impossible Things

Alice laughed. "There's no use trying," she said. "One can't believe impossible things."
"I daresay you haven't had much practice," said the Queen. "When I was your age, I always did it for half-an-hour a day. Why, sometimes I've believed as many as six impossible things before breakfast!"

—Lewis Carroll, *Through the Looking Glass*

This exercise is for awakening your imagination. Let your subconscious know you're going to have some fun. You'll be brainstorming at least twelve ways you can achieve your dream—six of them pure fantasy and six of them realistic. Start with the fantastic ones, as your creativity will be more fluid. Your ideas should at least make you chuckle. For example, you could imagine hitting the lottery with the numbers on your fortune cookie, being invited by space aliens to be an ambassador on another planet, or having your wedding on the moon. When you get to the more realistic ones, you could imagine opening a spa and retreat center, buying an airplane so you can travel easily, or having your own popular radio show.

After you do the brainstorming, rate your items on a scale of achievability, from one to twelve. Then choose the one that feels like the best vehicle for you—one that you can enjoy working on and that will lead to the achievement of your dream.

Manifestation Tip: Make it come true by seeing it through.

When traveling the path of manifestation, see your dream all the way through to the end and keep your vision on the goal. Every time you look at the dream within your mind, you strengthen the connection between the present moment and the fulfillment of your dream.

Visualizing Your Path to Fulfillment

After you've completed a trip across the country, you can trace your exact route on a map, showing each turn you made. The choices you made inevitably got you to your goal. When you began the journey, you may have planned an approximate route to follow, but there would be plenty of options going forward. "Should we take that smaller road, which will be more scenic or interesting? Or should we stay on the highway at that juncture, which will be faster but really boring?" "Should we stop in that town to shop and eat? What if someone tells us about a charming must-see attraction?" Once your trip is over, and you're looking backward, you will see that there was only one way you reached your destination—the way you chose. This is a trick known to sophisticated business planning experts: It's easy to remember your way back from the future, but it's very difficult to visualize the way forward, because there are too many choices along the way.

Enjoy this journey into your future, where your dream is fulfilled!

Exercise: Remember Your Way Back from the Future

Step 1: Now that your imagination is warmed up, close your eyes and go inside to your sacred center. Allow your breath to soften, slow down, and become even and deep. Gently relax in a comfortable sitting position.

Imagine roots at the base of your spine pushing down into the earth. Feel your whole body grounding into those roots. Let out a long exhale.

While keeping your roots pushing down, simultaneously lift your crown up, stretching the two ends of your chakra column in opposite directions simultaneously. Open your crown and allow yourself to align with your highest principles. Open to grace.

Bring your attention to your dream. Notice what images come to mind as you do so. What is the first image you see? Where are you? What are you doing? Who is there with you? What time of day is it? What season is it?

What attracts you about this image? Is this image an end point in your dream or a point along the way? Acknowledge what is important about this image.

If it is not an end point, then imagine a time and place in the future where you are experiencing the complete fulfillment of your dream. It could be walking down the aisle with your beloved, turning the key in the front door of your new house, making a deposit in the bank from your new business, or reading a newspaper article on how your dream has changed the lives of others.

See yourself at this point of fulfillment. How do you feel? What are you doing? What are you saying? Who is there with you—a friend, an audience, a community? Notice what time of day and season it is. See if you can perceive a date (it may not be apparent).

Allow your imagination to notice *all* of your senses, especially if visualizing is not your strong point. What are you feeling, hearing, sensing, or smelling? What does your body feel like? What are you wearing? How are you breathing? What are you thinking? Embellish this moment with as many details as possible, continuing to breathe slowly and deeply until your whole body feels immersed in this reality.

When you feel you have experienced the fullness of your dream in every sense possible, imagine a line of light, like a laser beam, between today's date and this point in the future. Imagine that the light cuts through all obstacles and charts a path of opportunity. Imagine yourself propelled forward in time along this beam of light until you reach the end point of your dream.

Say a word of gratitude for the fulfillment of your dream and bring the feeling in your body back to the room you are in now. Take a deep breath, open your eyes, and look around.

Take some time to write or draw in your journal any details that you would like to remember.

Step 2: After writing down as much as you can about your visualization, you are ready for the next step, which will help clarify your vehicle—that is, how you got there.

Return to your breath and a light meditative state. Imagine you are moving down that line of light from this present moment to your future end point again. Revisit the images you saw in Step 1. Then imagine turning around from this end point in the future and looking back toward what is currently the present. Look at the last thing you did before your dream was fulfilled. Soak yourself in that image—the feelings, your movements, the sounds, and any other sensations that were part of the end point.

Next, look at what you did right before your end point and really feel that experience on the time line. Notice how each action and activity led to the next action and the next activity, in a natural order. Then look successively at each point along the way, moving backward through time from your end point to the present moment of reading this book. Continue in this way, step by step, all the way back to the present moment. Look once again at the series and sequence of steps that led, logically and naturally, to the fulfillment of your dream.

When you're ready, come out of your meditative state. Write down the steps you saw yourself taking to get to your dream. These steps are the path your vehicle traveled to make it to that glorious end point.

These exercises and the writing you've just done will become more refined in the next chapter, where you will communicate your dream to others, integrate feedback you receive, and set specific goals that will move you inevitably forward toward your dream life.

Chakra Five:
Conversation Catalyzes

It is not what we learn in conversation that enriches us.
It is the elation that comes of swift contact with
tingling currents of thought.

—Agnes Repplier

Now that you have created your intention and brought it through consciousness in the seventh chakra and vitalized your intention into a vision in the sixth chakra, it's time to *communicate your dream to others.* The manifestation principle in the fifth chakra is *conversation catalyzes.* Although it is important to be clear about your vision and excited about its possibilities, now you must move it into the social world and speak about your vision effectively. The process of communication ignites sparks in others, who may get excited about your vision and offer help or advice. With feedback from others, your own clarity will be sharpened. Every time you communicate about your purpose and your dream, you get better at expressing what's most important to you. Whether you are writing advertising copy or a business plan, creating a proposal, giving a talk, or holding a meeting, good communication skills will amplify your ability to create on purpose.

At chakras six and seven, your dream is within you, taking shape. You can conceptualize, analyze, visualize, or imagine anything you like. There are no limits to consciousness. As long as your vision stays inside your head, there's no one to challenge you, criticize you, or steal your ideas. There's also no one to help you, nor can anyone offer suggestions, support, or feedback. You cannot bring your dream into reality from the upper chakras alone. When an idea remains in the imaginal realm and isn't brought down to grounded reality, it stays in fantasyland. A *fantasy* is simply a dream that hasn't been completed.

To move down from chakra six to chakra five, you must communicate your vision to others. As soon as you speak about your dream, you enter the social world of relationships. You are communicating *to someone*. It may be a friend, spouse, banker, coach, coworkers, potential clients, or investors. We'll deal with relationships in depth when we arrive at chakra four, the heart chakra. To maintain those relationships, you must be an excellent communicator, with skill and finesse, to inspire others and enroll them in helping you make your dream come true.

Chakra Five

An artist carries on throughout his life a mysterious,
uninterrupted conversation with his public.

—Maurice Chevalier

In this chapter, we look at many nuances of communication—both internal and external—and how to make it more effective. We examine the problems and blocks that occur at this chakra level and provide you with exercises to break through them. You'll learn about the power of storytelling and how to shape the story of your dream so you can optimize your impact on others. You'll also take a step down to the next level of reality, making your dream more doable by breaking it into smaller chunks—projects and goals—a theme that is repeated in upcoming chapters. The secret to getting great visions accomplished is to break big tasks into smaller and smaller bite-sized pieces so you can do one thing at a time.

In this chapter, you'll also learn the importance of keeping your word, both to yourself and to others. Many people do well when they're on their own but have difficulties managing projects or other people. We provide you with a framework for communicating effectively in a group setting, which is where most great things get accomplished. And we go into more depth about your inner voices and how to manage and benefit from the inevitable internal dialogue. Each of these fifth chakra elements is crucial to your success as you bring your life purpose, your dreams, and your intentions into the world. We'll follow these steps along the way:

- Telling your story
- Refining your mission through feedback
- Broadcasting your vision to others
- Setting goals to chart your course
- Turning inner voices into allies

These steps will help you master the fifth chakra challenge of communication—an essential element to successful manifestation! May all your conversations catalyze your dreams.

Telling Your Story

The Universe is made of stories, not of atoms.

—Muriel Rukeyser

Once upon a time, in a time before time, humans sat around the fire, warding off the darkness. On long winter nights, we told stories to keep ourselves connected to the past, to the future, and to each other. We told stories of how the world was created, why we were here, and where we were going. We told stories to our children, and they told stories to their children, on through countless generations. These stories have become real for us, and from this reality, we have created our world.

Today, we are seeking a new story about what our world could become and how we might create it together. Your dream is a part of that new story. What story do you want your grandchildren to tell about how you changed the world?

Stories have shaped civilizations; created religions, cultures, villages, and lives; and started and ended everything from wars to relationships.

They steer politics and policy. They lead to consumption of the planet and the potential of a new way. They are deeply embedded in our consciousness. They are teachers of meaning and morality. A good story can create a new world.

Consider the stories that have guided humanity since time began: the myth of a goddess's descent to the underworld, the myth of the virgin birth, the myth of the fairy goddess-mother who grants your every wish, the myth of the evil stepmother who wants you eliminated. We have myths of the Good King, the Wasteland, the Lost Grail, and the perfect love story of happily ever after. These may seem like tales from the distant past, but they describe the archetypal underpinnings of our collective psyche. Even now we are guided by myths, though they are subtler. We have the myth of the American dream, which says you can achieve anything you want; the myth of the good mother who nurtures her children perfectly; the myth of the hero who will save the world; and the myth that the goal of life is to accumulate as much money and power as possible.

Because we are storytelling creatures, the stories we take in become the basis for how we view ourselves and the world. They provide our motivation. They describe the journey from where we are now to where we are going, and they give us a picture of what we are becoming.

A good story needs good challenges—twists and turns, obstacles and disappointments. Difficulties develop character. When they happen to a civilization, they drive evolution. Hollywood producer Peter Guber said:

> There's a treasure trove to be discovered and it's inside you.
> Built into your DNA is humanity's 10,000-plus years of
> telling and listening to oral stories. . . . The business world
> has long ignored or belittled the power of oral narrative,
> preferring soulless PowerPoint slides, facts, figures, and data.
> But as the noise level of modern life has become a cacophony,
> the ability to tell a purposeful story that can truly be *heard*
> is increasingly in demand. . . . It's not the 0's and 1's of the
> digital revolution but the oohs and aahs of *telling to win* that

offers the best chance of overcoming fear—or compelling listeners to act on behalf of a worthy goal.[7]

Our world is longing for a new story about how to create our future. As you create your dream, you have a chance to contribute to this story. Consider the story that's guiding you in creating your dream. Is it the story of acquiring fame and fortune? Of pursuing a perfect love? Of fighting injustice, where you set a terrible wrong to right? Is it a mystery story with an ending unknown even to you, its author?

What stories have shaped your life, for better or worse? What were your challenges, and how did they shape your character? What story do you want to tell the world? What story guides your greatest desire, your dream for the world? Take time now to answer these questions in your journal—or at least write the questions so you can answer them later. Answering these questions begins an internal dialogue— perfect for the fifth chakra—that is a part of your story.

If you want to manifest something, you need a good story to support its manifestation. Tom Sawyer created a brilliant story—the privilege of being able to paint the fence—that inspired his friends to do his work for him. What story motivated you to create the particular dream you're working on now? Did it come from a childhood experience or trauma? What story would describe the full flowering of your dream's potential? How would you describe it to a person who will benefit from its manifestation in the future?

Storytelling is an act of creation and a function of the fifth chakra's aspect of communication. Your challenge is to create a compelling story that inspires others to support you, join with you, invest in you, and contribute to your cause.

Exercise: Tell Your Story

Step 1: Tell your life story to a friend. Find places or incidents where your energy, or "charge," becomes most alive. Notice the parts that reflect on or fulfill your life purpose.

Step 2: On another day, tell your life story from a fictional point of view. Make it symbolic of who you are by turning yourself into a hero on a quest. It begins, "Once upon a time, there was a . . ." What are the qualities of your character in this version of your life story?

Step 3: Every traditional story has a protagonist who valiantly attempts to accomplish something important and then meets obstacles that must be overcome. What have you been trying to accomplish, and what have been your obstacles? Who are your allies, and how will they help you as your story unfolds?

Step 4: Characters in a story have an arc of development, a trajectory in which they grow or mature in some way. Describe your arc. Where is it headed?

Step 5: Tell the story of creating your dream from your future—as if it has already happened. Describe how the world is different now, because your dream has been fulfilled, and what it took to accomplish it.

Refining Your Vision Through Feedback

As you enter the denser landscape of communication with other people, you encounter limitations. Some of the "anything goes" freedom of the upper chakras gets reduced by the hard realities of others' needs, desires, and positions. You have entered the territory of space and time, both of which are limited and both of which provide real limitations to what can be accomplished. In the social realm, everything is more challenging. And yet working through these limitations is great exercise, because it strengthens your commitment and brings more refinement and reality to your ideas. To sharpen a cutting tool, you must push it hard against something even harder. Similarly, you hone yourself and your dream on the whetstone of other people's realities.

Imagine that you have a dream of building your ideal house. You set your intention and envision it to be perfect—just the way you want it. You have developed a very clear picture of all the details in your mind.

But when you sit down to meet with your architect and communicate your vision to her, she may tell you that your vision is structurally impossible, or too expensive for your budget, or outside the building codes, or inappropriate for the chosen site. She also may have suggestions you hadn't thought of, such as changing the roofline to optimize solar heating, adding more windows for visual impact, using new building materials, or adding a water feature in the garden. Both positive and negative responses help you refine your dream, make it more specific, and bring it into better alignment with the world in which it will manifest.

At the fifth chakra, your dream hasn't made it all the way down to the physical world, so it's still easy to make changes to the idea and plan. Every person with whom you share your ideas will add refinement and possibilities, shaping it into a more realistic and exciting picture.

In systems theory, everything that's alive has four basic components that keep it growing and in balance: inputs, transformational processes, outputs, and feedback loops. Input is everything that comes into the system, and the transformational process is what happens to that input. Our food, water, air, and information are examples of inputs. Digestion and analysis are examples of transformational processes. Our output includes our work, our actions, and what we excrete. Feedback is the way we learn. Without feedback, a system either gets stuck doing what it has always done or goes off balance toward destruction. Think of your home heating system when your thermostat breaks. Depending on the thermostat's state when it broke, your house either gets colder and colder or hotter and hotter. Feedback is the mechanism that allows a system to find balance (homeostasis), change appropriately to the environment, and learn and evolve. In the manifestation process, opening yourself to feedback from others is crucial to your success. It can be one of the greatest catalysts for your personal evolution.

Communicating your vision to others elicits this kind of feedback, which will help you and your vision evolve. Students have asked us, "Shouldn't you keep your idea to yourself while it's in development?" Our answer is always the same: If you keep it to yourself, you're in danger of going off in the wrong direction. Feedback from others is crucial to making it more real. You don't have to implement every suggestion you hear, but you should consider everyone's opinion as potentially valuable. Even if you don't use a particular idea, it may stimulate other ideas. There are hidden gifts even in criticism and critique.

On the other hand, avoid sharing your dream with *dream killers*. These are people who say, "That's the most ridiculous thing I've ever heard! How could you even think you could do such a thing?" That kind of feedback can stop you in your tracks, especially when your dream is still new, tender, and unformed. However, if the feedback is negative but constructive, it can be extremely valuable: "There's a better way to go about this. Have you considered the possibility that you could do X instead? If you do, you'll save yourself a lot of time and money."

Sometimes the biggest dream killers are inside your own head. You might have an inner voice that says, "Nobody wants to hear about this," or "It's already been done," or "It's never been done, and what makes you think you can do it?" You may have beliefs about talking to others: "They're too busy. And besides, they're too important for a nobody like me." "I'm too small, too stupid, too old, too young, too inexperienced, too clumsy, too unattractive . . ." Do any of these voices sound familiar? These voices are just more crosscurrents. They can be cleared with the exercises we showed you earlier, such as "Declare Your Intentions" (page 37) or "The Belief Process" (page 70). You can also work with the voices themselves to see what they really have to say. Additional exercises in this chapter will help you express and integrate these voices.

As a first step, get clear on what you want to communicate. Sometimes you don't know what you think until you see what you've written.

Exercise: What Do You Want to Communicate?

Step 1: Journal on the following questions to clarify your dream and vision.

- What are the most important aspects of your vision that you want others to know? Why?
- What is the impression or impact you want to leave when you speak to someone about your dream?

- What feedback are you most afraid to hear from others? What is the most useful response you could hear?
- What action do you want others to take after they hear about your dream? How can you best ask them to take that action?

Step 2: Write a two- or three-paragraph "elevator pitch" about your dream. An elevator pitch is something that you could say to a crucial person, such as a venture capitalist, if you walked into an elevator with them and wanted to capture their interest between floors. You have their full attention for only ten or twenty seconds. What would you say to elicit the response, "Sounds interesting! Send me your business plan—here's my card"?

Manifestation Tip: Talk is cheap. Do lots of it!

The quickest way to manifest your dream is to talk about it to everyone you meet. Speaking about your dream, even to those who seem to have no connection to it, may elicit unexpected support.

Broadcasting Your Vision to Others

If you speak about your dream at a party, someone might say, "I know two people with expertise in that area who could help you," "A friend of mine just came back from Fiji and knows the island well," "I just spent time at my friend's incredible resort, and they're looking for programs like yours," "I know someone who has spent his life working in that field, and he's looking for a partner who can help him take it to the next level," or "I know the perfect agent/investor/editor/producer/retreat property/graphic designer/office worker/healer/single guy/gay woman . . ."

You can learn and master many essential fifth chakra skills, all of which will make you more effective in creating on purpose. As you talk about your dream to others, you want to incorporate these skills, such as connecting deeply to your own truth and authenticity, listening more empathetically, speaking from your heart, aligning with others energetically, marketing authentically, and enrolling others (which is called *sales* when you're disconnected from the person with whom you want to engage). In the pages that follow, we help you build some of these skills. For additional information on these skills, see Resources (page 261).

There are also many ways to broadcast your message electronically. People on Facebook and Twitter want to know what you're doing. Develop sound bites for your website and brochures. In the next chapter, we talk about creating a network. For now, practice telling your story and stating your dream in a way that enrolls other people's interest.

Setting Goals to Chart Your Course

Moving into chakra five also means refining your vision by breaking it down into smaller chunks: projects and goals. A project is a portion of your vision that you can complete in a reasonable amount of time. Achieving your full vision may take many years, but a project can be accomplished in two or three months. For example, the dream of building your ideal house can be broken down into subsets of these projects: (1) Find an architect and draw up preliminary plans, (2) present plans to the planning department and get tentative approval, (3) finalize blueprints and get them approved, (4) interview contractors and choose the best one. Each project is workable, as opposed to the big dream, which can feel unwieldy and overwhelming.

Goals are the basic unit of getting things done. A goal is much more specific than a dream or vision. It is a singular thing to be accomplished, and you know when you have accomplished it. Each project can be broken down into a set of goals. For example, the project "Interview contractors and choose the best one" can be divided into these goals:

1. Ask three friends who have used contractors for their recommendations—by March 1.

2. Do Internet research to find the top ten contractors in the city—by March 15.

3. Interview ten or more contractors by phone—by March 30.

4. Choose the top five contractors and interview them in person—by April 10.

5. Check county records on the top five contractors to make sure their records are clear—by April 20.

6. Choose the finalist, ask for references, and then check those references—by April 30.

The process of building your dream house may take two or three years to come to fruition. You'll know your dream is fulfilled once you've moved in, settled down, and felt that first "Ahhhh . . ." feeling. But when you break the dream into manageable projects, you can track your progress and feel good about each step.

Creating SMART Goals

Goals are solid, discrete, and specific in space and time. You know for sure whether a goal was accomplished. "I will lose some weight this year" is not a goal—it's a dream (or for some people, a fantasy!). "I will weigh 135 pounds on December 31" is a goal. On December 31, you can weigh yourself and know whether you achieved your goal. Each of your goals should be SMART:

- **Specific**
- **Measurable**
- **Attainable**
- **Realistic**
- **Time-based**

A complete goal includes a *what* (what the end result is), *when* (by when it will be accomplished), *who* (who is responsible for getting it completed or who will help you complete it), *where* (where it is to occur), *why* (the significance to you and your life and to others), and *how* (how it is to be accomplished).

There's a classic saying in business, which is also true about the process of manifestation: You can't manage what you don't measure. Measurement is crucial on the road to success, and a goal is measurable. You can see how far you've come and how far you have to go, and you can be certain whether you have accomplished it at any point along the way. If you haven't accomplished a goal, then there's more to do.

A good goal statement is both specific and significant. *Significance* describes the goal's relationship to your life purpose or dream. If a goal gets separated from your dream, it will feel like just another empty task you have to do. Remember the context—why is this goal important to you—and you'll be happy working on it. For example, "I will have my business plan completed and in the hands of the first investor by July 1" is a SMART goal. It is *specific* and *measurable*—meaning you will know whether it happened on July 1. It's *attainable*—unless you're starting it on June 15 (business plans take many months to complete). It's *realistic*—if you know how to write a business plan or if you have help from a professional. It's *time-based*—you have a specific amount of time in which to work and complete it.

As we said earlier, whenever you put a stake in the ground, it pulls you forward. You may have to move heaven and earth to reach your goal, shifting priorities and putting off things you'd rather be doing, but that's the power of setting a SMART goal. You can't fool yourself into believing you're making progress, but you also don't set yourself up for failure by being unrealistic. You can immediately see whether you are or you aren't making progress. It's a pragmatic wake-up call, telling your attention, "Hey! This is important! There's a deadline! Get to work!"

From SMART to SMARTER Goals

Some pundits have added an *ER* to the concept of SMART goals. The *E* stands for *Evaluating* and *Enthusiastic,* meaning that it's important to evaluate your progress periodically and make adjustments as necessary. And if you're not enthusiastic about your goal, you'll let it go as soon as it gets tough. This second *R* stands for *Resources* and *Rewards.* Resources are the money, time, information, and support you need to accomplish your goal. You also may need to make certain sacrifices in order to do so. Are you willing to give up that planned vacation or your social engagements so you can get done what you promised to do? The rewards are the goodies that come from accomplishing your goal. It may be the massage you've promised yourself if you get that document out the door or the sense of satisfaction (and short vacation) you get when it's done.

If you evaluate your goal and find that you need an adjustment, be sure to make your adjustments carefully. Your integrity is at stake here, and your changes will affect others. Don't let making adjustments become a way of slipping out of your responsibilities. Beware of accommodating sloppiness or sloth.

If your plan requires resources, be smart about it. Don't start spending money until you've secured the investment you need. Finding and securing investors is one of the most difficult and time-consuming tasks. Get support from wise elders who have already done something similar. Elders and professionals are valuable resources to tap into—perhaps the most important resource available to you.

When you're co-creating with others, it's very important that your collaborators agree on the specifics of each goal that you create together, including who will do what and by when. Then, agree to hold each other accountable. If you hire others, you can tell them what to do, but partners must create mutual agreements that work for all parties. We address broken agreements—the killer of co-creation—later in this chapter.

Exercise: The First Five Goals

Step 1: List at least five goals necessary to complete your vision. Make sure each goal is SMARTER, fulfilling all the requirements. Write each one as a declaration. The most powerful declarations begin with "I shall . . ." or "I will do whatever it takes to . . ." Writing your goals in this way helps you organize your thinking, adjust your priorities, and rally your commitment.

Step 2: Prioritize your goals by putting them in order of time. Which ones need to be done before the others can take place? Then, make a separate list, prioritizing your goals by putting them in order of importance to the fulfillment of your dream. Compare the two lists. What do you notice? Where will you begin? Choose one goal and begin taking steps toward its fulfillment.

Exercise: Get Feedback

With a partner, review your dreams and your goals. Ask your partner to help you define and refine your goals and to point out what you may not have seen. Have your partner ask you questions you haven't yet considered. Ask whether your partner is inspired by your dream and to give you any other kind of feedback you want. Be specific. For example, as we were writing this book together, one of us would share the draft with the other, saying, "This is still very rough. I don't want line editing, just a general reaction as to whether you find it interesting or whether it is understandable." If you're not clear about what feedback would feel helpful, you'll probably end up getting something else!

Skillful Communication

If you wish to be understood, seek first to understand.

—Stephen Covey

Conversation catalyzes. Through your words, you awaken and spread consciousness. You direct others' attention, you propagate your ideas, and you get things done. Through dialogue and conversation, you connect with another person, express your interior self, and meet the interior self of another. Clear communication is essential for manifestation. The bigger your dream, the more crucial clear communication becomes.

There are two types of communication:

- **Communication for Action:** Communicate to make things happen and get things done. This includes making requests, giving orders, negotiating deals, selling, enrolling, making promises, and implementing plans.

- **Communication for Intimacy:** Communicate to bring people closer together through speaking truth and listening deeply to others and to generate shared feelings. This includes expressing care, respect, welcome, interest, and intuition, as well as bonding through body language and tone of voice.

Because all creation is co-creation, co-creators must coordinate their actions through words. (In prehistoric times, this was likely done through pointing and grunting.) To *coordinate* means "to co-order" or "to put things in order." When you want to get something done, you need to coordinate the actions of many people.

Communication for Action

Communication for Action[8] is used extensively in business transactions. Business has come to dominate our economic environment in the same way that dinosaurs dominated our planet's physical environment for hundreds of millions of years. The reason is simple: Business is one of the most efficient and effective methods for getting things done. If you want to create a better life or a better planet, it's important to learn how business does things; then use those lessons to improve your effectiveness in the world. When people communicate to get things done, communication is a series of commitments that can be divided into four types:

- Requests—"I want a dozen roses."
- Promises—"I'll get them for you."
- Assertions or opinions—"That will be $22." "Gee, that's a lot for a dozen roses."
- Declarations, or assertions that carry vested authority— "My boss sets the price. I just sell them."

You already communicate in this way. When you call someone to make a date or an appointment, you engage in a negotiation—a series of requests and promises that end up with an agreement, a time and place to meet, and a mutual commitment. You've co-created a new future.

You now begin to shift your reality to accommodate your promise. You move some appointments and reschedule tentative plans so you can keep your commitment. You've begun to take action. But stuff happens, as it often does. You may be delayed by heavy traffic, or your car may break down. Something has prevented you from completing your promise as agreed (despite your good intentions). How you handle the breakdown makes all the difference. If you call and report the problem or breakdown as soon as possible, you preserve the trust in your relationship, and you can renegotiate the promise. If you don't communicate, your unkept promise makes you untrustworthy. The relationship is damaged.

Whenever we have broken agreements with someone (regardless of who caused the break), our tendency is to demean the other person, to reduce their importance in our life. Friendships that end suddenly can often be traced back to a broken agreement or an accidental betrayal that never got cleaned up. Even long-standing relationships can get broken easily.

When a relationship gets broken, it only takes one person to initiate the repair. You can restore and repair a relationship by reaching out and communicating your apology and your commitment to clean up any damage and make a new promise. Love, trust, and connection are restored.

In business relationships—and in any Communication for Action—it's important to make clear agreements about all requests and promises. Get very clear about what you want, and be specific about what constitutes the successful fulfillment of your request. Track promises in writing—because humans have faulty memories. Contracts exist primarily to help the parties remember later what they agreed to at the beginning of the relationship. A simple record of promises will prevent huge headaches later.

Another important element of Communication for Action is the feedback loop. When a promise has been made and completed, it's crucial that the one who made the promise circle back to the other person and state that the promise has been fulfilled. Every completed cycle (request, promise, action, completion, and feedback) builds trust and deepens the relationship. Incomplete cycles leave doubt. When you don't know whether a task has been completed, worry and uncertainty cause trust to be questioned, and the relationship weakens. When both parties know a task is complete, however, both can let it go.

If you analyze a relationship that isn't working, whether personal or professional, you're likely to find broken promises and incomplete cycles of communication. People generally do the best they can. If someone doesn't fulfill their promise, give them the benefit of the doubt, and don't judge them. But if you see a pattern of broken promises (on your part or another person's part), there's work to be done. Find the source of the pattern.

When a breakdown prevents you from fulfilling a promise, communicate what happened without excuses, shame, or blame. Simply take responsibility for what happened, even if it wasn't your fault. For example, you might say, "I didn't keep my promise. I apologize. I would like to make a new promise. I will complete this task by tomorrow at 1:00 p.m. Will that work for you?"

Integrity has been defined as keeping every promise you make and making only promises you will keep. Some people define it as keeping your promises 100 percent of the time. This is a high bar, but it's one you can shoot for. If you keep your promises, others can count on you. As trust grows, you're given more responsibility. Your "word" gains power. Relationships flourish when trust is present. If you break your promises and provide excuses instead of results, or if you stop communicating, then trust disintegrates, affinity dissolves, and the relationship gets devalued. You can build a life of integrity, strength, and power by keeping your promises and holding others accountable to theirs. With integrity, you can accomplish anything you set your mind to.

Finally, remember to take a moment to acknowledge and appreciate the completion of each cycle. Otherwise there's no joy in getting things done! To create anything great, you have to involve other people—sometimes, huge numbers of people. It's easy to focus on getting things done and to forget the human element. Work relationships need a great deal of care and feeding in order to get through the difficulties and all the way down to manifestation. Using these tips will save you endless suffering. In human relationships, we need an open heart and a clear head. The communication principles in this chapter will help you with both.

Exercise: Recover Lost Relationships

Think of people you have lost communication with or people you cared about at one time but don't any longer. Can you locate a promise that wasn't kept, an agreement that wasn't fulfilled, or a broken cycle of communication with that person? If so, it probably occurred just before the end of the relationship. With each instance you find, decide whether you want to repair and restore the relationship. If so, contact them and let them know how much you value and miss your relationship with them. Tell the truth. Watch magic happen.

Communication for Intimacy

Communication is where we let our inside out, and we let the outside in. Trust allows people to open up and be seen. When you see all the way into the inside of others, you see them as they are—precious and vulnerable human beings who (just like you) long to be accepted, heard, understood, and loved. We have wanted these things from the time we were infants, long before we had words. This desire doesn't go away when we're adults—it just gets more complex. Now our needs and desires often conflict: we want space, and we want closeness; we want to hide, and we want to be seen; we want to be successful, and we don't want to work harder; we feel good about ourselves, and we have doubts and insecurities. Do these dichotomies sound familiar? The truth is that we are all of it. As Walt Whitman wrote in his poem "Song of Myself," "We all contain multitudes."

Communication for Intimacy has the goal of bringing people closer together. It's as much about listening as it is about speaking. But *how* we speak is essential to how we are received. The Imago Dialogue Process, created by Harville Hendrix and Helen LaKelly Hunt, is a wonderful template for communicating to create intimacy with an other person. They have taught this method to thousands of couples, and it has saved countless marriages. The process has four major parts:

1. **Mirroring:** Mirroring helps you hear what others are saying and lets them know they are heard at a deep level. Mirroring is simply repeating back, *in your own words,* what you just heard them say. Then you follow with, "Did I get that right?" There is no mention of your own reaction, opinion, disagreement, or judgment at this point. It is a simple act of pure reflection.

   Here's an example: Your partner feels hurt because you didn't keep your promise to do the dishes. He expresses this hurt to you, either well or poorly. You might react to the complaint, feeling that you do the dishes all the time, or you've been busy doing other more important things, or you didn't even notice that the dishes hadn't been done. But why you didn't wash the dishes is irrelevant in this phase of the dialogue. For the time being, simply hold back all your reasons and feelings, and mirror what you heard: "I heard you say that when I didn't do the dishes last night, it resulted in you having some hurt feelings. Did I get that right?"

   Your partner might then respond, "Yes, that's exactly right," or "No, it's not really the dishes, but the comment you made when I asked you about it." Then you mirror that response, saying, "OK, you felt hurt because I didn't do the dishes and also because I didn't respond well when you spoke about it. Is that right?" When you hear back, "Yes, that's right," it's good to ask, "Is there more?" The goal is to "get" his communication fully, including all his thoughts and feelings. When your partner says, "Yes, that's all of it," he will feel truly "gotten" (not just heard) and can then move forward.

Here is a secret of communication for intimacy that will save you endless amounts of duress: If your partner repeats something over and over, it means he doesn't feel that you "got" his communication, which includes not only his words, but also his feelings, reactions, intentions, and the impact it had on him. If you pull it all out of him with mirroring, he can stop repeating himself and move on.

2. **Validation:** Mirroring goes even deeper when it includes validation, which shows others that you understand their point of view. Here's an example of validation: "I can see that you had a hard day yesterday, yet you cooked a nice dinner for me. From that perspective, I can see how those dirty dishes looked when you found them in the sink after putting the kids to bed." Again, it doesn't matter if you have a different point of view or are steaming mad on the inside about the whole thing. Just confirming that you understand and honor his point of view will help you both move forward in your communication.

3. **Empathy:** Whereas validation confirms how the other person *sees* the situation, empathy shows others that you can actually imagine what they might be *feeling*. For example, "I can imagine how you might feel hurt/scared/angry/sad/disappointed/_____ [fill in the blank] because you were left with the mess, and I got huffy when you asked me about it." Notice that you say nothing about whether the situation was fair or clearly communicated, or the fact that you were on the phone when you were asked about it, or that your partner sounded critical or angry when making his statement. Just stick to the facts and empathize with the other person's experience.

4. **Accepting otherness:** Here you acknowledge that the other person may have a different experience from you, that the person you are in relationship with is different than you are. Accepting these differences doesn't make your own point of view wrong or bad. It acknowledges that your partner, with whom you have so much in common, is a different person. When you see and accept someone's differences, it allows them to be who they are. It also fosters commonalities once those differences have been validated. "Having a clean kitchen isn't so important to me, but I realize it is actually very important to you. I realize you're different from me in this regard, and so the situation might land differently in you than it does in me." You accept that his point of view is different without making either point of view wrong.

When others have expressed everything and feel "gotten," they will let go, usually with a big release of breath, tension, or emotion. Take a moment to appreciate the release. It's a precious moment. No w, it's your turn to speak and be listened to in this way. You can now express your difference of opinion, your feelings, or any other truth. Practice these four steps with your partner so you can both bring this quality of deep listening to each other.

It may seem awkward at first to follow these four steps, but after a while, it will become more natural. The resulting feelings of understanding, closeness, and intimacy will be well worth the effort. When you master this communication, you will be able to have better alignment with your co-creators. They will feel heard and validated. If they learn this process, you too will feel heard and validated.

The fifth chakra is about effective communication with others, which is crucial for moving your dream down into social reality. These tools are essential to successfully creating on purpose.

Turning Inner Voices into Allies

You are not one, but many.

—Hal Stone

As you have seen, your dream and your daily work may involve communicating with a small number of people or a huge number of people on a daily basis. But there is one more area of communication that we must cover in chakra five, because it is the cause of more failure than any other: communication with your own inner parts.

If you're like most people, you can hear a chorus of voices inside your head. One voice says, "Eat some cake. It's delicious!" Another one chides, "If you break your diet now, you'll never lose that extra weight." Another says, "I wish I had better self-discipline!" A fourth purrs, "Yummy! Cake good! Eat!" The most powerful voice takes over, and your life feels chaotic, out of control. It's hard to manage your life—or your consciousness—as the many voices, opinions, and thoughts move you in different directions. Your ego, or personality, can be thought of as an inner committee composed of a variety of people. The committee works well some of the time, when everyone is getting along, but at other times it explodes into violent disagreements or gets deadlocked on decisions.

Somewhere along the evolutionary ladder, humans gained the ability to cordon off part of the brain and perform certain tasks automatically. This gives us the ability to multitask—to do many things at once, such as drive a car, drink coffee, and negotiate an important business deal on the phone. It also extends to the social task of *being somebody*. We separate off bits of ourselves to play specific roles. You know that one "you" comes out when you're at work, another appears when you're parenting your child, and another shows up when you're being a friend or lover. These parts are called by various names: *identities, subpersonalities, selves,* or *voices.*

Each of these subpersonalities acts like a real person. It has its own beliefs, attitudes, desires, and preferences. It has a specific strategy for being successful and issues with which it's most concerned. Some parts, such as your Inner Critic, are bold. They offer their opinions loudly during every waking moment. Some, such as your Hurt Child, wait quietly in the background, coming out only when something or someone triggers them. When you see a person undergo a sudden personality shift, acting completely unlike themselves, it's likely that one of their subpersonalities got activated and took control of the show; mature adults can suddenly act like spoiled four-year-old brats. This sudden takeover happens to all of us from time to time, especially when we're hurt or angry.

In their book *Embracing Our Selves,* psychologists Hal and Sidra Stone pointed out that most of these selves were formed when you were young and vulnerable. In the first years of your life, your body was tiny, your brain was still developing, and you were dependent on others—you couldn't even feed or protect yourself. You needed a mother to fulfill your needs until you were capable of taking care of yourself. But Mother couldn't be there for you all the time. Sometimes you woke up, and she wasn't there. You cried, but she didn't appear. You were filled with terror, feeling vulnerable and defenseless. It seemed your life was in danger. Even though you were young, your mind was wise, beyond age or experience. It adapted to these dangers creatively. It recognized that you needed protection, so it calved off a part of the psyche to come to your defense. That part took on a job and a strategy for protecting you. For example, it may have taken on the task of figuring out what went wrong and how to fix it, leading it to become an Analyzer-Fixer. Or it may have taken on the task of distancing you from the feeling of terror by retreating into a safe, isolated space, becoming an Isolator-Withdrawal persona.

Each self or subpersonality was created for a very good reason at the time, and each one helped you survive and thrive. The problem is they haven't changed much over the years; they're still doing the same jobs they were designed to do thirty, forty, or fifty years ago.

Consciousness can take any shape, and it's possible to call forward any part of consciousness and communicate with it. The Voice Dialogue[9] process, created by the Stones, utilizes this fact and enables us to have a conversation with any inner part. The exercises that follow are based on the techniques the Stones have developed over the past forty years.

Almost everyone can identify their Inner Child, their Inner Critic, and their Judge. The Inner Child can operate in any way a child can act—as a loving presence, a cranky tired kid, or a tyrant who throws tantrums and engages in sit-down strikes. If you have a strong Inner Critic, you probably internalized your parent's critical comments in order to survive and become more lovable. You reproduced your parent's voice inside yourself, and now it sounds like your own voice.

Subpersonalities can operate simultaneously, and they often have different opinions. It's common to hear people say, "I want to get my work done, but I also want to lie around and relax." Some people feel confused by this multiplicity of inner urges, desires, needs, and feelings. If we were simply one single, unitary being, it would be illogical or pathological to want two opposite things or to have multiple feelings simultaneously. The simple explanation is that we are not just one person. Each of our myriad subpersonalities has its own ideas and feelings.

As you explore and get to know your inner parts, you'll become more adaptable, more aware, and more effective at getting things done. Many of our students report that their conflicting inner voices interfere with their decisions and actions. But when you learn how to converse with your parts, you can align them with your dreams and goals. They then become internal allies, an unstoppable force in support of your forward movement.

Exercise: Voice Dialogue

There are many methods for making contact with your subpersonalities. Collectively these methods are called "parts work." Our favorite is Voice Dialogue. In this method, an inner voice is given a safe space to come out and speak directly, expressing its particular needs and desires. In Hal and Sidra Stone's original version of this method, a trained Voice Dialogue facilitator functions as a guide in the process until you are able to dialogue directly with your own inner voices. We've adapted this method so you can use it yourself or with a partner.

Step 1: Identify the Voices

Divide a sheet of paper into four vertical columns. Label the columns *Voice, Message, Job Description,* and *Strategy.*

Make a list of the voices you hear. In the voice column, give each voice a character name. Have fun with this. A voice might simply be the Critic, or it might be the Movie Critic if it provides continuous commentary on the movie of your life ("Two thumbs down!"). It might be the Harsh Critic. Or it might remind you of a critical family member (e.g., Aunt Gertrude). Identify both positive and negative voices. You may have, for example, the Cheerleader, the Coach, the Spiritual Advisor, the Tyrannical Child, the Pusher, the Perfectionist, the Manipulator, the Power Monger, the Rebellious Adolescent, the Mean Father.

In the second column, write down the main message you hear the character say. Some characters have only one phrase that they say over and over ("That's the wrong way to do it!"). Others are more creative—they deliver their message in many ways that make you feel miserable. The Scared Child might communicate its message as a tight, tense stomach, along with an urge to withdraw and isolate itself in social situations.

In the third column, write each character's job description. Even the most critical and vicious voices inside of you were originally created with your best interests in mind. A common job description is Protector. One subpersonality might be protecting you from embarrassing yourself in front of others. Another might be protecting you from feeling abandoned ever again. We usually have one or two Guardians at the Gate who protect us from those who might be dangerous. Controllers and Manipulators are other types of protectors.

The next step is to identify the strategy that the character employs to do its job. This is usually pretty simple. The Critic's strategy may be, "Criticizes my performance, providing feedback so I don't screw up again." The Annihilator's strategy might be, "Tells me I'm not worth anything, so I don't get an inflated ego." The Inner Child's strategy might be, "Stay silent, so I don't bother anyone," or "Be loving, so I get loved."

Step 2: Interview Each Voice

After you've identified your cast of characters, think of yourself as the director of a new play. Your job is to interview the characters to get to know them. Set up a chair across from yourself and pretend one of them is sitting facing you. Ask a character a question, and then change chairs. Become the character and answer from that character's point of view. Switch back and forth between yourself (which is called your *aware ego*) and the character until all of these questions are answered:

- What do you see from where you stand?
- What is your job? And how do you do it?
- What do you need?
- How old do I appear to you?
- What does success look like for you?
- What advice do you have for me?

Listen to each character as if it were a close friend with an important role in your life. Respect and honor it. Listen for its contribution to your life. Appreciate it. Like any person, when a subpersonality feels really listened to, it doesn't have to yell so loudly. This, alone, can provide some blessed relief.

When you do this exercise, you are separating yourself (your aware ego) from each voice, which naturally shifts your relationship with it. It is no longer *you,* but it is a *part of* you. There are no bad parts, but there are bad relationships with parts. When you resist an inner voice, it becomes stronger. When you accept it and honor it as an ally, it can serve your life as a trusted advisor. Each part really has your best interest at heart. The more you become aware of your inner parts, the less chance that they will interfere with your plans. Ask the advice of each part when you face a big decision. Over time, you can turn this annoying cast of characters into your trusted council of advisors.

Step 3: The Seven Voices

It's important to recognize that your inner voices were created long ago. The critical ones aren't intelligent judges of the truth. They're more like old tape recorders that have a loop of tape going around and around, repeating the same message over and over. They sound like authorities, so you think they're real. When you resist their message, they get bigger and more insistent. By allowing them to speak their mind, fully and enthusiastically, you'll recognize that they may have wisdom to offer. When you listen, without resistance, it's no longer a demon to push away—it's one of many advisors you've invited for a brainstorming session.

In this step, you're going to invite seven voices to speak out loud: your neutral self, three increasingly positive voices, and three increasingly negative voices. The purpose of this step is to allow you to hear, out loud, what you usually hear inside your head and to let it express itself. Everyone has these voices inside themselves to some extent. We have named them:

- The Visionary   (+3)
- The Dreamer   (+2)
- The Doer   (+1)
- The Neutral Self   (0)
- The Realist   (−1)
- The Doubter   (−2)
- The Annihilator   (−3)

The number beside each voice gives you a sense of the voice's charge and role in your life, from very positive to very negative. You will give each voice a chance to speak out loud. You can do this alone or with a partner (who will listen and encourage each voice to really let loose).

Stand up and begin in the most neutral position you can muster. State your first goal out loud, as a statement of fact. For example, "I will create my ideal relationship within the coming nine months." State it as a simple fact or affirmation.

Take a step to your left and take on the Realist's point of view and express the Realist's opinion. The Realist tells you what's important to pay attention to, because there are, after all, real things to consider. Think like a realist and speak like a realist. Your Realist might say, "Yes, I know you want a relationship, but there aren't that many good partners out there. You'll have to use every technique, including Internet dating sites. You resist that, so you'll have to find a way to make it fun or interesting. You'll have to go on a lot of dates with people who may not be right for you." Speak for a minute or two from this position.

Next, take another step to your left and stand in the Doubter's position. Express your Doubter's point of view. The Doubter doesn't believe you can do it. It tells you all the things you've tried in the past that didn't work and how disappointed you were. Become the Doubter. You may say, "Come on, you hate the whole dating thing. You've tried it before, and look what it's gotten you—absolutely nothing but heartache. Only losers use dating services. I don't think you're serious about this. You've made lots of promises before that you didn't keep."

When the Doubter has said enough, it's time to take another step to the left. Stand in the Annihilator's position. This is the part that's cruel, that demeans you and tells you that you're unworthy. Take the time to really move into this difficult place; you've probably suffered under its voice for decades. Really let loose and say out loud all the terrible things that you don't want to hear. You have an opportunity for real freedom here. Don't hold back. It may say, "You low life! How dare you even *want* a relationship? You're not worthy of the kind of person you want. Who would want to be with *you* anyway? As soon as they see who you really are, they'll run the other direction. Forget it!" As cruel as that voice might be, you will give yourself a gift by allowing it to have some airtime. Remember, don't take anything it says seriously. It's just doing the job it was given a long time ago.

Now take a step back to your right, back into the Doubter position, and feel its energy. Say one or two things as the Doubter about your dream.

Then take another step to your right, back into the Realist position, and feel its energy. Say one or two things as the Realist about your dream.

Then move back into the neutral position and state your dream again, just as a fact or a commitment.

Now take another step to the right and become the Doer. This is the action-oriented part that tracks your to-do list and keeps you moving forward. As you step into this practical part, consider what needs to be done to bring your dream into reality. It may say, "Well, there's a lot to be done. You need to write a new dating profile—that last one didn't produce good results. In fact, you should consult with an expert to really jazz it up. Then you'll have to post it on at least three sites. Five would be better. And, of course, you should begin telling everyone you know that you're looking, and you want them to refer the right kinds of people to you. That will be hard for you, but with the right support, you can do it."

Now take another step to the right and move into the position of the Dreamer. This is the "you" that bought this book. You have dreams for your life, and you know how good it will feel to fulfill them. Speak as the Dreamer: "When you meet the right person, you'll be *so* happy! You are built for relationship, and you deserve to be in a great one. That right person is out there, looking for you, too. You'll know it; you'll feel it when it happens. There will be a sense of rightness, and you'll feel supported like never before."

And step once more to the right, into the Visionary. The Visionary sees a great and prosperous future—not just for you, but for everyone. This part of you knows that when your dream is fulfilled, it will affect the whole world. It may say, "When you're partnered with that perfect soul mate, you'll grow together, work together, and create together. As a couple, you'll be able to help many other people, and you'll be a shining example of what's possible in a true co-equal partnership." Feel the glory of this kind of support.

Step to the left, back into the Dreamer position, and say one or two sentences from that position. Then take another step left, back into the Doer position and say one or two sentences from that position. Then step back into neutral and state your dream again, as a fact or commitment.

Now expand your awareness to include all seven voices. These are parts of you, and you are the space in which they live. You are a container, a whole, and each part of you is valuable and important. Even the harshest critic has some wisdom to offer. As you move out of the exercise, back to your life, recognize that each voice can become an advisor, like the grand viziers that served kings and queens.

How do you feel now about your dream? How can you use the advice from each character? When you hear each voice, what will you choose to do?

Exercise: Dialogue with Your Chakras

The Voice Dialogue technique is similar to techniques used in acting classes, psychotherapy, dream analysis, and playing make-believe with children. You can speak to any aspect of consciousness: a part of the body, a dream image, a universal energy, an ancestor, even a god or goddess.

You can call any aspect of yourself forward and give it a voice. When doing so, it helps to shift your physical position slightly. Move inside of the voice and feel what it feels like to be that part. Become it and speak as it would speak. When you're done, simply shift your position back and return to your normal, whole self. It's that simple.

In this exercise, you'll allow each chakra to speak about the dream or goal you want to work on. Choose one of your SMART goals. For example:

- "I will lose twenty pounds by the end of the calendar year."
- "I will live my life purpose and serve children as a teacher in a school."
- "I will help stop the destruction of the Amazon rainforest by contributing ten hours of my time each month to a nonprofit organization."
- "I will get all my debts paid off by June 1 of next year."

With paper and pencil nearby, bring yourself into a meditative state. Focus on your seventh (Crown) chakra. Feel it as an energy center, a part of you but separate from you. Say your declaration out loud. Listen to the voice of your seventh chakra, your voice of *knowing.* Note carefully what it has to say about your declaration, and write down what you hear.

If you do not get a response, direct your attention to that chakra, and say to it, "I want to hear your voice, your opinion, and your advice about this dream." Then say your declaration again and listen. Write down whatever you hear, whether or not it makes sense at the time. You may receive words, images, sensations, feelings, pictures, or a vision. Pay careful attention, and write down everything.

Be sure to express gratitude after your chakra has spoken to you. Even if you've received no information, say thank you before moving on to the next chakra.

Move down to the sixth (Third Eye) chakra and repeat the exercise. Ask this voice what it *sees* about your dream and wants to share with you. Acknowledge and write down whatever you receive from the voice. Say thank you and then move down to the next chakra.

The fifth chakra, being the realm of *communication* and voices in general, may have several voices that want to speak. Acknowledge each voice. Ask them to identify themselves, if possible. If they don't, that's okay; just record each communication. Don't be surprised if some of the opinions are contradictory. All of the information you get is valuable. Honor and respect all of the voices. Say thank you and move on.

The fourth chakra is the voice of the heart and *feelings.* Its voice may be the voice of love, or it may speak on behalf of your relationships. If your heart is not happy, you will experience resistance to moving your dream forward. Acknowledge the heart's voice by recording what it says. Say thank you and move on.

The third chakra relates to your power and what you must *do* in relation to your intention. This voice may be enthusiastic, resistant, afraid, confident, intimidated, or all of the above. Acknowledge and record each feeling. Say thank you and move on.

The second chakra has to do with *passion* and *commitment.* If you make decisions from your head and ignore the feelings in the second chakra, your efforts could be sabotaged. It's important for you to come into alignment and agreement with your intention and with all the parts of you. What is this chakra's emotional response to your intention? There may be more than one. You may feel excitement, fear, unworthiness, or power. Record what you hear, say thank you, and move down to the first chakra.

The first chakra's voices are generally focused on *practical considerations.* These voices calculate the nuts and bolts of time, money, location, and how to deal with obstacles. They must be honored, especially when they bring realism to your dream. These voices help us realistically evaluate our needs. Write down what you hear, say thank you, and move back to your normal, everyday awareness.

When you are done, read the statements from each chakra, and try to feel them as coming from that aspect of yourself. See them working together in harmony, with each voice having its say and being acknowledged for its wisdom. Share your results with a friend, mentor, coach, or teacher. This exercise can be used to diagnose inner conflicts and identify important blocks or beliefs that may get in the way.

Every voice, like every person, wants to feel respected, honored, and appreciated. Voices can be reassured, just like people. Treat them like precious friends, and you can't go wrong. When this internal group-therapy session reaches resolution, your chakras will be more aligned with your intentions. All of your chakras can now work together harmoniously and cooperatively, ready to help move you toward the fulfillment of your dreams. This harmony is what makes the act of conscious creation ecstasy.

Exercise: Proposal to the Gods

Your SMART goals have given you a clear idea of what you have to *do* to manifest your dream. With these goals in place, you are more realistic, and you're ready to take your dream to an investor, agent, business advisor, or the gods themselves.

In the next exercise, you will bring your dream to God, the gods, Spirit, your Higher Self, or whatever form or essence of the Divine that resonates with your belief system. What is most important is that you feel comfortable relating to this universal force or archetype and that you can imagine speaking directly to it.

Write a proposal to the deity (or deities) of your choice. Describe your dream, what you need, and what you will deliver. A book proposal sent to an agent would contain what you're going to write, how long it will take you, and who the book is written for. Write a similar proposal to your own divine Source. This proposal should state the following information:

- The thrust of your idea and the way your dream fits with your life purpose (chakra seven)

- A description of your dream in its completed form—your vision (chakra six)
- The story you are trying to convey and the intended impact on others (chakra five)
- What you love about your dream and how your dream will benefit others (chakra four)
- What you will do to help your dream come true (chakra three)
- What you need, including resources, support, expertise, guidance, time, coincidences, and agents, to make your dream come true (chakra two)
- What the completed form will look like and when you intend to complete it (chakra one)

The very act of writing this proposal helps you clarify your vision, goals, and needs. Take it through many drafts as you refine your vision and work your way through the lower chakras in this book. Read it to others and get feedback.

Then meditate on your divine Source. Approach it reverently and offer your proposal from your heart. Read it and offer it up. Be receptive and accept what comes—be it advice, praise, grace, or blessings. Remember that divine advice is still only advice for you to consider; take it as additional information, not necessarily instructions or marching orders.

Save your written proposal for later. When we get down to chakra one, it will become a seed you can plant for your future success.

Chakra Four:
Love Enlivens

*Our task must be to free ourselves . . . by widening our circle
of compassion to embrace all living creatures
and the whole of nature in its beauty.*

—Albert Einstein

———————————————

Everything around you came into being through relationship: the clothes you're wearing, the home you live in, the book you're reading right now. Each of these manifestations is the result of many hands, hearts, and minds, working together toward a shared vision, from conception to completion. These interactions exist within a larger web of relationships, one that is so complex that it's a wonder things flow as smoothly as they do. Countless transactions occur from the birth of something to the end of its life, when it is consumed by something else. Food, for example, travels from the farm to the store to your table; newspapers are printed on former trees, with ink from a factory that tells stories written by many hands and minds; a bus made in a huge manufacturing plant takes children to school on roads built and maintained by work crews; hardware stores gather supplies and parts from around the world, just in case you need them. All of these things, which we take for granted because they're available for our use, involve countless people interacting with one another. Relationships are the backbone of co-creation, and the core of successful relationships is love.

Love enlivens is the fourth chakra manifestation principle. Love makes the ordinary extraordinary. Love is contagious and can inspire others. It enhances every step of the manifestation process. It may be cliché to say, "Do what you love," but the heart chakra's core principle advises us to turn it around and say, "Love what you do." You may have spent a significant amount of time clarifying and visualizing your completed dream. This chakra tells you that it is not the destination that is important, but the process—the route, or *how* you get where you're going. If you bring love to all of your transactions, you will be rewarded all along the way. If you have a positive effect on others, you will leave the world better than you found it. Whatever brings you more deeply into loving relationship—with yourself, with others, and with the world around you—will enhance the manifestation of your dream.

As you enter the heart chakra, you consciously take your dream into the realm of relationships. Having developed the arts of communication, you now have the tools to enhance those relationships. At the heart, we introduce the following steps of the manifestation process:

- Highlighting your service to others
- Finding the right relationships
- Establishing your network
- Co-creating with beauty and love
- Fulfilling your heart's desire

When you approach life with your heart chakra open, you interact with love. Your manifestation power will be enhanced by everyone you touch.

Chakra Four

A bit of fragrance always clings to the hand that gives roses.

—Chinese proverb

Love is something we can't live without, yet the world is crying for lack of it. It is what most of us ultimately seek. And yet love isn't found by merely seeking; it is something we create—or more accurately, co-create with others. In creating on purpose, we want to make sure we bring love into all of our relations, both casual and intimate. What is created with love has the capacity to last, to shine, and to inspire.

Chakra four is the middle chakra in a system of seven. It is the balance point between spirit and matter, mind and body, heaven and earth. Balance is the underlying foundation of longevity in all things, especially in relationships. What has balance lasts longer. Think of a finely tuned automobile engine, in which every component works smoothly with others, compared with an engine that is badly out of tune, in which parts rub against each other.

The heart chakra is also the integrator of polarities. Opposites interact through relationship. Through the heart, your mind integrates with your body, your spirit is brought into relationship with matter, and your dreams are balanced with reality. Through this integration of opposite poles, the unexpected can spring to life—your dreams can soar to levels beyond your expectations.

The element of the fourth chakra is air, signifying the way this chakra relates to the breath, to spaciousness, and to sacred reciprocity with our environment. We breathe in and we breathe out in a constant give-and-take with the atmosphere around us; we are in constant exchange and co-creation with others. You would not have oxygen to breathe if it were not for trees and plants, and they would not get the carbon dioxide they need were it not for you. Focused on balance and reciprocity, the fourth chakra teaches us that we are served by our service to others. Even the word *deserve* means "to come from service." The basic principle of love applies to all of manifestation: the more we give, the more there is for all. This is the law of abundance.

In the downward path through the chakras, love comes before will. When we create from the highest, bringing heaven down to earth, we want to make sure we don't put our will and power—or even our purpose—ahead of the way we treat others. In the descending current, we are *strengthened by our relationships;* we actually gain power through them. When our purpose serves others, our creativity is enhanced and our vision empowered. We learn from others and are held by others in our most tender places.

Above all, the heart chakra tells us this: We don't have to do it alone. Through partnerships and collaboration, we can do more with less effort. To live this principle in the world is to create a social revolution, a shift from the *love of power* to the *power of love*. The love of power is based on a belief in separation. One part is pitted against another, one nation against another; even parts of ourselves attempt to control other parts. The power of love, however, harvests abundance by bringing people, communities, and nations together in cooperative and collaborative co-creation. Working *with* others saves an enormous amount of energy that may have previously been used to compete and protect ourselves. Competition in which both parties are strengthened and enlivened, as in sports, is healthy, but competition in which the goal is to take out the other is destructive to the life force. War is the most obvious example. When competition and cooperation are served by life-enhancing principles, vision is vitalized, truth is shared, and the resulting co-creation brings into manifestation the best possible option.

What we love is enhanced by that love. When you take loving care of your home, it becomes a harbor of beauty and grace. Loving your children fosters their highest possibilities. At work, relationships that include positive regard and genuine care bring out the best in your employees and coworkers. Loving your partner encourages them to do their best. It follows that loving our world is the way to bring heaven down to earth—and, in doing so, creating a world that works for everyone.

Earlier, we expressed the need to shift from being children of God to being adults of God. As children, we accepted care from our parents in the form of having everything supplied for us—our home, food, education, clothing, and guidance. Through this care, we learned our first lessons about love. But for most of us, our imperfect parents demonstrated imperfect love. We became confused about what love really is and how it behaves.

Raising a child is a universal initiation into adulthood. You enter into a lifelong relationship that is founded on unconditional giving without thought of return. Your role as parent and provider lasts at least two decades. Despite the enormous amount of work parenthood entails, most parents would say they received far more from the experience than they gave. And most would say that if they could do it over, they would have given even more to their children!

We are the parents of the future society that our children and grand-children will inherit. This is our initiation into adulthood. It begins with every transaction we have with others and everything we create with others. The heart chakra asks what you can give, not what you can get. Your life is God's gift to you. What you make of your life is your gift in return. Your creation is your gift to the world. It will be your legacy.

The heart chakra invites you to discover its secret: You are an agent of love in the world's dream. The more you love yourself and share your love with others, the more creation becomes ecstasy.

The breath of love in the fourth chakra symbolizes the air that is required for the fire of the third chakra to burn. When your heart is fulfilled by love, your joy empowers your will at the third chakra. The fire of will in the third chakra is necessary for you to burn through the inevitable obstacles that will appear on your path as you manifest and act on your dream.

What Do You Love about Your Dream?

When you consider your dream job, dream relationship, or dream community, it should be something that you *love*. If it doesn't fill your heart to overflowing, it's not your dream—it's somebody else's. A student in our workshop said, "My dream is to have a job I don't hate." Our response was, "That's not a dream. It has no love in it. There's nothing positive to draw you forward or reward your efforts. It's merely avoidance of what's negative."

Every dream creates its own obstacles, challenges, and difficulties along the way, so it's important to remember what you love about it. When we get up at 4:00 a.m. to catch a plane after only a few days at home, it's easy to forget how much we love teaching. We grumble to ourselves, "There must be a better way to make a living." Once we arrive at our destination and start to teach, however, we remember how much we love our work, our life, and traveling to new places.

What do you love about your dream? Do you love being on stage and making people happy? Do you love what happens when your clients awaken to a new realization? Do you love to make things beautiful? Does the face of a joyful child fill you with joy? Do you love bringing people together? Let's examine all the things you love about your dream.

Exercise: Ignite the Heart in Your Dream

Write down all the things you love about your dream. Make sure everything on your list resonates with your heart. Notice whether what you have written gives you an uplifting or expansive feeling in your chest. Let your heart speak more loudly than your mind. Post this piece of paper on a wall where you will see it often. It will be a helpful reminder when the going gets tough.

Highlighting Your Service to Others

The greatest good you can do for others
is not to share your own riches, but to reveal theirs.

—Anonymous

We stated earlier that when people seek only their personal dreams, it creates a collective nightmare. If every person were to strive to get a bigger house, a newer car, and every material good available, the planet would run out of resources, and civilization would die an ignominious death. We would have blown the chance to create heaven on earth. Unfortunately, the American dream has been warped by the idea that people should be free to pursue their own desires, regardless of the consequences. Although this belief fuels our economic engine, it's bad for people as a whole—not to mention bad for a planet with limited resources. If your dream does not serve the whole of life in some way, then the energy behind it will be limited. In keeping with the heart chakra's element of air, imagine that serving others puts wind in your sails. You will be supported by a web of relationships, and natural forces will urge you forward.

Manifestation Tip:
What serves the greater good puts the wind in your sails.

Open your heart to all that is around you and speak to the needs of humanity. You will be assisted by the evolutionary impulse embedded in the creative process.

Compare these two simple statements:

- "Come buy my services; I need to pay my rent."
- "My services can ease your pain and help you become the person you've always wanted to be."

No one would use the first statement in an advertising campaign, but the truth is that your own needs are often your primary motivation. This ego drive can get in the way of what you are trying to sell or establish. If you focus instead on the benefit to others, you can get your ego out of the way and live into the possibility you're creating. This is like opening the door to let the breeze blow through or positioning your boat so the wind can fill your sails. You get into harmony with something larger than yourself. The Universe notices and rewards you with unseen support.

Even if your dream is to have the perfect relationship, a healthy body, or better finances, find a way to see that outcome in relationship to the whole. You'll be better able to serve others if you have a healthy body and the right relationship to support you. If you receive adequate financing, you can better contribute to the greater good. If you have enough business and cash flow, you'll be able to offer your skills pro bono to nonprofit organizations or at reduced fees for people with low incomes. When you feel prosperous, you can give more money to worthy causes.

Imagine your dream in its fulfilled form. Notice how it bene-fits others and makes the world a better place. Then write in your journal at least five ways your dream serves others and the greater good. Put yourself in the place of someone receiving the gift of your dream and notice how it feels.

Then, align your dream with others by asking these questions of your heart:

- What parts of my dream match the dreams of others?
- How can I find like-minded co-hearts who are already working toward dreams that will accomplish most (or all) of my dream?
- Am I willing to sacrifice some of my ego needs in order to contribute to the accomplishment of a larger vision, such as a world that works for everyone?
- Can I adjust my dreams so that the shared dreams of every-one can be accomplished?

Exercise: Give and Receive

Co-creation happens when two or more people commit to helping each other and to accepting each other's help.

Step 1: At least once this week, offer help to someone in your life. Offer it selflessly, without expecting any return. (Make sure you are offering help they actually *want!* Be careful of codependence and meddling.) Notice what it feels like to offer this help selflessly. Notice what it does for the other person and how it affects your relationship. This step is a warm-up to the next exercise, which you may find more difficult.

Step 2: At least once this week, ask someone for help in accomplishing some aspect of your manifestation. Ask for support, a favor, a referral, physical assistance, or whatever you might need. Practice asking and accepting. After you receive help (graciously), feel the gratitude in your heart. Does it make you want to give even more? If you asked someone for help and were refused, how did it affect you? Was it easier or more difficult to ask the next person?

Step 3: At least once this week, give an unexpected gift. You may decide to give a panhandler ten or twenty dollars, write a poem or romantic card for your mate, buy flowers for a coworker, do a favor for someone without being asked, or create beauty where it can be seen by many others. Notice what happens, both inside your heart and in the hearts of others.

Finding the Right Relationships

*There is one word that may serve as a rule of practice
for all one's life: reciprocity.*

—Confucius

Creativity isn't just making something out of nothing; it's also creating new relationships between elements that already exist.

A huge number of relationships are required in order to actualize your dream and fulfill your destiny. You may need support, mentorship, playmates, employees, customers, clients, an audience, investors, agents, or designers. You may have to deal with building departments, school systems, government bureaucracies, or corporate ladders. You may be creating your dream within the context of a marriage or family, a community, or a company that is already full of people in complex relationships. Navigating this realm is an all-chakra experience, integrated through the heart. It includes understanding (chakra seven), clear seeing (chakra six), good communication (chakra five), strong will (chakra three), a wide range of feelings (chakra two), and embodied presence (chakra one). If you ignore the heart (chakra four), you will eventually fail, for only what is created from the heart is truly sustainable. When you serve from the heart and your dream serves others, the Universe supports you and rewards your efforts.

Knowing how to navigate the web of relationships is a necessary skill. For better or worse, it matters more *who* you know than *what* you know. Even more important is who knows you. According to Jeffery Gitomer, author of *Little Black Book of Connections,* "To climb the ladder of success, you don't need more techniques and strategies, you need more friends . . . All things being equal, people want to do business with their friends."[10] If people like you, they want to work with you—they want to include you, invite you to events, and help you out.

Friends are made by connecting with others and caring about them. Your power to create is multiplied by the number of those caring connections. One measurement of your power—your field of influence—is the distance that you have an impact. Consider the reach of the president of the United States or of the wealthiest individuals. They can influence events around the globe, affecting millions of people. How far do your loving connections extend? The only way you can create something larger than yourself is through your web of relationships.

Exercise: Who Do You Know?

Make a list of everyone you know (or would like to know) who could help you on your path to fulfill your dream. Next to each name, write down what you could offer that person as a way of cultivating your relationship. Think about how you could do that and what specific actions you could take. Then, begin to take those actions. Develop the relationship without asking for anything. A good relationship is like money in the bank: It is social capital. It creates interest by your being *interested.*

Next, make a list of all the relationships that are necessary to create your dream: *all of them.* For some, you will know their names; write them down. For others, you may only know the roles, such as graphic designer, office organizer, coach, angel investor, real estate agent, publicist, editor, or architect. In addition, make a note of the relationships that will be affected by your dream—either directly or indirectly—such as your spouse, children, neighbors, coworkers, or customers.

When you name what you need, you plant a seed in your consciousness. If you nurture it with attention, it will grow in strength until it becomes magnetic. Then it will draw what you need toward you. When I (Anodea) decided to create a foreign-language version of my DVD *The Illuminated Chakras,* I knew I needed to find several different translators for the European languages. I wrote down the languages I wanted, did a brief Internet search, and was quickly overwhelmed by too many choices and high prices. Two days later, I went to a party and met a woman who handed me her card, which said, "Voice-over recordings and translations." She spoke fluent French and Italian and had colleagues who spoke Spanish and German. In fact, her German colleague was my housekeeper! Within a week I had found everyone I needed and secured translation contracts for all four languages. Naming my needs and writing them down brought those needs into focus. Giving the seed a chance to grow allowed it to draw what I needed to me, easily and effortlessly.

Exercise: Create Your Dream Team

This exercise offers you the opportunity to build relationships with a specific set of people—a group we call your *dream team.* This is a group of people who will do the following:

- Listen carefully to your dream and support you in achieving it
- Add their particular expertise, wisdom, or coaching to your efforts
- Meet with you regularly as a group to help you move your dream forward
- Be available to meet with you in person or by phone
- Love you through the ups and downs of creating your dream

Your dream team will be your most important allies during the manifestation process. They will help guide you through the rigors and rough waters that lie between your current reality and your dream life. Here is a sample request you can send to potential dream team members:

Dear _____: I'm putting together a dream team, a group of people who will support me in creating my dream. My dream is . . . [Describe your dream—especially the results your dream will produce.] I thought of you as a person who would be really helpful because of your _____ [contacts, wisdom, love, support, enthusiasm for the greater good—whatever is appropriate], and I want to invite you to become a member of my dream team.

What I'm looking for is a group of _____ [three to seven] people who will meet with me in person [or by phone teleconference] once each month for two hours. This meeting would be like a board of directors meeting, where I report my progress and get your feedback and guidance. I would also like to be able to call on you for specific help every once in a while. Of course, I would be happy to serve on your dream team as well. I'm looking for a commitment of around twelve months or so.

I would love to have you as a member of my dream team. Are you willing and able to do so?

You can set up monthly teleconferences on a service such as freeconference.com, which allows you to have as many people on the conference call as you wish. It records your conference automatically for those who can't attend. The format of your monthly dream team meeting should include the following:

1. Welcome, check in, and come to order
2. Set and review the agenda
3. Review your dream, goals, and projects, with any clarifications since the last call
4. Old business 1: commitments you made in the last call that you have completed
5. Old business 2: commitments you made in the last call that you have not yet started or have not completed
6. Blocks: what got in the way and prevented you from following through and completing your commitments; request help with the blocks

7. New business 1: next steps you know need to be taken
8. New business 2: feedback from your team about those next steps
9. Additional items: brainstorm, requests from any team member to other team members, miscellaneous business and personal issues, and so on
10. Commitments: the specific commitments you're making at this time and through the period until the next meeting
11. Schedule and confirm the next conference call
12. Give appreciation and thanks; close

Modify this basic outline to fit you and your dream team. You can also use this format for one-on-one dream support when you ask for mentoring or coaching from individual dream team members.

You may be saying to yourself, "I couldn't possibly ask anyone to help me this way. It's selfish to ask people to take time out of their busy lives to help me. Why would anyone want to take time to help me?" First, know that most people are afraid to ask for help, and this fear prevents great and important ideas from coming into existence. The truth is, *none of us can do it alone.* Busy and important people know this. If your dream truly serves others, people will join your dream team to accomplish the good that your dream represents. They are not just supporting *you;* they are also getting value for themselves, such as the good feeling that comes from helping others and the chance to extend their own web of relationships. Be bold. Be courageous. Let those you ask have the pleasure of saying "yes." And if they say "no," ask them who they would recommend.

Establishing Your Network

When we try to pick out anything by itself,
we find it hitched to everything else in the universe.

—John Muir

The world has become hyperconnected. Social networks, online communities, cell phones, and media connect us like never before. More than two billion people are online at any given time—nearly a third of the world's population. The production of computing devices is expected to quadruple in the next ten years. As technology advances faster and faster, each of us becomes more connected to more points in a vast and complex web. An average person today has interactions with more people in a week than our ancestors did in a lifetime.

This web of connectedness is linking the consciousness of the entire planet. Long before the Internet, Pierre Teilhard de Chardin named this web the *noosphere,* from the root *gnosis,* meaning "knowledge." He wrote about a sphere of knowledge, or consciousness, surrounding the earth, as if the entire globe were a single group mind. As a species, we are learning to think with this web of connectedness, and through its shared information, we are becoming collectively smarter. Intelligence and connectivity are inextricably linked.

As you communicate into that web, your truth vibrates its strands. What you create can be propagated and multiplied faster than ever before. You have access to more people than at any time in history. An essential part of creating a new world is fostering new connections.

What attracts attention on the Internet is what you *offer,* not what you can get. More and more is being given away free. Even though Google is free to users, it has become the largest organization of knowledge in human history. Mark Zuckerberg, creator of Facebook, was adamant about building his network without charging people to join. Facebook is now one of the most highly valued networks on the planet. We have entered a new world of economics—one based more on giving than on taking. This philosophy creates more abundance than the old system of competition for market share. When you use this principle of generosity, you expand your network. It is a faster route to success than anything else you can do. The more you give, the more likely you will be remembered and valued. When you do offer something for sale, it will be bought by those who trust you, because they already received something of value from you.

Every event you attend is a potential networking event. When you are in a room full of people, do you scan the crowd to look for someone who might offer you some benefit? Or do you look for those who might benefit from what you have to offer? When you come home from an event, whom do you remember? The people who tried to sell you on their project or the ones who paid attention to your needs, who listened and gave *you* something of value?

When you meet someone new, is your focus on your own short-term advantage or the potential of a long-term relationship? Will that person want to see you again, remember you for what you did for them, for taking the time to see who they are? The quality of your relationships determines how you are regarded and remembered and whether people are open to you and what you are doing.

Many people feel timid when it comes to meeting people and talking about their vision. Often it's because they are trying to *get* something (approval, attention, or support), instead of trying to *offer* something. When you offer a gift from your generous heart, you are rarely rejected. Your offer may be rejected because it's not right for the other person, but it won't be a personal rejection. You will be remembered as a generous person, even if your offer isn't accepted. It leaves the door open for future possibilities.

In the first few minutes of speaking to others—whether one-on-one or in front of a group—your listeners do not evaluate your content. They are deciding whether they like you. If they do, they will listen to your content. If they don't, it really doesn't matter what you say, because little of what you tell them will be remembered or considered.

Seek first to be friendly and to make a connection. Establish rapport and offer value to others. Create a reputation out of this practice. The reason we, as teachers, get asked to teach all over the world is because we're friendly, are easy to work with, and give value not only in our workshops but also in all of our connections. We realize that everyone we work with is a person worthy of honor and respect. They are doing their job and doing the best they can. When you genuinely appreciate others, their hearts open to you. The *real* work (for all of us) is to make every moment of connection with another person a moment where that person feels seen and valued. This makes for better relationships, a better life, and a better world. A smile and a kind word improve the day for both people. It makes people want to come back for more. It is said in the business world that a happy customer will tell three of her friends about the great service she received, whereas an unhappy customer will tell ten of her friends about the lousy experience she had.

If you want to successfully bring your dream to fruition, ask the following questions as you expand the web of your relationships:

- Who do I know? Who do I want to know?
- How can I connect with more people? How can I make deeper connections?
- Who knows me? Who *should* know me?
- Who are my ideal clients or customers? What are their needs, wants, and desires?
- Who would benefit from being connected to my dream? How would my dream serve them?

Co-creating with Beauty and Love

We live only to discover beauty. All else is a form of waiting.

—Kahlil Gibran

None of them knew what they were beginning on that warm evening in 1978, when the first pickax dug into the foothills of the Italian Alps. Yet they tirelessly dug all night. By dawn, only three feet of dirt and rock had been removed—a tiny fraction of what was to come. But one man, Oberto Airaudi, had a vision, as well as the ability to inspire others to join him in its creation: a series of underground temples that would rival anything seen for thousands of years. His vision was so strong that it inspired dozens of people to spend thousands of nights covered in dirt, doing hard manual labor for a dream that was, by all logical reasoning, preposterous. He envisioned that tunnels would be dug in secret—by hand, at night—unseen even by fellow community members. They used only shovels and pickaxes to dig through mud and hard rock. The work was difficult, yet Airaudi's vision persisted, and it continued.

Five years later, with more than a million buckets of dirt passed along human chains lining underground corridors, the Hall of Water was completed. It was the first of many chambers of reverence dedicated to various aspects of spirituality. Many obstacles had been overcome, structural and otherwise, to achieve this goal, and the first chamber was consecrated. This holy site was the first major accomplishment in what is today one of the great wonders of the world—and the center of the spiritual community of Damanhur.

Today Damanhur's underground temples rival the Sistine Chapel in scale, beauty, and detail. A series of seven chapel-sized chambers are ornately adorned with murals, sculptures, mosaic floors, and exquisite stained glass art. Visitors come from around the world to be amazed and blessed by this holy place, and a spiritual community of more than a thousand members has grown around the area. Airaudi's vision has inspired hundreds of thousands of people. He began with a vision, he communicated it to others, and he inspired others to help him create a miracle of awesome beauty and exquisite artistry, with the wisdom of many spiritual traditions depicted on the walls.

Damanhur is a place where a dream has been realized, where beauty abounds, and where the impossible became a reality. The temples are a testament to the power of a dream. The community's vision continues to grow and is an inspiration to others all over the world. This is an example of heaven brought to earth, of vision made manifest.

Rumi said, "Let the beauty we love be what we do. There are a hundred ways to kneel and kiss the ground." What makes you kneel and kiss the ground? What brings heaven down to earth for you? What fills your soul with inspiration and lets you know you are in the presence of the Divine? How does your beauty shine in the world?

Beauty opens the heart. It commands our attention, inspires awe, and radiates grace. It is present in a natural landscape, wildflowers on a hillside, the sparkling night sky, and the rise and fall of the ocean waves. It beckons to us through a child's laughter, a lover's eyes, and a vulnerable tear running down a cheek. Beauty speaks of a deeper order, a composition in which everything is placed in its best relationship to everything else, in such a way that every part's unique essence is magnified and harmonized with the whole.

Beauty is an essential archetype of the soul. It touches us somewhere deep inside, moving heaven and earth closer. If we are co-creating heaven on earth, then beauty is essential, because it lets us know we are close to the Divine. If we are gods and goddesses in training, and if our job is to co-create with the Divine, then one of our prime design requirements is to create more beauty. Beauty is what we were given to start with. Could we create any less? Unfortunately, in Western culture, the answer is "yes." We have come to value efficiency much more than beauty. We have turned the archetype of beauty into a commodity to be sold. Beauty has been diminished to a stereotype of appearance at the surface.

Caring for beauty has fallen primarily to women. They express their love of beauty through their appearance, clothing, adornments, and home environment. For many men, appreciation of beauty appears to be effeminate, gay, or threatening to their masculinity. As a result, we have failed to include beauty in the design of our cities, our buildings, and our products. With this loss, we have created a world full of objects and commodities, and we have fallen out of love with the world. The resulting dissociation is both dangerous and destructive.

Whatever your project or dream, take time to embellish it with beauty, for doing so will attract love. What is truly loved becomes beautiful, as does the one who loves deeply. Whatever you create, create it to have lasting value, so that it may be appreciated and worthy of the resources used to create it. Your enjoyment will be deeper and longer lasting, the value of what you created will be greater, and you will be brought closer to the Divine. To create heaven on earth, beauty is a requirement, not a luxury. Nothing less will do.

To explore your relationship with beauty, consider the following questions:

- What do you feel when you are in the presence of beauty? What does it inspire in you?

- What aspects of beauty touch you most deeply? How do you seek these qualities?
- What about your dream is beautiful to you?
- How can you court beauty and have more of it in your life?
- What do you believe about beauty? Are these beliefs yours, or were they indoctrinated into you through advertising and modern culture?

Exercise: Practice Beauty

Beauty is not just something to entertain in your grand vision. It is an everyday practice with your environment. Some cultures, such as Japanese, Thai, and Balinese, create beauty in every plate of food, believing that food's attractiveness is as important as its nutritional value. The following are easy-to-implement suggestions to increase your beauty quotient:

- When you sit down to eat, take a moment to notice your food. See the colors and textures. Notice the smells and tastes. Find beauty in your food and appreciate that beauty with every bite. Notice your level of satisfaction when you are done. Set your table with an eye for beauty and see how your meal is enhanced.

- When you get dressed in the morning, find some way to bring beauty to your attire—even if you're a man! Notice the colors and textures of your clothing. Notice how they make you feel. If you feel beautiful, notice how it colors your day.

- Do something to beautify your workplace, whether you work alone at home or with others in an office.

- Write something beautiful to those you love. Leave it in an unexpected place where they will find it.

- Listen to beautiful music at least once this week. Stop doing everything else and listen with your whole attention. Music feeds the soul.

- Visit a place you consider beautiful—either natural or human made. It may be a forest or meadow, an art gallery or concert hall. Notice how you feel in such a presence.

- Make a point to verbally appreciate someone else's beauty, whether it's in their clothing, their way of speaking, or their actions. Complimenting others makes their efforts worthwhile and inspires them to keep creating beauty—which makes more beauty for all of us. We become more beautiful when we are seen and appreciated. What we appreciate appreciates!

- Notice the beauty that exists even in difficult things: disagreements that move us into our truth, losses that open new realms, and even destruction, such as forest fires that stimulate new growth.

- When you find something beautiful, study it. What makes it beautiful? How can it teach you to create more beauty in your own life?

- Give thanks for beauty wherever it occurs in your life. This invites more of it to occur and opens your attention more widely.

Fulfilling Your Heart's Desire

There is a longing within each person's heart. Even if life is good, the future is calling us to the next level of fulfillment. We may feel this pull in our hearts as a subtle or not-so-subtle longing for more, for different, for better. This is not the desire for a new car or a bigger house or even for the affection of someone you just met. Such "ego goodies" tend to carry a hidden price—they often bring more frustration than fulfillment in the long run. Longing is different than desire—it tends to be rooted in the soul rather than in the ego. We long for a life of generosity, not just abundance. We long for happiness for all people, not just for ourselves. We long to fulfill our life purpose, which always involves benefits to others. We long for more truth, beauty, and goodness.

The following guided meditation is based on a little-known element of the heart chakra called the *Anandakanda Lotus,* which translates as "coiled bliss." This lotus of eight petals is said to reside just beneath the heart chakra and contains within it the *Kalpataru,* or Wish-Fulfilling Tree, one of five trees said to be located in the paradise of the god Indra. The belief is that this tree will grant the fulfillment of whatever you wish in its presence. But a word of caution: This tree is likely to give you *even more* than you wish for! Be careful what you ask. Consider Oscar Wilde's statement: "When the gods choose to punish us, they merely answer our prayers!"

The idea, however, is that the natural world is abundant and wants to say, "Yes, dear" to anything we ask for. If you're like most people, this tendency has gotten you into trouble more than once. Woven into this meditation is reciprocity, meaning that something must be offered in order for you to receive your wish. We advise you to wish from the deepest essence of your heart, for the fulfillment of your highest vision and purpose, and for the benefit of all. When you do that, you won't regret the outcome.

Exercise: Guided Meditation on the Wishing Tree

Before beginning the guided meditation, take time for some inner contemplation and journal work to explore your wish:

- What do you really wish for? Drop down inside your body. Pay special attention to the area of your heart chakra. Allow your heart to speak of its deepest longing. Rather than looking for some kind of *thing,* go for the *essence* or *outcome* that would bring you fulfillment. Examples: "I wish to find more joy in my work." "I wish to know my life purpose." "I wish to find deeper love with my partner." "I wish for dynamic health and vitality." "I wish for a more profound relationship with Spirit." Focus on how it would *feel* if your wish were granted and what it would bring to your life.

Avoid trying to picture the form it would take, as that limits the Universe's ability to grant your wish.

- In exchange for having this deepest wish of your heart fulfilled, what are you willing to offer? You could offer to cultivate virtues such as loyalty, compassion, generosity, or perseverance. Or you could offer the willingness to study and train in a discipline that will strengthen your body or your will. You may offer to give up something dear to you for a period of time, such as watching television or eating chocolate. You could also choose to offer a sacrifice—something you are willing to give up, such as tobacco, alcohol, or another destructive habit.

Once you have determined your wish and your offering, have a friend read the following meditation, or read it aloud and record it so you can play it back when you can be totally relaxed. Follow the words into an inner journey. (Note: It should be read slowly.)

Find a place and time where you won't be disturbed for at least fifteen minutes. Find a comfortable position for an inner journey. Lie down or sit comfortably in a way that allows your body to deeply relax, yet not fall asleep. Have your journal nearby so you can write down anything you wish to remember during or after the meditation.

Begin to focus on your breath. With each inhalation, imagine you are filling your heart with abundance; with each exhalation, you are entering more deeply into a state of peace. Continue to focus on your breath as you breathe in abundance and breathe out peace. With each breath, you move deeply into a state of relaxation and harmony with your body. Allow your muscles to relax more deeply with each breath. Allow your face to relax. Allow your mind to let go of all thinking and merely follow the guidance of these words, as you prepare to go on an inner journey.

This inner journey begins by you stepping outdoors into the natural world. Imagine you are stepping across the threshold of your home. You smell the fresh air outside. It is a beautiful day. The sun is shining and feels warm on your skin. There is a light breeze gently blowing through your hair. Your body is full of energy and excitement as you prepare to go for an afternoon stroll along your life path.

Looking down as you walk, you notice that your feet are on natural ground. The earth feels solid beneath you, yet it is moist and fertile. You may decide to take off your shoes and walk barefoot. The path before you unfolds clearly as you walk into a large meadow with high grasses blowing in the breeze. You can hear the sounds of birds singing and bees buzzing as you walk merrily along your path. Trees dot the hillside. As you walk, the trees become more numerous, and the forest becomes more verdant. The air is moist and alive.

Soon you see in front of you a grove of very tall trees. They call to you, as if their very branches are beckoning you as they sway in the wind. Following that call, you walk toward the grove, feeling a deeper sense of purpose with each step.

When you get to the middle of this huge grove, you spot an enormous tree at the very center. This tree appears to be very old, with a wide trunk and large, gnarly roots. It has many branches extending outward in every direction. It is so tall that it's difficult to see the top. You marvel at its age and enormity as you begin to walk slowly around its massive base. You touch the bark with reverence.

When you get halfway around the tree, you notice a low altar made of stone and covered with leaves. You brush aside the leaves and find a large, leather-bound book. It appears to have been there for a very long time. Gently, you open the book and notice that it is filled with writing. Each page contains a name and a pledge; each person who has come to this place has written an offering to the tree and sealed it with their name at the bottom of the page. You turn the pages, amazed at the reverent offerings that have been made. You come to a blank page and notice that there is a writing instrument tucked into a pocket of the leather cover. You pull it out and face the blank page. You remember your pledge and carefully write it down—an offering to the Wish-Fulfilling Tree in exchange for fulfilling your deepest longing. You sign your name to seal your pledge, and then you close the book.

As soon as the book is closed, something very strange begins to happen. The leaves of the tree begin to rustle, there is a crackling sound, and the branches begin to rotate, moving into a spiral pattern, creating a kind of staircase spiraling up and around the trunk. You feel beckoned to climb. Stepping onto the first branch, you find that it holds you solidly. You take another step, then another, continuing up and around the trunk in a spiral pattern. You climb higher and higher, feeling safe and secure, until you reach the very heart of the tree.

Here you find a natural place to sit, as if a comfortable chair had been carved where two branches split. It is an inviting place to sit, and it fits your body perfectly. You are now in the heart of the Wish-Fulfilling Tree.

Sitting in this sacred spot, you begin to meditate on your heart chakra. You breathe into it deeply. With each breath inward, you feel the essence of your longing. Your soul is calling for fulfillment of its true purpose. With each exhalation, you breathe out this longing into the leaves that surround you. You listen deeply to your heart, and if it comes naturally, you may name this longing, though it is not necessary to do so. Breathing into the tree transmits your message. Continue to breathe the essence of your longing into the tree, as if you are whispering a secret to its very heart.

When you feel that you have expressed the deepest longing of your heart, and the tree has absorbed it fully, you notice a bird flying into the tree. It perches on a branch near your heart. The bird cocks its head from side to side, as if listening intently. It is receiving the message of your heart and the longing that the tree now holds. You look at the bird and say, "Thank you for delivering my message." With one final look into your eyes, acknowledging your thanks, the bird flies away into the forest, singing your message as a song, informing and activating the natural powers and forces that inhabit this forest.

Knowing that your message has been delivered, your heart fills with gratitude. You open your heart and your body to receive the fulfillment you have called for. You express your gratitude to the tree. You know with certainty that your wish will be fulfilled at the right time and in the best possible way.

As you complete expressing your appreciation for this gift in your life, the wind stirs again, and you know it is time to climb back down the branches to the ground. You take each step carefully and reverently.

When your feet touch the ground, the branches shift and the staircase disappears. You walk around the tree again until you catch sight of the stone altar with the book. You remember your pledge and recommit yourself to that offering.

The leaves rustle once again as if to say goodbye. You turn in gratitude to walk out of the grove. The birds are singing, the wind rustles through the leaves, and you sense the harmony and connection all around you.

You return to the meadow and walk once again upon the dirt path, step by step, back to your home. Your heart is open and fulfilled. When you get to your home, you step across the threshold and enter the place where your body is now. With one final word of gratitude, you let go of this meditation with the knowledge that your wish will be fulfilled in the right time and in the best form possible. Open your eyes and return to this place.

Chakra Three: Power Produces

Life shrinks or expands in proportion to one's courage.

—Anaïs Nin

At twenty-six years old, Mohamed Bouazizi would not live to see what happened after he set himself on fire in the streets of Tunisia. This young man had been unable to find steady work and was eking out a meager living by selling vegetables in order to support his family. On the morning of December 17, 2010, Tunisian police seized his vegetable cart and beat him mercilessly because he didn't have a permit. This wild act of abuse resulted in tipping the balance of power in a new direction. Whether setting himself alight was an act of incredible courage or the result of momentary insanity, the sparks of his burning body kindled a flame that burned across the Arab world in a movement that has now (as of January 2012) overthrown three dictatorial governments and produced uprisings in at least a dozen more. Some say the sparks of his sacrifice and the ensuing Arab Spring ignited the Occupy movement that began in the United States and spread around the world. As we activate our individual and collective will and align with our higher purpose for a better world, we use our power to make change.

One never knows the impact that a personal act of power will have. We stand on the shoulders of those whose courageous acts changed the course of history. Rosa Parks refused to move to the back of the bus, and after a yearlong citywide bus boycott, the segregation of the Montgomery, Alabama, bus system was lifted. Mahatma Gandhi, a barefoot man in a loincloth, united an entire nation against British domination. Nelson Mandela spent twenty-seven years in jail, inspiring a generation to rise up and end apartheid. Whether your acts of courage are large or small, they make a difference. They are needed now to change the course of history toward a sustainable future, a peaceful world, economic justice, a culture of kindness—in other words, heaven on earth.

You are now more than halfway through the manifestation process. You have created with your consciousness, vitalized your vision, catalyzed your life with communication, and enlivened your relationships with love. Now it's time to produce results. This is the *active* part of manifestation, the place where you actually have to *do* things—like get up in the morning, make phone calls, write reports, and send emails. You need power to accomplish these tasks, and power is associated with the third chakra. Our core manifestation principle at this level is: *power produces.*

To create on purpose and to manifest heaven on earth, you must claim your personal power and use it for a higher purpose. But how can you develop the personal power required to truly create, on purpose, the world that you know is possible?

In this chakra, we invite you to take command of your power and to strengthen your will. When you take responsibility for your life and your world and take actions that bring you closer to your vision, you will feel your power as pure aliveness. Then, when you get down to the second chakra, you'll be fully open and available to experience pleasure beyond your wildest dreams. To make this possible, we'll explore these steps:

- Becoming proactive
- Strengthening your will
- Planning your steps to success
- Handling distractions and obstacles

Humans are the only animals who control fire, the element of the third chakra. We are the only animals with this degree of free will—and we are still learning how to use it wisely. Our climate is heating up from burning fossil fuels. Is this symbolic of too much fire or of power misused?

In his book *Kinds of Power*, Jungian psychologist James Hillman wrote:

> Among the ideas of business, "power" rules the roost. It is
> the invisible demon that gives rise to our motivations and
> choices. Power stands behind our fear of loss and desire
> for control; it seems to offer the ultimate rewards. Power
> does not appear nakedly as such but wears the disguises of
> authority, control, prestige, influence, fame, etc.[11]

As Hillman unpacks the complex concept of power, he clarifies the many ways the word can be used:

> If you say you "want more power," are you asking for more
> vital energy, or for more opportunity to dominate messy situ-
> ations, or for more recognition, or for more tough endurance
> to bear your burdens? Do you want a more prestigious office
> and title or to have more authoritative input in decisions?
> Do you want to lead or to command? Do you want to be
> loved for your support or respected for your fearsomeness?
> All these ideas enter into a differentiation of power.[12]

Most people would prefer to have more control over their lives, and there is a direct correlation between the amount of control people feel they have and the amount of happiness and satisfaction they feel. Dr. Gabor Maté, a Vancouver physician and social medicine expert, has pointed out that most modern afflictions—including heart disease, cancer, attention deficit hyperactivity disorder, and addictions to alcohol, drugs, and food—can be directly attributed to an excess of stress in our lives. The cause of stress can be found in the deadly combination of our culture's worst features: alienation and isolation, fear and uncertainty, lack of control over our lives, and the inability to express ourselves fully. According to Maté:

You can't separate the body from the mind, and you can't separate the individual from the society. Capitalism itself causes stress, and every aspect of our culture seems to add more stress to the human system. The only solution is to return to our human values: relationship and connection, self-control and self-determination, taking care of each other in community, and fully expressing ourselves.[13]

Here's a prescription for the cure to your own powerlessness: Master the manifestation process. When you take charge of your reality and create what you want, you reduce your fear and uncertainty, because you recognize that you're in charge. When you reach out to others, establish stronger connections, and express yourself fully, you not only bring your dreams into reality, but you also increase your health and vitality. When you imagine something you want and use the manifestation process to create it in reality, you feel the true power of a creator. Your self-esteem soars, and you recognize that you can make any dream come true.

We become most aware of *power dynamics* when we see an obvious difference between someone else's power and our own. Power and responsibility are closely tied. Compare, for example, the power differential between workers and bosses inside a company. Bosses have the power to call the shots and the responsibility to produce the results. Workers have less power—they get told what to do—but they have less responsibility; they don't have to worry about making payroll or keeping stockholders happy.

As a child, you knew that your parents held far greater power than you did (although you found ways to exercise your own—starting with the word "No!"). How this power differential was handled in your family in large part determines how you handle power in your life now. Were you allowed to assert your will? Were you dominated, controlled, or humiliated when you took a stand? Were you encouraged, empowered, and supported in your efforts to define yourself as a unique individual? Or were you told how to look, how to act, and how to be?

Power comes in many forms in the external world, such as economic power, political power, intellectual power, military power, and media power. In the United States, and in much of the rest of the world, we live in a submissive paradigm. We are taught to submit to authority figures, turn our power of choice over to those who know what's good for us, seek satisfaction through purchasing things made by others, and vote for the lesser of two evils. If you have any doubt, watch people going through airport security. We are subjected to X-ray screening and intimate frisking by strangers in uniforms, and we stand patiently in line for it, like sheep walking toward the slaughter.

The opposite of having power is being *disempowered*. This is what occurs when someone or something controls you, dominates you, forces you, or overwhelms you. It happens whenever a power differential leaves you feeling powerless—at the mercy of another's choices or whims. We all experienced this disempowerment as children. We wanted to do something, and Mom said, "No." We wanted to have something, and Dad said, "I'm not buying that for you." They said, "Go to bed." You said, "I don't wanna." They said, "If you don't go to bed right now, you're going to get a spanking." The threat of violence cowed you. You turned sadly away, feeling small. They were bigger than you, and you couldn't run away. You were dependent on them for your survival. You had to do what they said.

In school, you may not have been able to go the bathroom without getting permission from the all-powerful teacher. If you rebelled, you got in trouble. If you attempted to become your own authority, you were quickly brought back into line. When you expressed your will, you were told you were being obstinate. Is it any wonder that most of us have issues with power and authority?

In order to re-empower yourself, you must retrain yourself at the deepest core. You need to find and exercise your will and your decision-making apparatus. You need to know your truth and learn to express it fully and unabashedly. When you plan your actions and then act on your plan, you gain personal power. You find that you can make things happen. You gain control over your reality. You are no longer a victim of circumstances, not subject to others' whims.

In this chapter, you will learn what successful businesspeople have known for hundreds of years: Planning pays off. We will teach you (or remind you) of the basic steps of planning. It's the best way to make things work in the real world and to make things real in the work world. When you express your power in a clean way, people respond positively. When you blend your fourth chakra heart with your third chakra power and act in service to the divine will in the seventh chakra, you are sure to succeed—and will have fun doing so.

Chakra Three

Nothing is impossible. The word itself says, "I'm possible."

—Audrey Hepburn

We have now descended past the halfway mark between matter and spirit. As we enter the lower half of the chakra system, things get more physical and more practical. Setting intentions, visualizing, communicating, and loving are necessary for a full life, but they won't get the work done. For every dream, there are things you have to do. *Doing* characterizes the realm of the third chakra. Many of us fall down in this realm. We want our dream, but we don't want to do all the things necessary to bring it about. When things don't go the way we want, we drop our goal and give up, returning to our old habits, our old patterns, and our old life.

Chakra three relates to will, personal power, self-esteem, strength, energy, vitality, focus, discipline, freedom, purpose, effectiveness, and ultimately *mastery*. The third chakra is ruled by the fire element—the element that brings transformation. If you followed all the directions for baking a cake—mixing together flour, sugar, and eggs—but you never put the batter in the oven, it would just be a mixture of flour, sugar, and eggs. The oven's heat transforms batter into a new form— one that holds its own shape and tastes delicious. In the same way, the fire of your *will* heats your vision into tangible form. It forges your vision into a vessel—a cup that can receive in chakra two and be completed in chakra one. Your fiery will acts like a kiln, turning the clay you've worked with thus far into a solid, usable structure.

If your third chakra is strong, you stay on task. You live deliberately. Your actions are in accordance with your intentions. You make a plan to do something, and you do it—without resistance, apology, or complaint. The Nike motto is pure third chakra: *Just Do It!*

Most people set an intention, visualize what they want, talk about it in their relationships, and begin by taking some action. But when the going gets tough, their fire in the belly goes out. They may begin a diet with good intentions but then find themselves facing temptation: "Well, weddings don't happen every day. I'll eat the wedding cake because it's a special occasion—and I'll restart my diet tomorrow." They may begin a task that *must* be done but then come to the conclusion, "This is too hard. I'd rather be doing something else. Maybe I'm not supposed to do this." We've entered the realm where the rubber hits the road, where actions get done, or they don't. Either you keep your commitment, or you don't. Strength in this chakra is one of the essential keys to being successful in life. If you learn to navigate this difficult third chakra terrain, you can achieve success in anything you put your mind (and manifestation process) to.

Exercise: Measure Your Personal Power

Step 1: How can you measure your own personal power? Take some time with your journal and rate yourself on a scale of 1 (barely detectible) to 10 (mastery) in the following facets of personal power:

- I am able to control and focus my attention.
- I manage my physical energy throughout the day.
- I have control over my circumstances and environment.
- I set and defend my personal boundaries when necessary.
- I manage my money, finances, and resources."
- I keep my promises to myself and do my daily practices consistently."
- I keep my promises to others and communicate when I can't.
- I open my heart when appropriate and feel my feelings fully.
- I am able to manage my thoughts, beliefs, and reactions.

- I create and maintain positive and productive relationships with others.
- I am able to connect to Source/Spirit/God/Goddess easily and at will.
- I can choose my attitude and responses in the face of adversity.
- I am organized in my work and I accomplish my goals.
- I am able to create on purpose joyously.

Step 2: Pick the weakest area of personal power on your list and work to strengthen it for a designated period of time: a week, a month, or a year. If you're not sure how to strengthen it, ask for advice and suggestions from someone you know who is really masterful in that area.

Becoming Proactive

The future belongs to those who prepare for it.

—Ralph Waldo Emerson

A student in one of our courses presented this problem: "My boss continually interrupts what I'm doing. He gives me more work to do. I don't know what has priority. Everything gets stacked up, and I get derailed and stressed out." Her passivity turned her into a victim of her circumstances. When you believe "I have no power," it becomes true. We suggested that she own the problem as her own, get proactive, and make an appointment to speak with her boss to address it directly. She began to see it as a joint issue between them. Her lack of productivity affected her boss as much as it did her. We recommended that she speak what was true for her: "I really want to do a good job here and fulfill your wishes, but I don't know which tasks have priority, and I don't know if I can tell you that it will take longer than you expect. I'm afraid you'll get upset and yell at me. Let's come up with a priority-making system where you can get what you need done, and I know the order to do things." Speaking her truth this way is co-creation at its best. It deals with the problem proactively rather than reactively, and she could see her boss as a co-creating colleague instead of a powerful father figure towering above her.

When you're *reactive,* you allow others to determine how you respond. Your third chakra is firing on its own, devoid of higher consciousness. Being *inactive* is to remain passive, without energizing your third chakra. A balanced third chakra is *proactive* and *responsive,* rather than reactive. *Pro* means "first" or "before"; thus, being proactive is an invitation to act before something becomes a problem, rather than reacting to the problem later. If you want a promotion in your company and you passively wait until there is an opening, it will likely be filled by someone more proactive. If you establish a relationship with the head of the department *before* there's an opening and discover what they will be looking for in the future, you can shape your own destiny. Too much third chakra energy produces bullies; too little produces victims.

Strengthening Your Will

We gallop through our lives like circus performers balancing on two speeding side-by-side horses—one foot is on the horse called "fate," the other on the horse called "free will." And the question you have to ask every day is—which horse is which? Which horse do I need to stop worrying about because it's not under my control, and which do I need to steer with concentrated effort?

—Elizabeth Gilbert, *Eat, Pray, Love*

The most important skill to develop in the third chakra is strengthening your will. The primary purposes of your will are (1) to decide where to direct your attention, (2) to focus your attention in that direction, and (3) to make changes in your circumstances in accordance with your intention. Most human beings have not adequately developed their will. We are taught that power exists outside of us—it is in the hands of parents, teachers, religious leaders, elected representatives, institutions, the boss, or another authority. Our schools reinforce passive behavior and punish those with a strong will or a drive toward independence (which teachers often equate with obstinacy). When the will of the people is weak, those who have a strong will (and desire for power and control) can easily take the helm. When you're unsure of yourself or don't know what you want, you are easily influenced by others.

People without willpower operate as if their attention is on automatic pilot or directed by outside forces. They don't make clear decisions, or they make decisions based on momentary feelings. Whatever appears next in a stack of wants and desires becomes the next object of attention. Most people live their lives as victims of their circumstances, allowing the winds of influence to determine their direction. As Henry David Thoreau said in *Walden*, "The mass of men lead lives of quiet desperation." It's easier to let someone else steer while you relax and enjoy the ride—but you don't get to determine the destination.

The greatest leverage you can gain for your life is the cultivation of willpower. To reclaim the power of your will, begin by realizing that everything you do is a choice. Even if someone told you what to do, *you* chose to do it. Even *not choosing* is a choice. Unless someone is holding a gun to your head, *you* are the one deciding what to do (and even if there is a gun to your head, you're choosing life over death). If your boss tells you to do something, or if your wife, kids, or friends want you to do something, you are choosing that action because you have chosen to please others. Doing something because you think someone else is making you do it puts power outside of yourself, creates resistance, and exhausts your third chakra.

Here's a good third chakra strengthener: "I don't *have* to . . . I *choose* to . . ." Saying this gives you back your will. It allows you to realize that you can do something if you decide to, but that nobody is forcing you. From that place of freedom, you can choose actions that are aligned with your purpose, your vision, and your will. There is less resistance. You'll feel more aligned with yourself.

This past week, how much have you been in charge of what you did? Were you living from your own choice and decisions? Or have you been living someone else's intentions, desires, needs, or expectations?

Doing things out of obligation is like driving with the brakes on. We call it "outer compliance and inner defiance." Think of the way children stomp up the stairs when sent to bed during a favorite TV show. They do what they're told, but broadcast their resistance loudly. Many of us get stuck in this mode, but we pay a steep price. Resisting what you're doing is like pushing against something you're pulling. It's exhausting. Choose your actions consciously, use your will wisely, and let go of resistance while you do what needs to be done.

The will is a combination of intention and energy. Intention comes down from consciousness through chakra seven, at the top of the manifestation path. Your idea is an arrow, and the direction in which you shoot it is your intention. Your intention meets physical energy coming up from chakras one and two. Chakra one represents solid matter, and chakra two is movement. Energy is a combination of matter and movement. Rub your palms together rapidly and feel the heat that gets generated. Rub two sticks together long enough, and you get fire, the element of the third chakra. Your will brings intention and energy together in the third chakra, creating the power to accomplish tasks required to fulfill your intention.

Energy without a clear intention is squandered. Children use their energy to do whatever feels right in the moment, which is why so much adult energy is spent on controlling children in schools. Dogs wander around wherever their nose leads them. If you don't have a clear intention, your will is only whim. Whims are fine, but they don't get things done.

Are the following thoughts familiar? "I wanted to clean my house (make the calls, write the ad copy, set up appointments, etc.), but I didn't have the energy." "I wanted to do it, but I just couldn't get to it." Intention without energy is empty—a fantasy. As the saying goes, "The road to hell is paved by good (but unfulfilled) intentions." You can strengthen your will by focusing on one clear intention, fueling it with your energy, and doing whatever it takes to fulfill it.

Whenever you fulfill an intention, you get a kick of energy back into your system, plus you gain a sense of satisfaction and power. Your self-esteem rises. It feels good to cross something off your to-do list. Mastery happens when you repeatedly practice using your energy to fulfill your intentions. Mastery is the ultimate goal of the third chakra.

It's the only kind of power that really serves you without making you a slave at the same time. A task becomes easy and effortless when you do it without resistance or grumbling. As you fulfill your intentions, one by one, you come to recognize that you can accomplish anything you set you mind to. That's true power.

We are surrounded by thousands of distractions. They come at us from every direction, all day long. The sheer volume of things wanting attention is getting larger and faster. For this reason, it is crucial to strengthen your ability to focus your attention. Those who can are able to do marvelous things. Those who can't, flounder.

On the other extreme, it's possible to live *too much* from the will. Some people have such a strong will that they dominate everyone around them. They even dominate themselves, working too hard and losing the joy in life. There is a balance point between creating and accepting that allows creation to be easy and ecstatic.

Disorders of the Will

We've diagnosed a number of third chakra disorders that cause distress and distraction. If you suffer from any of the following, apply the healing solution.

- **Intention Deficit Disorder (IDD):** "Gee, that looks more interesting. I'll switch to doing that instead." If left untreated, IDD can lead to **Add-nauseum Deficit Disorder (ADD)**, a variation of IDD that constantly adds new things to what you're already doing, resulting in overcommitment and a feeling of being overwhelmed. These feelings, in turn, lead to scattered energy and doing everything poorly.

  Solution: Learn to prioritize and make a plan; then work from the plan. Do one thing at a time, and stick to it until it's complete. When that one task is complete, you can start the next one on the list. You'll actually get more done this way.

- **Shoulding (also known as Oughta-gotta):** "I *gotta* go pick up my mother-in-law." "I *should* spend more time with the kids."

"Tomorrow I *oughta* clean out the garage." "I *gotta* get this done." "Should I or shouldn't I . . . ?"

Solution: Notice what happens to your energy when *should, oughta,* and *gotta* come into your thinking. It places power outside of yourself. Change the operative words to "I choose to," "I want to," or "I decide to," and feel the shift.

- **Never Enoughism:** "I don't have enough _____." You might fill in the blank with *time, money, skills, knowledge, friends,* or *support.* Whatever you're missing becomes your convenient excuse for not getting something done. A great excuse for nonaction is "I don't have what it takes."

Solution: Remember our manifestation tip: Never let your reality define your reality. Ask yourself instead, "What will it take to get to my goal? Am I willing to do whatever it takes?" This is a good place for "The Belief Process" exercise (page 70), since your "lack" is actually based on a belief. Or use Step 3 of the "Declare Your Intentions" exercise (page 39) and exaggerate your crosscurrents. Ask yourself, "What do I need to do in order to get what I don't currently have?"

- **Distractomania:** "With all the emails, the phone ringing, the kids, the dog, and the house to take care of, I just can't get to my dream." On your deathbed, will you remember the emails you responded to or the dreams you fulfilled?

Solution: Make your energy bigger than your distractions by using the "Remove Obstacles with Your Will" exercise at the end of this chapter (page 187).

- **Otherizing:** "Others do it better, faster, and smarter. And they can do it cheaper. I can't compete with them." The real difference between you and "them" is that they got into action, and you didn't.

Solution: Practice the declaration "I do it," and clear out all crosscurrents. If it's *really* true that they can do it better, faster, and cheaper, then hire them to do that part of your project! If they were part of your team, what could you accomplish?

- **Distended Trying:** A person with a well-functioning third chakra makes solid commitments and takes responsibility for following through. A person with a weak third chakra says, "I'll *try* to get that done for you." This is not a commitment. Remember Yoda's advice to Luke Skywalker in *The Empire Strikes Back:* "Do or do not. There is no try."

  Solution: If you're not sure you can do it, say "no." If you say "yes," don't try—just do. Here's a trick to convince you: Try to pick up a pen off your desk. Don't actually pick it up—just try to pick it up. Try harder. Harder! Notice that all the trying you can muster doesn't actually get the pen into your hand. You can only pick it up by picking it up. *Just do it!*

- **Tomorrow-crastination:** "Tomorrow's a better day. I'll feel more rested (more ready, in the mood, clear headed, etc.). The kids will be out. The weather will be better." Or: "I'll start my exercise program as soon as my workload decreases." (Notice that it never does.)

  Solution: Do something every day that moves your dream forward, even if that something is small. Make one phone call, write one page, talk to one person. Doing just one thing will make clear that there is always *something* you can do now. Your will gets strengthened by small steps forward.

- **S'posed-to-ism:** People often ask, "What am I supposed to do?" They hire psychics or coaches, use Tarot cards or the *I Ching,* or consult astrologers to find an answer. The problem is, it's the wrong question. The only answer lies within: *You decide what to do.* Living from what you believe you are "supposed to do" puts power outside yourself. It leaves you waiting to be told what to do, second-guessing other's expectations, and figuring out what's right and what's allowable.

Solution: What if there weren't any "s'posed to"? What if that, too, were arbitrary—just somebody else's good idea? You might as well go with your own good ideas. If you can't decide or don't know what you want to do, pick *something* and do it. The results will provide you with more information. Either you'll move something forward, or you'll learn a valuable lesson, which will move you forward.

- **Respond-Addiction:** When you open your computer, a hundred emails request you to respond. The phone rings at an inopportune moment, and you must pick it up. The kids walk in to ask for something, and you stop what you're doing to respond to their needs. Your boss asks you for something while you're working on another project, so you drop what you're doing. At the end of the day, you've responded to everything but your own agenda. Responding to everything and everyone runs down your third chakra and exhausts you. Be careful, because the more successful you get, the more invitations there will be to respond to.

Solution: Consciously choose what you will respond to—in advance. Get clear about what's most important. Respond first to what fits into your agenda and leave the rest until later, instead of leaving your dream until later. Choose your response based on what actions are aligned with your life purpose, dreams, and vision. Learn to say "no" to anything that is not a clear "yes."

Exercise: Strengthen Your Will

Pick an object near you and focus your attention on it for one minute. Put all of your attention on the object. If you notice your attention going elsewhere, gently bring it back to the object you're focusing on. Continue to practice, using different objects, until you can effortlessly keep all of your intention on an object for a full minute.

You can also pick a task to do for one week, such as meditating for twenty minutes every day, flossing your teeth every night, counting your breaths for five minutes every hour on the hour, or avoiding one particular food you like. Make your task somewhat arbitrary and train your will to do what your mind decides.

Creating vs. Accepting

There are two major schools of thought in spiritual and self-development circles. We call them Creation and Acceptance. Many traditional spiritual and religious paths teach that accepting things as they are brings peace and happiness. On the other side of this polarity are the success-oriented, you-can-do-anything teachers of self-development and motivation. They say that happiness comes from creating what you want or attracting it into your life. Are these two points of view really in conflict?

We see them as complementary paths rather than a battle for "the right and true way" or "the only way to be." *Acceptance,* which we refer to as the Path of the Buddha, is a journey toward allowing, appreciating, and letting go of attachments. It is a valid path to inner peace, and it's just right for some people. It is called *yin* in the Taoist system and is the more feminine and receptive of the two paths. In the chakra system, it is *mukti,* the upward current through the chakras, the path of liberation. Sitting quietly, you leave the physical world behind and tap into spacious, universal energies and divine consciousness.

On the other side is *creation,* the Path of the Avatar. It is a journey of actively making life the way you want it, manifesting your dreams. It is *yang*—the masculine, penetrating force that makes things happen. In the chakra system, it is *bhukti,* the top-down current we're following that brings your ideas into reality. The focus is on declaring what you want, changing old patterns, and moving the world with your attention and energy. This is a valid path leading toward a life of empowerment and enjoyment, and it is just right for some people.

Our view, and the view of the Tantric sages, is that life is a balancing act between the poles of creating and accepting. Sometimes a little

Path of the Avatar	Path of Purpose	Path of the Buddha
Creating	Integrating ego	Allowing
Choosing	and essence	Receiving
Making		Accepting
Manifesting		Appreciating
Willful Action		Letting Go

Figure 2 Three paths

more creation is needed, and sometimes a little more acceptance is needed. You decide which you need, based on your circumstances, feelings, and intuition. *Balance* can be seen as static, like equal weights on a scale, or as dynamic and ever-changing, like the balance you need for surfing, skiing, or teeter-board acrobatics. It's a dance between polarities. Sometimes, the world pushes you more into one pole or the other. Can you accept that fact, allowing your own strong will to dance with the world's will, or with divine will? Dancing is the right analogy—watch how dancers shift direction and move with each other and how much they enjoy doing so!

People who insist on shaping reality to their own desires can become controlling. People who live exclusively in the realm of acceptance can become victims of their circumstances. But there is a third option, which Tim Kelley, author of *True Purpose*, calls the "Path of Purpose." In this option, you establish a direct connection with your own Trusted Source—this may be God, Spirit, the Divine, your Higher Self, an angelic guide, your soul, or whatever spiritual source you trust implicitly. Through a two-way dialogue with this source of wisdom, you ask questions and get specific guidance. You come to know your soul's purpose with great specificity and clarity. Your choices are influenced by balanced information from both your ego *and* your Trusted Source. Standing this way—with a foot in both worlds—allows you to make better decisions and to live and work in alignment with your life purpose.

Which path is right for you? What is the right balance for your unique life? What do you need in this moment? And this one? And this one?

Personal Will and Divine Will

When we talk about this balance between creating and accepting, we are often asked, "How can I tell the difference between my personal will and Divine will?" We use the metaphor of sailing across a large lake. Your intention is to sail to a particular beach on the other side. You have a map, and you know the direction you want to go. In order to sail you need the wind, which represents Divine will: "What Source wants for me." You have no control over which way the wind will blow, how hard it will blow, or even whether it will be windy that day. If you have a motor (your own internal motivation and power), you're not reliant on the wind. You can go anywhere you want without the Divine, but you won't be aligned with universal forces. If you work with the wind, you can get to your destination naturally and joyfully.

You set your sails based on the direction you want to go (your intention) and the direction the wind is blowing (Divine will). *Attitude* is how you face into a force. If you have no intention in particular, the wind will simply blow you around in whatever direction it's going. If you want to achieve your goal, you have to control your sail and tack back and forth. You keep your eyes on your goal, your vision of where you want to end up, and you make periodic corrections. When your personal will works in harmony with Divine will, you get where you're going while having a good time.

The sailboat represents your vehicle for getting from where you are to where you want to be. But a sail must be hitched to a mast, which is your purpose. You can then catch the power of Divine will. The larger your mast and sail (the greater your purpose), the more Divine will you can harness. The sailboat also has a keel, or a downward-pointing fin, beneath the boat. This is your ground, anchoring you in what you know—both in your body and in your environment. It keeps you steady and stable. This is your faith and integrity.

If the wind doesn't blow, you can choose to sit on the beach, sip a margarita, and enjoy yourself, waiting for things to change, or you can fire up your motor. Bringing your personal will online will move you out into the game until Divine will comes back online. Without a motor, you can get caught in the doldrums. (The original meaning of the word *doldrums* was "a boat caught without wind.") If you use only your motor, you miss out on the vital source of power that is free and clean. You'll feel like you're working too hard, pushing a big boat. Ideally, you use your motor only when you need to. The rest of the time, you use your personal will in harmony with Divine will to get where you want to go. It's a great way to co-create—and an enjoyable ride!

> Manifestation Tip: If you don't plan, it won't withstand.
>
> Your dream can be accomplished, but only if you plan. The more carefully you plan, the more you can accomplish. It is said in business that every hour spent planning pays off tenfold in productivity.

Planning Your Steps to Success

Everyone is trying to accomplish something big,
not realizing that life is made up of little things.

—Frank A. Clark

Chakra three focuses us on the fire of doing, on actions that move you and the world. If you don't plan what you need to do, it probably won't get done. Every large project—even saving the world—can be broken down into smaller and smaller bits, specific actions that someone can do. Before the Industrial Revolution, things were made by craftsmen—people who had apprenticed for many years to learn all the steps necessary to create that thing. The Industrial Revolution asked the question, "Why take so long to train craftsmen and do things one at a time? We can make many things simultaneously, and more cheaply, by dividing the labor into tasks small enough that an idiot could do them." Efficiency became more important in business than did craftsmanship. The key was planning—by planning tasks well in advance, they could be done more efficiently.

If you spend time planning your week, you'll get twice as much done than if you do no planning. The more complex your project and the more people it involves, the more planning is necessary. When other people are involved, a project turns quickly to chaos if it hasn't been planned well in advance.

From Planning to Action

Projects can be large, complex, and unwieldy. The more complex they are, the more ways there are to go wrong. Now that you've clarified your dream, defined your project, and established your SMART goals, it's time to break it down further into an action plan. Every goal can be defined by the specific actions that must take place in order to reach that goal. Efficient planning involves identifying the actions required, organizing them in time and space, and detailing them sufficiently so that you can delegate them to others and have those people know exactly what they should do. Every action taken moves you a little closer to your goal.

To bring all these ideas together, we'll use as an example one of our students, David, and his dream. He identified his financial dream this way: "I will live my life in abundance, without worry about money or finances." Within this dream, he came up with a vision, a vehicle that would take him toward his dream. "I will reduce my debt to zero and increase my income so I can feel free to live as I choose." His most important goal became: "I will be free of debt, except for my mortgage, by the end of next year, on December 31." He then broke his goal down into three major projects, which he felt he could get his arms around: reducing his expenses, refinancing his mortgage, and adding income through coaching others (Figure 3).

Using the art of project planning, David then broke down each of his projects into an action plan, with time lines for each action. In business, this is called *project planning,* and it's the best practice for being effective and productive.

David took his first project, "Reduce my expenses," and broke it down into specific actions he could take:

Figure 3 David's first goal and its three major projects

- Eat meals at home instead of at restaurants except for two meals per week
- Sell the second car so I'm not spending money on maintenance and insurance
- Give up the extra cable channels I don't watch and reduce my monthly fee
- Go over my insurance policies with my agent and see where costs can be reduced
- Take a driving vacation this year instead of flying somewhere exotic
- Refinance the mortgage to lower my monthly payments

Each task could be detailed further, but for David, this was sufficient. He knew what to do and who to call, and he could put each task on his calendar so he knew when to do it. He then broke down the rest of his projects in this way. With an action plan, he could track his activities and know whether each action was done. In this way, he was able to accomplish his goal, which led him further toward manifesting his dream.

From Action Plan to Your Calendar

An action plan is essentially a detailed to-do list, a compilation of all actions required to accomplish your goal. Each *action item* should contain the *who, what, when,* and *how* elements that would enable you to assign the task to another person. For some items, add where it is to be done. And remember to know why you're doing it!

The next step provides the real power that moves a good idea into action: Assign each task to a specific time on your calendar. When you do this, you are making a commitment—to do *that* action at *that* time. This commitment is what brings an intention closest to completion. Of course, you still have to *do it at that time.* Each action you take moves you closer, a step at a time, to your goal and ultimately to the life of your dreams.

Figure 4 shows an excerpt of David's action plan for his second project, "Refinance my mortgage."

✔	TASK LIST (My Action Items)	Due
✔	Call the bank and discuss their Home Loan Modification Program	May 15
	Download loan application and complete it	May 18
	Meet with CPA to get updated financials for this year, and copies of last two years' tax returns	May 21
	Send in complete application	May 23
	Follow up with bank on a weekly basis until I get the modification	Weekly on Fridays
	Explore alternative financing with three other banks	May 25 to August 20

Figure 4

David's action plan for completing Project 2 in support of his goal of being debt free

Transfer each action item onto your calendar. Identify the particular day and time you will do each task. Consider this item an appointment with yourself—as important to keep as an appointment with your doctor, dentist, attorney, or important business contact. This time on your calendar is reserved for doing that task. The more you can control interruptions and keep your appointments, the more your inner critic will back off—and your self-esteem will soar.

If you keep your appointments with yourself, you will get each thing done. Act as if your boss will fire you if you don't get them done! Here's an important secret to making this work: Remember that breakdowns happen. Something important will come up, and you won't be able to do what you promised yourself you would do at that time. Instead of shrugging your shoulders and saying, "Oh well, I guess I can't do that now. I'll do it later," STOP! Just as you would change an appointment with someone else, move this task to another date and time on your calendar, and keep that appointment with yourself. Don't just let it slide off your calendar. This one tip will help you get more done than you ever thought possible and will enable you to accomplish your long-hoped-for goals.

After you accomplish each item on your action plan, cross it off. Keep the action plan visible—on your desktop or taped to a mirror—in order to remind yourself that you are making good progress. Take time periodically to feel how good it feels to move forward, step-by-step, toward living your dream life.

Here are some project-planning tips that will help you manage this phase of the manifestation process:

- Start with the end in mind. Be clear about what success looks and feels like when you have completed the project and about the benefits it will bring to yourself and others.

- Use project-planning software, such as ProjectManager.com, Microsoft Project, ConceptDraw project, or Project KickStart. If one of your projects is to write a business plan, we recommend BizPlan Builder by Jian.com, as it comes with easy-to-use templates you can just fill in. ConceptDraw.com has a very educational online project-planning manual that you can study on your own.

- Create a giant wall-sized time line showing all the tasks related to your project and how they relate to each other in time. This is called a Gantt chart (named after Henry Gantt, who developed and popularized this form of project planning). The software products listed above can create these time lines for you.

- Use Communication for Action principles (page 115) with your co-creators to convey a clear understanding of what constitutes the successful completion of each item. Create a separate action plan for each co-creator, including a check-off list they can hand back to you, thus completing the cycle of communication.

- Create a group-wide communication and feedback system with everyone on your team, so they can track the progress being made on each front. This system keeps your team inspired, honest, and productive.

- Decide on the five most important action items you will do every day. Do those first, no matter what. This one technique is guaranteed to increase your productivity and effectiveness by 20 percent or more (or your money back!).

- Prioritize your action items on the basis of both importance and urgency. Do the important/urgent items first. Do the important/not-urgent items second. Do the not-important/urgent items third and the not-important/not-urgent items last. Most people reverse the second and third types, so they never get to the important items.

- Remember to celebrate and take time to enjoy yourself every time you accomplish a significant action item, project, or goal. Celebrating will allow you to experience the happiness and joy that comes from manifestation. It will energize you for the next phase.

Handling Distractions and Obstacles

Distractions are another form of crosscurrent. They come in every flavor, from important to trivial, and from every direction. They tempt you, cajole you, and promise you a good time. The important thing to remember about distractions is that they are *someone else's goal.* Your attention is the most precious commodity in your life. If you don't take charge of where you place your attention, there are thousands of other people who will happily control it. Remember that one of the main jobs of your will is to direct and focus your attention.

Advertisers talk about *eyeballs* as their most important resource. That's *you* and *your attention* they're talking about. If they can grab your attention, they can sell you something. Everything that's offered for free, including websites, blogs, and television programming, has a hidden cost. The cost is that your attention will be sold to an advertiser as a commodity. That's actually the game in advertising and marketing: *You* are the commodity they're selling; it's not the product, service, or entertainment they're offering.

If advertisers are willing to pay for your attention, doesn't it make sense to protect your attention as a precious resource? Make a list of distractions that take your attention away from the things that you need to do in order to fulfill your dream. List as many as you can. Here are some common distractions that may appear on your list:

- Exercise and yoga
- Television and movies
- Interesting websites
- Email from people you know
- Email from people you don't know
- Emails offering interesting workshops, trainings, and classes
- Phone calls

- Laundry or housecleaning that must get done
- Mail sitting in a pile on the desk

Note that some distractions, such as exercise and yoga, are actually self-care, an important priority. Others, such as communications from friends, are in the important category of relationships. Laundry and housecleaning are priorities for health and a pleasant environment. Put the items in your distraction list into categories such as these. Note the value of each one. Even television has value at times—we need entertainment and relaxation, and we need to be informed. The key to controlling distractions is to *choose them carefully so they support you.* To stay informed, for example, a digest of news on the Internet may be a better choice than television. To be entertained, it may be better to give your attention to a book, which uses your will and imagination, than to a television program, which drags your attention around where it wants you to go. When you look at a distraction and examine it carefully, you'll see what it may offer that is good for you and what it may offer that is bad for you. Remember: You can't manage what you don't measure.

There are many kinds of obstacles in addition to distractions. Each kind has to be dealt with in its own way in order for you to take back your attention and focus it on your goals. For example, if you live in a very noisy environment, and the noise is a constant drag on your attention and energy, moving to a quieter neighborhood may be the best way to handle it, since you can't change the neighborhood. If you have children, it's not possible to move away from them, so you have to make other adjustments to their constant needs. You may need to arrange special "Mommy time" or "Daddy time," during which they are not allowed to disturb you, or you may need to *buy* focused time by paying for a sitter. But in many cases, what you need is stronger willpower—the willingness to say "no!" to the offers, needs, and pleadings of other people for your time and attention. The following exercise can strengthen your will directly.

Exercise: Remove Obstacles with Your Will

This exercise involves getting other people to step in and represent your obstacles. We highly recommend it for empowering your third chakra and disempowering your obstacles. You will need to gather some friends or co-hearts to fully experience it.

Step 1: Identify Your Difficult Tasks

There are many things we *have* to do but don't *want* to do. Children protest when they have to do things they don't like doing. You could say that one measure of maturity is the willingness to do that which is unpleasant but necessary. Adults who refuse to do what is distasteful rarely succeed in the world of economic reality.

Let's examine this phenomenon and find a way through it. Look at your action plan and list five things you have to do but which you find distasteful, difficult, or daunting. Examples might include making cold calls, cleaning out the garage, working out at a gym regularly, writing every day, or asking for letters of recommendation.

Choose one item that you've had problems accomplishing and frame it as a SMART goal: **s**pecific, **m**easurable, **a**ttainable, **r**ealistic, and **t**ime-based. It should have sufficient detail so you know exactly what you need to do. For example:

- Do Internet research on May 11, look up literary agents, and send out three query letters every day for seven days, starting May 12
- Work out at the gym with a trainer four times each week and drink a healthy smoothie instead of eating lunch six days a week until I weigh less than 180 pounds

Here are examples that won't work for this exercise (or for your life):

- Find a literary agent (it doesn't say what you have to *do* to find one)
- Lose weight (this is not specific enough and not actionable)

Step 2: Choose the Most Difficult Task

Write that specific commitment on a sheet of paper, beginning with "I will . . ." For example, "Starting next Monday, I will work out at the gym four times each week with a trainer and drink a healthy smoothie instead of lunch, and I will continue until I weigh less than 180 pounds." Beneath that commitment, write down all the crosscurrents you can think of. They can be real or imagined. They may be distractions, obstacles, beliefs, or internal voices.

- There's not enough time in the day
- The gym is too far away
- I gotta do email
- I like to lie in bed in the morning
- I'm too busy
- I'm too old
- It won't make any difference
- Work is more important
- I never stick to anything anyway
- The last time I worked out, I hurt myself
- I'd rather spend time with friends
- The kids need more time with me
- I'm on a deadline
- I'm too tired

Step 3: Throw an Obstacle-Removing Party

Invite friends over to do this exercise as a group. Promise them a really fun and interesting two hours. Everyone should do Steps 1 and 2 on their own and bring the list to the gathering. When you come together, have each person pick their top difficult task and as many crosscurrents as there are people who have joined you for the exercise. The more, the merrier!

Tape a large piece of paper on a wall. Clear any furniture away so you have fifteen or twenty feet of open space in front of the wall. Write down your commitment at the top of the paper.

Beneath your declaration, write down the crosscurrents you've chosen, one for each friend who's helping you.

Before you begin the next part, do some third chakra–energizing physical exercise, such as running in place, pushing against a wall, or digging your heels into the ground while roaring with a big sound. You'll want your third chakra very awake for the next step.

Step 4: Have Each Friend Represent One Obstacle

When you're all ready, pick one person at a time and give each person the job of representing one of the obstacles on your list. Instruct each person how to embody this obstacle. (For example, "I'd like you to be my child, interrupting me every five minutes, asking me to play with you or feed you or help you with your homework." Or "I'd like you to be the part of me that never sticks to anything and thinks it's hopeless.") Tell them how the obstacle or distraction appears to you and what to say or how to act to represent how that obstacle shows up in your life.

Line up the people representing your obstacles in a direct line between you and where your goal is written, facing you, one after the other. You have to move past each person to get to your goal. Your line-up should look like this:

You ➤ Obstacle 1 ➤ Obstacle 2 ➤ Obstacle 3 ➤ Obstacle 4 ➤ Goal sheet on wall

Step 5: Clear Each Obstacle with Your Will

Declare your goal out loud and begin moving toward it. The first friend faces you, preventing your movement toward your goal—just as your obstacles do. As you approach your obstacle, your friend begins to imitate that obstacle or distraction in your life. Your job is to physically, energetically, or verbally deal with each obstacle by making your energy even larger and feistier than your obstacle's energy. Your friends may give you a hard time, making you really raise your power to overpower them. Get permission from them in advance to be able to touch them physically, to shove them out of the way if necessary (without doing them any harm, of course). Your obstacles should not move aside until they feel your power fully engaged.

Remember: Don't *reason* or *plead* with your crosscurrents. That just gives them energy. Many people try to convince their obstacles to move aside. They say things like, "If you just let me work a little longer, then I'll get to you." Crosscurrents don't listen to reason; they are emotional, not reasonable, elements of your psyche. In this exercise, you have to get bigger than they are. Use your will!

When the person representing the obstacle feels your power fully engaged, he or she gives way to you, allowing you to move the obstacle physically out of your way (but not too easily—your obstacles are tough!). Then you come face-to-face with the next obstacle, and the game continues until you have moved all the obstacles out of the way. When you've moved through them all, touch the piece of paper and say your declaration out loud. Feel the power!

Congratulations, you got there! Now you know how to use your energy and willpower to clear those obstacles and distractions out of the way.

Step 6: Overcome Kryptonite

Some obstacles are the equivalent of kryptonite, the green stone that robbed Superman of his super powers. When you hit kryptonite in this exercise, you can feel your third chakra collapse. You collude with your crosscurrent ("You're right, I'm a quitter. I'll never get there."), and your power vanishes. Watch for the things that turn your will to jelly. There is usually at least one that will take you down. If that happens, use the following technique:

The obstacle, in the guise of your friend, says the phrase that triggers the collapse. For example: "You're a quitter. You'll never do it for three months. You won't last two weeks!"

Put a finger to your lips and say, "Shhh!"

The obstacle repeats the phrase a little louder.

Say more firmly and loudly, "Be quiet!"

The obstacle repeats the phrase louder still.

Raising your voice, say very loudly, "Shut up!"

The obstacle repeats the phrase even louder.

As loud as you can, yell, "Bug off!" (Stronger words are highly encouraged!)

This last, strongest command often causes the obstacle to shrink and back away, leaving you feeling great, because you've finally overpowered a countercurrent that's had power over you.

If the obstacle still doesn't leave, breathe, feel your feelings, and use the "Declare Your Intentions" exercise (page 37) or "The Belief Process" exercise (page 70) to reprogram your belief about it. Take time to go deep. What you glean from these exercises is precious information for your growth. You will be more aware of the issues blocking your success. Your will is strengthened and your awareness deepened. If obstacles are still standing in your way, there's more work to be done. Do it happily!

Strengthening your third chakra and your will may feel difficult at first, but the more you practice, the better it feels. It's similar to working out with weights in the gym, because the will is like a muscle. At first, it's a pain. But over time, your stamina and strength build, and you recognize that what was once hard is now easy. You want more. You feel good about yourself. You feel your power flowing through you. You are alive! Your strengthened willpower will serve you well, allowing you to complete each goal until you accomplish your dream. Your life will never be the same.

Chakra Two:
Pleasure Pleases

*We may affirm absolutely that nothing great in the world
has been accomplished without passion.*

—Georg Wilhelm Friedrich Hegel

Once your third chakra engine powers up and you take action, results start to appear. You get excited! You have set a course, and you now have momentum. To sustain that momentum through all the hard work to come, it's important to engage the second chakra's attribute of pleasure. Our core principle at this level is *pleasure pleases*. What is done with pleasure—and what results in another's pleasure—is pleasing to all. Pleasure oils the gears of manifestation and lets everything flow more smoothly, and it lets you have fun while you're at it!

This is the flow through the waters of the second chakra:

- Riding the river of passion
- Enhancing your pleasure principle
- Combatting seriousness
- Balancing masculine and feminine
- Attracting what you want and need

To flow down a river, you need the right type of boat, the right equipment, and an experienced guide who knows how to steer through the dangerous thrills of the rapids to come. The river of the second chakra flows in the direction you chose with your intention, and it moves you toward your destination. Enjoy the ride! You still have some work to do, though—you need to bring your dream to completion through the root chakra, which we'll discuss in the next chapter.

Chakra Two

Welcome to the realm of passion and pleasure! Chakra two is associated with the juicy element of water and is related to emotion, need, desire, sensation, pleasure, sexuality, and passion. Whew! That's a lot of power you can use to move your dream forward. This is where creation becomes ecstasy.

As we said earlier, the ancient texts on chakras called the downward current *bhukti*, which translates as "enjoyment." When the Divine manifests, it brings enjoyment in infinite forms: flowers, mountains, waterfalls, autumn foliage, children laughing, sensuality, and the human ability to manifest divinely. Enjoyment produces pleasure, which is one of the strongest attractors in the world. Our bodies are wired for pleasure. People want to buy, experience, or participate in pleasurable activities. Next to sheer survival, pleasure is humanity's most effective motivator.

Motivation, at its root, means "to move." Motivation moves you into action. Strong motivation moves others, as well. People enjoy being moved, whether it's by a great piece of music, a touching poem, a grand story, or a great love. To be moved means that you feel something deep, down to your core. When someone is moved internally, they are inspired to move externally in the world. An inspiring speech by a great orator such as Martin Luther King Jr. or Mahatma Gandhi can move an entire society in an inspired direction.

Riding the River of Passion

To achieve your dream, you need to remain passionately connected to it and also stir passion in others. What is created from passion has the power of a strong current. It moves things along. What lacks passion gets caught in the shallows and doesn't complete its journey all the way down to earth. By the time you get down to the second chakra in the creation process, you should see signs of your dream beginning to manifest, even though it's not yet complete. You've done the work: You honed your intention, clarified your vision, created SMART goals, and completed many of the tasks that move your project forward. You've cleared many obstacles out of the way. Your dream team is excited about what you're doing and is giving you support. You've gotten over some hurdles and received feedback that helped you plan your next steps. You may have attracted your first clients, made a few sales, had your first dates with someone special, or lost those first ten pounds. You may have an agent interested in your book, your first performance lined up, or the go-ahead from the building department for your house construction project. Your dream is picking up momentum. With evidence of results, you get more excited. It's happening! You can *feel* it!

There's nothing like success to get your passion going. With smaller projects and SMART goals, you can experience many little successes along the way. Your internal dialogue shifts: "Hey! I'm doing it! It's working! If I can get this next piece done, I'll be even closer." With this confidence, you talk about it even more. People see the results you've created and are more likely to believe in you and to support you. The fire of the third chakra hits the water of the second chakra and picks up steam. Hurray!

The current of manifestation has become a river of passion. Now it's time to really go with the flow. By this, we don't mean laying back and just letting it happen. It means actively paddling through the rapids—getting up early every morning to do what needs to get done, whether it's making cold calls, filling orders, or doing more of whatever you've been doing that's working. Positive feedback makes doing those things a lot easier. This is the time to stick with it, to dip your paddle back into the water, and to press forward. Enjoy the journey, but don't forget to paddle!

Enhancing Your Pleasure Principle

The element of chakra two is water. Although water can put out a fire, fire can heat water to make steam. The fire of your will can burn out if it's not tempered with the waters of pleasure. If you work all the time and never play, your work will suffer. Pleasure actually makes your work flow more easily. So it's important to nurture yourself with pleasure periodically while you are working on your purpose. This might be as simple as scheduling a weekly date for dinner and a movie, getting a massage, taking a trip out of town, enjoying sexual pleasure, or just hanging out with friends.

How much pleasure do you allow yourself in a given week? What percentage of your time do you spend in pleasurable pursuits outside of your purpose, goals, and accomplishments? What happens when you take pleasure? Do you feel guilty or renewed?

Both of us have the tendency to be workaholics. When we're in a work burn, such as preparing for a workshop or writing under a deadline, when lots of things are vying for our attention, we curtail the pleasurable activities that renew us—playing piano, dancing, gardening, kayaking, doing yoga, visiting with friends, going out to dinner and movies. Recently, when I (Anodea) was getting ready for a big trip, I looked out at the water that is my backyard and longed to take a sunset paddle in my kayak. Sadly, I didn't think I could take the time. But then I noticed that a piece of my wooden dock had gotten loose and was floating on the other side of the lake. I knew I had to go retrieve it before it got lost. The next thing I knew, I was paddling out at sunset, just as I had wanted. I laughed because I obviously *did* have time for this pleasure, but I wouldn't give it to myself until something happened to justify taking the time. It was a good lesson for me—don't wait for something bad to happen to take time off!

Guilt is the demon of the second chakra. We're told that we shouldn't need anything, shouldn't want so much, shouldn't feel this way, or shouldn't have *that* sexual fantasy. Our culture has loaded the second chakra with guilt and then sold it back to us piecemeal through advertising. Guilt checks the flow of pleasure and blocks our passion. It dams up the stream. Guilt is an appropriate feeling when you've harmed another person or violated someone's boundaries; but in our culture, guilt takes the upper hand over everything pleasurable and diminishes our pleasure even when we're engaged in it. The dieter who feels guilty about eating may not really taste her food. Guilt about sex interferes with its ease and enjoyment. I feel guilty if I skip my morning yoga or workout, but if I do my workout, I feel guilty that I started my workday late!

What beliefs lie behind your feelings of guilt? Are these your own beliefs, or did your parents or culture indoctrinate them into you? Are they true? Do these guilt-inducing beliefs serve your well-being? What would life be like if you had another belief? Use "The Belief Process" exercise (page 70) if you want to eliminate beliefs that interfere with your life. Replace them with beliefs such as, "Pleasure is a signal that I'm on the right path. Pleasure is healthy. Pleasure is good."

Manifestation Tip: Make it fun until it's done.

Fun greases the gears of manifestation and helps it flow smoothly. Make the process as enjoyable as achieving the goal, and everyone involved will be happier, more productive, and more creative.

Jason was working on a screenplay. He'd outlined his plot, chosen his characters, and begun writing dialogue, but somehow the characters weren't coming alive. He felt stuck. His screenplay was supposed to be a comedy, but he wasn't feeling very funny.

In a brainstorming session, we focused on the second chakra and looked at how he might make the whole process more fun. We suggested that he have a party for a few of his friends, loosen them up with some wine, give them silly hats, and then have them improvise skits based on his characters. His friends were bound to think of things that hadn't occurred to him. It would take the pressure off his shoulders and would be fun for everyone. The result would be a fresh stream of inspiration and pleasure that would make his job easier.

It worked. They had fun and came up with surprising scenes, and Jason was re-inspired to complete the screenplay. That screenplay became the basis for a hit television series.

If you're not having at least *some* fun at what you're doing, you'll eventually burn out or divert your attention to something that is more fun. Fun engages the most basic part of you: your inner child. If your inner child is left out, he or she will sabotage your success. If you bring the joy and enthusiasm of your inner child into your activities, life becomes a playground. Playing is the most direct line to your creativity, as well as to your productivity.

What can you do to make your dream or project more fun? *Think outside the box.* Doing something ordinary in a different way can make it more fun. Imagine cooking dinner in your hot pink underwear or practicing your voice exercises while standing on a table. Imagine that aliens from another planet are spying on you at the gym and are trying to figure out what the hell you're trying to accomplish. If you're stuck in traffic, imagine what other people are thinking about as you see their faces; put their thoughts inside cartoon thought-balloons. If you hate doing the dishes, imagine you're actually Cinderella and there is a handsome prince waiting to rescue you, except he forgot your name and you have to come up with a new one that will make him laugh when he finds you. If you want to read poetry to your lover, get under the covers and read it with a flashlight, as though you were kids staying up late to read comic books.

My (Anodea's) brother used to watch TV with the colors distorted so everyone's face was bright pink and their hair was green. Then he'd turn the sound off and make up the conversation. (He became a very successful comedic television actor in Hollywood.) With a little twist, ordinary things become extraordinary. Making it fun to manifest your dream is like oiling the gears of a machine so everything flows more easily.

Combatting Seriousness

Taking yourself too seriously takes the fun out of life and makes manifestation into a chore. If you find yourself mired in seriousness, be amused at yourself. Instead of typing a question into Google, turn your inquiry toward Giggle. Look at your life as if it were a sitcom. Find the humor in it. Our friend Steve Bhaerman (a.k.a., Swami Beyondananda) says that the opposite of gravity is levity. If you're feeling grave, you'll end up there much too soon. Laughter is the medicine that cures seriousness. We need a dose of *silliousness* to counteract seriousness. As Swami says (in an exaggerated Indian accent), "Be a fundamentalist. Make sure the fun always comes before the mental. Realize that life is a situation comedy that will never be cancelled. A laugh track has been provided, and the reason we are put in the material world is to get more material. Have a good laughsative twice a day, and that will ensure reguhilarity."

Remember: *Enlightenment* means to lighten up! Give your inner child the official job of Fun Advisor. Ask what he or she would like to do today. See if you can match his or her energy and playfulness. If you can't make contact with your inner child, play with some real children. You might feel awkward at first, but if you let go of expectations that you have to be any particular way, they'll teach you all about play. It is said that the work of children is play. Through play, experimentation, and make believe, they come to know the world. But at some point, they're taught that life is supposed to be serious. Bring the belief "Life is serious" into "The Belief Process" exercise (page 70) and eliminate it. Try on "Life is joy." Do you prefer to wear that belief instead?

The root of *enjoyment* is *joy.* Ramone Yaciuk, author of *Enjoy the Hell Out of Your Life,* says that joy is a choice. When we choose joy frequently, it becomes a habit. If you're in a state in which you can't find joy in the moment, get out your map and drive to another state. Close your eyes and think of a time when you felt joyful or playful. Bring that state into your body. Or mimic someone you know who is frequently playful. Yaciuk says that when he's feeling stuck, he sits down to interview his inner Robin Williams, who answers his questions in a wide variety of funny voices.

Here are two short, easy exercises to help you combat the dreadful disease of seriousness:

- Lift the corners of your lips toward your ears, put your hand on your belly, and repeat the sound of "ha" while exhaling rapidly and rolling your eyes. See what happens.

- When you first get up in the morning, walk into your bathroom and look in the mirror. Find something funny about the person looking back at you and begin to laugh at that person. What a silly goose! Look how seriously they take everything! What a riot! Make faces at them. Continue until you feel lighter than you did when you woke up.

Balancing Masculine and Feminine

Although every chakra has a masculine and feminine quality, nowhere is this polarity more pronounced than in the second chakra, which represents duality, sexuality, and the attraction of opposites. We find that men and women tend to approach manifestation differently, and they have different challenges in bringing ideas down into reality. Both masculine and feminine exist within each one of us as qualities and as ways of being. To be balanced and whole, we need to be able to embrace the masculine and the feminine forces within us. Our greatest growth comes from embracing qualities that are less familiar to us.

Some people have used the term *femifesting* as a balance to the word *manifesting*. In manifesting, you follow the steps we've outlined in this book: Choose an intention, make goals and plans, take action, deal with the obstacles, and get to your goal. It's a tried-and-true method, and it could be considered masculine in nature. Femifesting, say our women friends, works by sitting in the middle of the reality you want (even if it's imaginary) and saying "no" to anything that's not in alignment with what you want. Manifesting reflects king energy, while femifesting reflects the power of a queen.

Biologically, men have a *thing,* and women have a *place.* The masculine way of living life has given us many things: cars, stereos, airplanes, buildings, roads, houses, computers, . . . the list is endless.

These things are great gifts to society. But in the process of producing so many things, we've trashed the place. Industrialization has created pollution, scarcity, and clutter—in short, an environmental mess. We're out of balance. At this point in time, we don't need more *things;* we need to clean up the *place* and make it a more pleasing and pleasurable place to live our lives and raise our children.

Speaking in broad generalities, men produce, and women attract. Men are more likely to doubt their ability to produce, and women tend to doubt their ability to attract. In our ancient brains, a man's ability to attract a mate depended on his skill at seeking, hunting, and producing food. Women attracted mates with their sensuous beauty and their skills of gathering, nurturing, and making babies. Hunting required a single-pointed focus of attention, bonding with other men in silence and stealth and facing danger with courage. Gathering required a wide focus of attention. Women worked together, looking across the landscape for subtle colors of plants and talking with each other to stay connected and to scare away beasts. Women attract with their radiance and beauty; men attract with their power and presence.

Our sexual organs tell the same story. Men have equipment to penetrate; women have a place to receive. The archetypal energies are yang and yin, masculine and feminine, active and receptive. Together, as the Tao, these energies are a balanced whole. The manifestation process requires the embodiment of both polarities. There are times to gather and times to hunt. Sometimes we rely on the power of attracting what already exists, and other times we have to go out and create what doesn't yet exist. To master manifestation, you need to get good at both attracting and creating.

Attracting What You Want and Need

The Law of Attraction, popularized through the book and the movie *The Secret,* has taken center stage as a cultural meme for manifestation. Workshops, books, and websites about it abound. This law states that like attracts like, that your thoughts will draw toward you a reality that matches. If you have negative thoughts, you will attract negative results. If you believe life is hard, it will be hard. If you focus your thoughts on abundance and prosperity, you will attract it into your life.

We see it a little differently. What you think and believe is not so much an *attractive* force that draws preexisting conditions toward you, but rather a *creative* force that actually creates reality out of the raw elements of the universe. As we explained in chakra seven, consciousness creates. If you change your beliefs, you will change the reality you experience.

In the second chakra, pleasure and passion are primary attractive forces. The success of a venture depends on people being attracted to you and to what you are doing. People are attracted to what brings them pleasure (or what promises to), whether that pleasure is healthy, such as the pleasure that comes from good food and music, or unhealthy, such as pleasure that leads to an addiction to drugs, alcohol, cigarettes, or unhealthy foods. When you experience pleasure, you become more attractive. Your excitement is contagious, and your enthusiasm sparks others.

In the business world, it's said, "Enthusiasm sells." The root of the word *enthusiasm* is the Latin *en theos,* meaning "in God." Enthusiasm is what we feel when we are infused with God or Spirit. Let your passion move you, and it will move others!

Desire is another important aspect of the second chakra. Our desires draw us toward things, people, and situations. At the biological level, desire causes us to move toward that which we need in order to survive and thrive. Desires can be divided into *wants* and *needs.* In the manifestation of any dream, there are things you want, and there are things you really need. It's important to get clear on which is which. Both are important; the difference is that your needs are necessities. You *need* to put gas in your car (unless it's electric), or it won't go anywhere. Your body *needs* sleep and food, and you *need* money to pay your bills. You may *want* more money to fuel your project or a famous designer to help you create your website. You may *want* to have your book reviewed in the *New York Times.* But none of these wants are necessary for your success.

It's easy to confuse wants with needs and sometimes they are in conflict. You may want a better job, but you need the income from your current job. You want to hurry and get things done, but you need more time for research or training. You want to make more money, but you need more time to rest.

Most of us were taught as children—by family members or friends—that it's bad to be needy. Being called "needy" is terribly humiliating. So we try to move forward without having needs and without having what we need. And then we wonder why things don't work out the way we wanted them to. If you feel guilty about having needs, then you may not be acknowledging your needs as real necessities. You may not make fulfilling your needs a priority. Unmet needs can turn into obstacles later, stopping your progress.

The first step toward clarity is to identify what you really need and what you want. You'll do that in the "Distinguish Needs from Wants" exercise (page 204). You can fulfill some of your wants and needs yourself, but most desires require the cooperation of other people. Learning to ask for what you need and want is the next step. However, merely asking may not get your needs met (as you've probably learned from life). You have to be able to express your needs and wants in such a way that it brings results. This includes saying *exactly* how you want them met. In many cases, it also means expressing what you do *not* want or need. Because we all have delicate egos, we need to learn to speak our truth authentically and kindly. For example: "Thank you for your input, but I don't need help with that aspect of the project—can you work on this one instead?" "Right now I need to finish doing this without adding any more to it. Can we schedule another time to talk about your other ideas?" When you learn that you can express your needs clearly, specifically, and kindly, you can gain the cooperation and support of others to help you fully manifest your vision.

When you express your wants *knowing* that they are not needs, you can remain unattached to the outcome. A want is a "nice to have," not a "must have." Not getting what you want won't stop your progress. You can ask for anything you want, knowing that if you don't get it, there's no harm done. If you do get it, you can celebrate!

Another crucial skill for manifestation mastery is the art of negotiating. In business, it is said, "You don't get what you deserve; you get what you negotiate." Some people are naturally good at this skill—they began by negotiating with Mom to get a cookie before dinner. Those of us who did not learn as children have to study and practice this important life skill. Negotiation turns a yes-or-no decision into myriad possibilities, most of which you weren't aware of when you began. Negotiation is a mutual discovery process, not a wrestling match. It's especially important when negotiating with others that you see *their* wants and needs as being equal to your own. Otherwise you're merely using them to get what you want, which demeans them, turning them into a mere resource for your personal advantage. If the result of a negotiation is a win-win situation, both parties walk away happy with the outcome. If the game is played so that you win but the other person feels like a loser, the negative consequences can last a lifetime.

Exercise: Distinguish Needs from Wants

Take a piece of paper and draw a vertical line down the middle. Write "Needs" on the top of one column and "Wants" on the top of the other. Make a list of everything you need and everything you want in order to complete your dream. Note carefully whether each thing is a need—that is, a real necessity—or a "nice to have" want. Your list may include money or funds, time, support, friends, connections, education, miracles, skills, products, or supplies. Also note which items you can obtain yourself, without the help of others, and which ones you need help with from other people. For extra depth, add the names of people (or their roles, such as "a lawyer") you could ask to help you obtain each item on your list.

Making your needs and wants clear and exact helps draw them to you. The Universe wants you to have what you want, but it can't help you if you aren't clear about your wants. Clarifying your wants and needs is like typing a word into Google and having websites come up that are relevant to your inquiry. If you could have anything, what would you ask for? The clearer you are, the fewer options there will be, but they will be easier to fulfill. (Remember: You can have anything, but you can't have everything. Besides, if you could have everything, where would you put it?)

Exercise: Express Your Desires

In this exercise, you'll practice asking for exactly what you want. This is an important second chakra skill. It's crucial for the process of creation—and for a good life!

Try this exercise with at least one other person; it's better with two or three others. Decide who will go first. That person is designated the Asker-Receiver. The others will be Givers for an agreed amount of time—twenty to thirty minutes is a good place to start. Givers will respond to the Asker's requests. During this precious period of time, the Asker may ask the Givers for anything he or she would like to have—whether it be food, drink, entertainment, touch, and so forth. The Asker must specify *exactly* what they want and how they want it. Of course, Givers have a right to say "no" if responding to the request is inappropriate for them. Hearing "no" has to be okay with the Asker, because not everyone will say yes when they are asked for something. Givers also have the right to negotiate. However, the spirit of the exercise is to serve the Asker and give them what they want as much as possible. Remind the Givers that their turn to be the Asker is coming up!

As the Asker, you may want to have your feet rubbed, or you may want the Givers to listen to your poetry. You might want a cup of tea brought to you or to be tucked in with a blanket and told a story. Look inside to discover what you really want. Pay no attention to the voices that say, "I shouldn't ask for that," or "Others will think less of me if I appear needy." Express your wants as the precious gifts that they are. Feel what it's like to receive exactly what you want!

If you receive a "no," take a moment to feel what that feels like and observe your reaction. Then, look at the deeper need beneath your request. For example, if you want skin-to-skin contact, the deeper need might be to be held and rocked like an infant. You can then ask for the deeper need to be fulfilled, to see whether the Givers can respond. Your need may or may not get met in this exercise, but identifying it and verbalizing it is important. When you know your deeper needs, you can ask your partner or someone with whom you can be more intimate.

The second important skill to practice during this exercise is feedback. If the person rubbing your feet is not giving you the exact pressure or style you want, tell them what you *do* want. Many people tend to criticize when they're not getting what they want instead of providing feedback. If something isn't working for you, be specific. Say, "I like how your fingers feel on my foot, but I need more pressure. I'd like you to press harder here, on the bottom, then move with a circular motion that moves all the way up to the tips of my toes." Is your tea too hot? Ask your Giver to blow on it to cool it down. Is the music too loud? Ask your Giver to adjust it to the volume that's just right for you.

As an Asker-Receiver, feel how glorious it is to ask for what you want and to actually get it. This is your opportunity to be truly selfish. Most of us were told as children, "Don't be selfish!" But that's the job of children—to be self-oriented and to learn, slowly, how to care for themselves. Our families may have needed (or wanted) us to grow up too fast, so they made selfishness bad or wrong. Release this belief using "The Belief Process" exercise (page 70). Experiment with the belief, "My needs are good, and I deserve to have them met," or "Asking for what I want is healthy." Self-care and self-nurturing are positive virtues. Your responsibility as the Asker-Receiver is to be clear about what you need to be happy—and then to be happy when you get it.

It is said that in relationships, a man wants to make his woman happy, and he will leave a woman if she doesn't become happy. Happiness and pleasure are your responsibility—it's not the responsibility of others to make you happy. You don't get what you deserve—you get what you ask for—and negotiate! Learn the skill and be happy!

When you take the role of Giver, feel the satisfaction that comes from giving someone *exactly* what they want without needing anything in return. This is the beauty and pleasure of pure service to others.

Extend this experiment into your personal, intimate relationship. Talk to your spouse, mate, or lover about this exercise and get his or her approval for an evening of giving and receiving. The feedback loop during sensual and sexual play might sound like this: "That's really good. Now move a little slower and lighten (or increase) the pressure." Asking for what you want is even more important in the bedroom than in the world of business, projects, and tasks. The flow of asking and receiving creates intimacy. Many people get only a tiny fraction of the pleasure they are capable of receiving because they don't ask for exactly what they want. Take this assignment seriously! Bring more pleasure to yourself and your intimate partner. Opening the second chakra in this way makes manifesting your dream—and life itself—a whole lot more fun. Here's a manifestation tip, and a life tip: Fun is good!

Chakra One:
Matter Matters

Hidden beneath your feet is a luminous stage
where you are meant to rehearse your eternal dance.

—Hafiz

W hen you get right down to it, matter matters. It matters what we do to the earth. It matters what we put into our bodies and how we treat them. It matters whether wooden boards are cut to the right length before they're nailed together. It matters how a bridge is built, that a chair is strong enough to hold us, that the hardware in our computers is assembled in a precise way. It matters that our farms produce food and that the earth's biosphere continues to thrive.

It matters what we put into our foundation—whether it's the foundation of a building, a relationship, or a business. A foundation is not just physical—it is also ethical, moral, and philosophical. If a building's foundation is faulty, the whole structure could fail. If we do not live our lives with a foundation of integrity, our relationships fail.

If we do not build and sustain our society on a solid foundation that honors the world of nature, our bodies, and the people within it, then the structures of society will eventually collapse at the most fundamental level. Consider the great empires of the past. Each one failed at some point—some fell into chaos, some were overrun by invaders, and some shrunk to a more manageable size. Collapse, by definition, pulls us downward toward the earth.

When we were writing this book, citizens around the world were demonstrating against long-standing economic and political inequities. Millions of homeowners lost their homes. Sovereign nations went bankrupt. The middle class, built up over the past sixty years, has been disappearing. The "1 percent"—which is really the 0.01 percent of the world population—continues to consolidate its wealth and power, but revolution is in the air. Without a foundation of fairness and balance, the institutions we rely on cannot hold. Yet we fear collapse because it brings chaos and danger.

The last step in our manifestation process brings us down to the first chakra, the element of earth, where we ground all our hard work into the material world, into the final resting place of manifestation. If you do everything else in this book but fail to ground your work in your earthly reality, your dream will not manifest—or if it does, it will not hold solid. As you work your way down to the ground, you'll step down through these elements of the first chakra:

- Fulfilling your commitments
- Making sense of your dollars
- Having your dream
- Inhabiting your body
- Touching the earth
- Completing every cycle

This level of manifestation creates the greatest resistance of all the chakra steps, because you are now hitting solid ground. Resistance is the tendency of matter to prevent change, and it is a useful principle. If the earth had no resistance, you couldn't walk on it. Your feet would slide around as if you were walking on slippery ice. If the ground had no resistance, you would fall through it, and you wouldn't be able to build anything on it. During a massive earthquake, the earth turns to jelly in some places, and that liquidy state allows great buildings to fall. When you're bringing your dream into reality, you have to use force to shape the world in your direction, similar to an artist chiseling stone into a sculpture or pressing porcelain clay into a the shape of a cup. You have to bring the third chakra's fire and power into play with the water of the second chakra and the earth of the first chakra to make something useful.

When you ground into the first chakra, the earth holds you steady and solid, and it allows your energies to build. A leaky cup can't hold water, just as a small or shaky foundation limits what you can build on it. It's understandable if you have some resistance to the exacting nature of the earth plane, because it's so demanding! But if you can accept the demands and work with them, they will hold you and support your dream, all the way through to completion. The hard work that's required will make you strong and your dreams real.

Chakra One

The first chakra is a very exacting and unforgiving realm. You can't throw boards together without measuring them and expect your house to hold up. You don't go to a bank and say, "Give me some money!" (unless you're robbing the bank). Instead, you fill out a form that says you want to withdraw an exact amount: $1,374.75. You're allowed to take it out only if you have that much money or more in your account. Accounting is an exacting process, balancing income and expenses down to the last penny. If you say to a waiter, "Just bring some food," he doesn't know what to deliver to your table. Exactness matters in the first chakra.

The Sanskrit name of chakra one, *Muladhara*, means "root support." The roots of a plant support its growth upward and outward. The deeper the roots, the higher and bigger the plant can grow. It's not deep pockets that we need in order to manifest, but deep roots. It's quite simple: The more grounded you are, the more easily you can manifest.

Roots have both a masculine and feminine quality. On the masculine side, they *penetrate* the earth, pushing their way downward between rocks and soil. The feminine aspect of roots is *receptive*, drawing nourishment and moisture up from the earth to feed the plant. You must be able to do both—to hold your ground, deeply penetrating "what's so" with your intention to create "what's possible," while also receiving support and nourishment from the world.

You can view your body as a temple in which your chakras are the inner chambers. The root chakra is your foundation, which must be solid enough for the temple to hold the divine energies that come down from above. Your body temple exists in the physical universe and operates by the laws of physics, chemistry, and biology.

Psychologically, the root chakra represents the urge toward survival, materiality, security, money, and possessions. It is ruled by primitive instincts, which at times interfere with our common sense. When we get reactive, we want to fight or flee. But what we really need at such moments is to be grounded and practical, open and aware, and able to deal with whatever comes up—whether resistance from within or external obstacles and circumstances.

Fulfilling Your Commitments

Concerning all acts of initiative,
there is one elementary truth, the ignorance of which kills
countless ideas and splendid plans: that the moment one
definitely commits oneself, then Providence moves too.

—W. H. Murray

As you bring heaven down to earth, each chakra's activities feed and inform the chakra below it. When you receive guidance and clarify your intention in the seventh chakra, it is easier to create a clear vision in the sixth chakra. When your vision is clear, it's easier to define your SMART goals and communicate and convey your excitement to others in chakra five. Clear communication is the foundation for good relationships, both personal and professional, in chakra four. Enlivening your love feeds you and others, generating the energy from which you derive your power and the motivation to do the things that need to be done in chakra three. With each step forward, you feel the spark of pleasure in chakra two, and you recognize that creation is ecstasy, so you keep going even when the going gets tough. Fun greases the gears for a smooth journey.

Each step is important. But if you are not fully *committed* to fulfilling each one, your dream cannot be birthed into physical reality. Commitment is more than just uttered words or even a signed contract. It requires fully showing up—being committed in energy, heart, and mind. It is the willingness to do whatever it takes to fulfill your commitment in the best way possible. You can be outwardly committed in a relationship but not fully present. You can commit to showing up at work every day but spend your time daydreaming or chit-chatting with coworkers. Commitment is an alignment of all your chakras, following through on all requirements of each level, *down to the last detail.*

Bringing things into the physical world and making them real requires time. We all know that time is hungry—it eats whatever we give it. It is a little-recognized fact that tasks will always expand to fill whatever time is given to them. Cleaning a closet can take an hour or a day, and for some people, it can take a lifetime. If you say to an acquaintance, "Let's have lunch sometime," they will usually respond, "Yeah, sure, I'd love to." And it never happens.

Your SMART goals are time-based, which means you have a "by when" date for completion. But that is not enough. It doesn't tell you exactly what parts of the task you are committed to doing when. Most of us are deadline driven—we wait until the last minute, until it *must* be done. In chakra three, we showed you that making appointments with yourself is one key to getting things done. It can be difficult to manage your internal to-do list because your mind is fluid, flexible, and always changing. An appointment on your calendar, however, fixes that to-do item in space and time, making it more real. You bend the rest of your life around that commitment in order to show up or do that thing on time.

How you keep your commitments—to yourself and to others—defines your integrity. How often do you let yourself off the hook after making a commitment to another person? Does it depend on that person's position in your life? You're not likely to let a commitment to your boss slide, but you may treat an appointment with a salesperson with less conviction. Do you keep your promises to your children? Did your parents do so with you?

If we could make only one recommendation that would improve your life, it would be to hone and improve your integrity—that is, your willingness to make and keep commitments to yourself and others. If you can be counted on to keep your word, others will value you. If you do what you say you will do, you can count on yourself to create the life you want. Examine your life deeply and determine where you can—and can't—be counted on. Then, do whatever it takes to improve your count-on-ability. This is the final filter that separates those who can manifest from those who can't. Keeping your commitments is like putting screws and bolts into the parts of a car to hold it together. Without the nuts and bolts, all you have are pieces. With them, you have a vehicle that can take you wherever you want to go.

Exercise: Make a List of Your Commitments

Step 1: Make a list of what you are going to get done in the coming thirty days to forward your dream, goal, or project. Place these promises to yourself on your calendar, on the dates and times when you commit to doing them. Do this step *now*!

Step 2: Make a list of what you are committed to doing in the next seven days to move your dream, goal, or project forward. Place each item on your calendar for the coming week. Find an accountability partner—a friend, partner, or colleague—and ask your partner to check in with you at the end of the week to ensure that you have kept your commitments.

Step 3: Make a list of five things you are committed to doing tomorrow. When tomorrow comes, do those five things first—before you do anything else. Cross off each item after you've done it. At the end of the day, look at the list and celebrate the things you accomplished. If you didn't accomplish something, analyze the reasons and handle it as a crosscurrent. Then make five new commitments for the next day. Repeat every day until your dream is fulfilled completely.

Making Sense of Your Dollars

*Too many people today know the price of everything
and the value of nothing.*

—Ann Landers

No discussion about manifestation or the first chakra would be complete without talking about money. For some people, money is the beginning and the end of everything important. Their chief limitation is that they don't have enough of it, and their sole goal is to get more of it. But we see money merely as a means to an end. It's often a necessary means, but it's not an end in itself.

Money and prosperity are universal concerns in teachings about manifestation. The people who have more than enough money rarely buy books on how to manifest; they have the means to just go out and create. For the rest of us, money can be a stumbling block or a stepping-stone, an uncomfortable limitation or a foundation that supports and liberates us.

To create heaven on earth, we must first recognize that the natural state of the universe is abundance. There are hundreds of billions of galaxies, each with hundreds of billions of stars. In all likelihood, there are billions of planets supporting life. Apple trees produce an abundance of apples, regardless of whether the fruit is eaten, and they don't hold a meeting when there's an economic downturn and decide to produce fewer apples. Flowers in the wilderness cover the ground regardless of whether anyone is there to see them. Scarcity is a uniquely human condition, a sign that we are not in harmony with the natural flow of abundance.

The Industrial Revolution maximized the exploitation of resources and people. It produced abundance, but at a cost. It has mass-produced stuff (more than we know what to do with) while simultaneously producing massive waste and cheapening the value of that stuff. After World War II, the field of advertising began to exploit the emerging principles of psychology and propaganda to encourage consumption and to manipulate people into buying what they didn't need. Our economic system isn't a fair game. The playing field is not equal—it's designed to make the wealthy and powerful more wealthy and powerful. The amount of money we make is not proportional to how hard we work. Not everyone can earn a decent living. The economic downturn makes it even more difficult to achieve the prosperity that everyone wants. But all of this is based on belief. In any economy, there are people who prosper. There are many ways to do things, and many things to do, without money. Since your beliefs determine your possibilities, examine your beliefs about money. If you feel limited in your ability to live a prosperous life, find out where your limitations are coming from.

We're really seeking value in our lives, not money. There is real value in human relationships, love, and community. And yet the economy has focused our attention on green pieces of paper. Almost everything has been reduced to a commodity to be bought and sold on the open market. We have been trained to focus on money and security, and we have been so well trained that we don't even know we've been trained well.

Regardless of the state of the economy, you can use first chakra principles to live a life of integrity in your personal economic system. Doing so aligns you with the physical world. In addition, when you have integrity with the physical, you'll get support from the world.

Money is a very exacting realm, which is fitting for the first chakra. Banks count your money to the last penny. Cash registers have to balance at the end of the day. Cars, houses, clothes, and food all cost specific amounts. Money represents one measure of exchange with the universe. Love can't be measured, but dollars can.

People who have difficulty with money often have difficulty being specific. Have you created a budget? Do you balance your checkbook? Do you keep track of your expenses and know exactly what you spend? If money is an issue for you, deal with it by focusing your attention on specifics. Use the "Evaluate Your Financial Foundation" exercise (page 217) to get down and dirty—or clean—about your money flow. Where are the leaks in your money system? If your boat is leaking, it doesn't matter how much wind is blowing into its sails.

I (Anodea) once had a client who had made millions of dollars several times, through different projects. He had lost his entire fortune each time. He was good at making money, was comfortable handling huge sums, and could negotiate big deals. But something within him couldn't hold onto his wealth. I had him visualize his chakras, one by one. When he got to the first chakra, the root foundation, he discovered that it looked like an unfinished construction project. It was full of missing pieces—places where his money leaked out. We worked on grounding exercises first, giving him a connection to the material plane. Then we looked deeply into his family dynamics and the beliefs he held about money. Through changing his beliefs, he was able to clear out his shoddy foundation, establish solidity, and get back on the road to sustainable financial success.

Exercise: Evaluate Your Financial Foundation

How much money do you spend each month on basic necessities? On extravagances? On your health? On your business? On paying interest on your debt? What are your beliefs about money? Where did they come from?

To get grounded and be successful in the world, you need to be specific about your money, your assets, and your liabilities. When money moves through a system, it's called *cash flow*. Think of a river flowing through a steep canyon. If you put a turbine in the water, you can generate electricity from the flow. If the river is healthy, it provides a rich source of food for plants, animals, and people. Prosperity comes from flow, but only if that flow continues. If the river dries up, everything dies.

Step 1: Your flow is determined in large part by your beliefs. Take time to answer these questions in your journal:

* What do you believe about money? Write down your beliefs, repeatedly completing these sentences: "Money is . . ." and "Money should . . ."

- Review each belief. How has that belief served you? Limited you? Hurt you?

- What did your parents believe about money? What did their parents believe? How many of your beliefs are the same as theirs?

- Do you have doubts about your own worth or value? If you charge for your services, do you charge what your actual value is?

Take the beliefs that no longer serve you into "The Belief Process" exercise (page 70) and create new beliefs that will serve you better.

Step 2: Reflect on the following questions and be specific in your answers. If you don't know the answers, spend time researching what's true.

- My monthly income ranges from _____ on the low end to _____ on the high end.

- In each of the past five years, my yearly income totaled _____, _____, _____, _____, and _____.

- In each of the past five years, my yearly expenses totaled _____, _____, _____, _____, and _____.

- My monthly expenses are . . .

    _____ for necessities.

    _____ for wants.

    _____ for extravagances.

    _____ for savings and investment in the future.

    _____ for everything else.

- I want to earn _____ percent more next year than I earned on average in the past three years. I intend to create this reality by _____ [date].

- My biggest obstacle to earning more money is _____.

- My biggest obstacle to reducing or controlling my spending is ____

  _____ .

- If I won the lottery or had sufficient abundance and never needed to worry about money again, this is what I would do with my life:

  _____ .

- To achieve my dream, the amount of money I need to manifest is

  _____ .

- I will do whatever it takes to manifest this amount by _____ [date].

- I will manifest this amount by doing the following: _____

  _____

Address your obstacles, weaknesses, beliefs, and crosscurrents by using any of the techniques we've taught, such as "Declare Your Intentions" (page 37), "The Belief Process" (page 70), or "Voice Dialogue" (page 124). Find a coach, a friend, or a colleague who can help you work through your money issues. When you clear your path of obstacles, you'll experience more flow, more prosperity, and more freedom around money. It will become a resource for fueling your dreams, rather than a burden or problem.

First Chakra Principles

An entire book could be written about the grounding principles of the first chakra. As you come down from the seventh chakra to the first, you confront more and more limitations—limitations in time, space, resources, ability, energy, and bandwidth. We brought this book into reality by following the same principles that we've presented. As we come down to our first chakra, the physical form of the book, our publisher gave us limitations in both space and time. We made adjustments to align with their standards in order to bring our project to fruition. Here, we've summarized some of the additional principles that will support you in bringing *your* dream to reality:

- **Ground, by definition, is hard.** This is a good thing; you need hard ground to make a solid foundation. Every bit of matter has specific edges and boundaries. Physical things can be quantified, measured, and counted. A knife blade is sharpened when it's pushed against a hard stone; in the same way, you are honed by the difficulties you push yourself up against. Surrender to the discipline of things that are hard. Learn to work with what *is* and discover the laws that govern the way things are. Then, you can create what might be.

- **To manifest, accept limitations.** The first chakra is the most limited realm of all the chakras. Thoughts are infinite, but you have only one body. Accepting limitations gracefully is an essential key to maturity—and to manifestation. Containment allows you to hold and solidify: A covered pot boils faster. Becoming financially solid gives you a solid ground from which to grow. Be willing to accept the limitations of time and money. Remember, you can have anything, but you can't have everything.

- **Integrity preserves value.** Keep your word, fulfill your promises, pay your debts, charge a fair price, and be honest in your dealings. All of these actions keep your money "clean." Lack of integrity hinders the flow of prosperity.

- **Caring for what you have demonstrates that you're ready for more.** Be thankful for whatever level of abundance you have already experienced. Avoid comparing what you have with what others have. Care for your possessions, whether they are abundant or meager. How you care for what you have is the best measure of whether you are ready to have more. If you loan something to someone and they take good care of it, you are more likely to share with them again. If your home environment is simple but well cared for, you are showing the Universe that you will preserve the value of what you have been given. You become a good investment. Take good care of your car, your home, your clothing, and your possessions. Care for other people's things with the same respect. Honor the physical world of the first chakra, and it will honor you in return. In his book *Kinds of Power,* James Hillman wrote, "Not only persons call for service; things do, too—the oil changed, the VCR cleaned, the dryer repaired, the message transmitted. . . . Objects have their own personalities that ask for attention. . . . Treating things as if they had souls, carefully, with good manners—that's quality service."[14]

- **How you care for yourself reflects how you care for everything else.** Lack of financial health often results from a sense of deprivation, unworthiness, guilt, or low self-esteem. Examine your beliefs around these issues and develop deep self-respect and methods of self-care. Get your basic needs cared for first, then your higher needs, then your wants. "One step at a time" is a first chakra mantra.

- **Generosity breeds abundance.** The wider you can open your tap, without being foolish or unconscious, the more prosperity can flow through you. Tithe a portion of your income to a cause you believe in or give generously to someone in need. Keep your ground, but open your flow.

- **You are not your money.** Who would you be if you gave up all your money mania and lived a life of voluntary simplicity? If this idea creates feelings of shame or unworthiness or if it seems completely crazy, you may be identifying too much with your financial worth. Who you are is not defined by what you have. You are much greater than you can possibly imagine, unlimited in scope and possibility. Money doesn't define you.

- **Each want and need has a monetary value.** Go back to the "Distinguish Needs from Wants" exercise (page 204) and put a monetary value on each item. What would it cost to have everything you need? What would it cost to have everything you want? Few people recognize this important fact: Everything you own has a mouth, and it needs to be fed. All things require maintenance. Expensive things require protection and insurance. Your family, clients, and customers all need to be held, loved, and serviced. It takes time, money and resources to do so. Are you prepared to spend what it costs to have what you want?

- **Manage your money so your money doesn't manage you.** In the same way that your third chakra power has to be bigger than your obstacles, you have to be bigger than your finances. Choose real value over monetary value. That might mean that you don't buy the cheapest tool or product, but instead pay more for something that lasts.

- **Planning for the future changes your financial priorities.** How much do you need (and by when) in order to pay your bills easily and to feel comfortable financially? How much do you need in savings to avoid bankruptcy in case you lose your job or if someone you love becomes ill? (Most people who go bankrupt have one or both of those two scenarios.) How much do you need for retirement? How much will it cost to send your kids to college, and how much do you want to leave for them when you die? Planning for the future changes your priorities in a very healthy way.

- **Your values determine how you spend your money and time.** If money were time and each dollar you spent represented time off your life, would you still buy that expensive item? (Check out the excellent movie *In Time* to see this philosophy played out in action.) Don't waste your time where you are not appreciated or adequately compensated, whether financially or in some other form. Likewise, don't waste your money on anything that doesn't have lasting value.

- **Attention is like money. It needs to be paid.** Our friend, visionary activist Caroline Casey, advises, "Build an altar to your troublesome gods." This means you should pay attention to whatever is troubling you. This is obvious when it comes to your body, as frequent health problems require you to pay closer attention to your body. But it also applies to anything that troubles you. If money is a constant issue for you, it is asking you to pay closer attention to it on all levels. Spend time focusing on the deeper issues and needs that underlie the reality that's showing up in your life.

- **Perfectionism is a way of not having anything.** If what exists is never quite good enough, you'll get zero satisfaction from having it. Perfectionists believe that 99 percent is not passing. People who are seeking the perfect mate tend to remain single. People who want the perfect body have trouble enjoying the body they actually inhabit. If you allow things to be *sufficient* or *good enough,* you'll have more to enjoy. Perfection lies only in the here-and-now as an intrinsic *is-ness:* Everything is perfect just as it is. When Harry Palmer, creator of the Avatar Course, was asked by a cynical student, "So, are you perfect?" he responded, "I'm a perfect me." Zen master Suzuki Roshi said it well: "Everything is perfect. And it could use a little improvement."

Having Your Dream

The first and second chakras represent the *having* aspect of the three aspects of life: being, doing, and having. In the downward flow of manifestation, first figure out how you need to *be* in order to create your dream. Then *do* the things that need to be done. Finally, you get to *have* your dream in your life and enjoy its fulfillment. But can you really have it?

The ability to have is basic to our nature, but early childhood programming can convince you otherwise. You may believe that having too many things is not okay. Or you may believe that what you have will be taken away at any moment. Like any skill, the ability to have can be developed with practice. Your inner sense of self-worth, in large part, determines your ability to have. You can't have more than you think you're worth. Studies of people who win the lottery have shown repeatedly that most of those who win large sums of money lose their fortunes within a few years.[15] It's likely that their self-image wasn't large enough to hold that much fortune. It has also been shown that income disparity between men and women is not just a result of a male-dominated society, but also a result of the fact that women more readily accept lower pay. Women aren't as skilled at negotiating on their own behalf, they are less likely to trust their worth in a man's world, and they fail to hold out for the pay they really deserve.

To examine or clarify your sense of worth, use the "Declare Your Intentions" exercise (page 37) with the intention: "I am worthy." Clear out crosscurrents that interfere with that intention. Or conduct "The Belief Process" exercise (page 70) on any hidden beliefs you discover about your self-worth. Other people's estimations of your worth and value are directly influenced by how worthy you believe you are.

Another aspect of the ability to *have* is related to trust. If you don't trust something, you won't let yourself have it. Even if you're thirsty, you won't drink from a stranger's bottle of water. You don't trust that the water is clean and safe to drink, so you won't let yourself have it. If a close friend offers you water, however, your trust allows you to quench your thirst.

When you distrust the world around you, it's difficult for you to have what it offers. The Universe tries to give you gifts every day, but if you believe you don't deserve them or if you don't trust the source, you aren't able to receive them. Your receiving pipe is crimped, and everything that's available to you shrinks to fit through a small opening, limiting your abundance. When you feel truly grounded and safe in the world, on the other hand, you can trust, open, receive, and *have*.

Those who manifest easily have these qualities: (1) They have a basic trust in themselves *and* in the world, (2) they do the planning and work that is required, and (3) they know how to handle the inevitable blocks and barriers that will appear. Master manifestors have confidence that their work will be rewarded. But the ability to have goes even deeper. It includes the ability to fully allow something in, to truly experience it. Have you ever eaten a meal quickly and then realized you didn't let yourself have the experience of savoring your food? Some people don't really let themselves have intimacy with their partner or quality time with their kids. To really have something requires slowing down, turning your attention toward it, and experiencing it fully with all of your senses. Look at areas of your life in which you hurry through experiences. Experiment with slowing down and savoring the moment. Life is a limited resource—enjoy its precious offerings.

Your ability to *have* is an essential first chakra element in your manifestation process. To bring your dream into reality, you need to be able to have the time, money, support, and resources needed to follow your plan all the way through to completion. If your first chakra energies are contracted, the fullness of your dream cannot flourish.

Exercise: Measure Your Havingness

Havingness is a term that represents your ability to have. How much do you allow yourself to have particular things, such as money, success, time for yourself, friends, love, pleasure, adventure, play, or nurturing? This exercise will help you determine (and increase) your havingness in any area.

Step 1: Imagine a pressure gauge that measures from zero to 100 percent. Zero represents the state of "cannot have," and 100 percent represents your ability to have something fully and completely. Without thinking too much, let your subconscious come up with a gauge reading in response to each of the following questions. Close your eyes and imagine the needle on your gauge resting at zero. Then observe it jump up to a number when you ask each question. Reset the gauge to zero after each question.

- How much material prosperity do you allow yourself to have?
- How much pleasure can you let yourself have?
- How much love do you allow in your life?
- How much positive attention from others can you handle?
- How much time alone do you give yourself out of what is possible?
- How much time do you dedicate to contributing to the world?

Add your own questions in any domain you're curious about.

In which areas did your gauge read above 50 percent? Above 75? Where do you allow yourself 100 percent? If the gauge was stuck under 25 percent, do some self-inquiry to find out what beliefs are underneath your limited ability to have.

Step 2: For each area that had a low reading, close your eyes and imagine the needle being raised another 5 to 15 percent—whatever amount you think you can handle. Then imagine what your life would feel like if you were living at that level of havingness. If you were low on physical prosperity, for example, imagine what your bank account, house, clothing, spending, and earning would be like if you could live at a level 15 percent higher than you do now. As you visualize, feel the feelings in your body. Gradually increase the number on the gauge until your *ability to have* matches your *want to have.*

When I (Anodea) first started doing this exercise, back in my twenties, I registered readings of about 10 percent in the financial department. By gradually raising my willingness and ability to have a prosperous life, my readings are now up to 90 percent, and my income went up proportionately. I'm now working on that last 10 percent!

If you don't care about money or time for yourself, there's no need to push your ability in those realms. What's important is to increase your ability to have your needs met. From there, you can work on having what you want and desire.

———————

Inhabiting Your Body

Your body is the physical manifestation of your being. It is "where you matter." If you are a person who lives largely in your head, learning to inhabit your body fully could be your ticket to manifestation. It is through our bodies that we bring heaven all the way down to earth. Your legs and feet are the link between your first chakra and the ground itself. Action requires moving forward, and, unless you're in a wheelchair, moving forward always requires using your legs and feet. When you take a stand for something or stand up for someone, you use your legs to plant yourself on the ground, stand erect, and make a commitment to do whatever it takes to accomplish your purpose.

To ground your vision is to bring it fully into the material universe. At the material level, things have solidity, edges, boundaries, and weight. They operate by known and tested physical laws. You can operate in the material universe only through your body, so grounding your vision cannot be done unless you also ground through your own body. Embodiment is an essential and final aspect of manifestation.

Your body also has limitations: It needs to eat and sleep and stretch from time to time. Honoring your body's needs keeps your temple in good repair. Grounding your body is like plugging in a television set. Even though electronic signals pulse through the air at all times, you can only receive them when you've plugged in the television and tuned into the waves at a particular frequency. In the same way, you can tune into the energies of each chakra, receive what they have to offer, and become more alive. But to do so requires that your first and second chakras be plugged in and turned on.

Grounding happens through the legs and feet. Achieving your goal happens one step at a time—steps taken on the earth itself. When people tell us they haven't found their path, it's usually because they're not grounded in their legs. How can you find your path if your feet don't touch the ground? Use the following exercise to powerfully open the energy channels in your legs. This will help you make firmer contact with the ground, which, in turn, will make you feel more secure. The more grounded you become, the easier it will be for you to manifest.

Exercise: Grounding

Plant your bare feet on the earth or floor, shoulder width apart, with your heels slightly wider than your toes. Bend your knees a bit, so they're just over your feet. Be careful to keep both feet fully engaged, alive, and feeling what's beneath them. To check for proper alignment, look down and spot your big toes on the inside of your kneecaps.

Now, push firmly into both feet with a down and outward motion, as if you were trying to push the floorboards apart or push a boat away from a dock. Feel how your feet and legs grip the ground and feel the power in your pelvic area. Your whole body has become more solid. This is a basic grounding stance that represents the rooted aspect of the base chakra.

Next, charge your roots by inhaling, bending your knees more deeply over your feet as you do. Then, exhale as you push through the core of your legs, slowly pushing the floor away from you. As your legs straighten, don't come all the way into a locked-knee position, as that would shut off the charge you're building.

Repeat this movement several times, inhaling as you bend your legs and exhaling as you straighten them. Continue pressing down and out with your feet as you inhale and exhale.

If you are doing this exercise correctly, you might begin to feel a subtle trembling in your legs. If so, you're doing great! The point of the whole exercise is to increase the charge in your body and to open the flow energy, or *chi*. Continue bending and straightening, inhaling and exhaling, until your legs are really shaking. For some people, this trembling happens within a few minutes; for others, it takes longer.

Discover which position and how much effort gives you the *most* trembling. Use a combination of muscular energy and surrendering to gravity. You will also discover—someplace on your journey between bent legs and straight legs—where the energy flows the strongest. Make little adjustments and movements around this spot. See how much energy you can channel through your legs.

Practicing this exercise over time will increase your ability to ground. It employs both the masculine and feminine aspects of rootedness. You find stability by pushing into the ground, and you nourish yourself by pulling earth energy up through your body into your chakras. You may notice blockages in the flow of your energy, but if you stick with it, the vibrating energy may dissolve those blocks.

Touching the Earth

Our bodies and nervous systems were designed to live in the natural world. Connecting to the earth in its natural state of beauty has an effect of recalibrating our energy body. It grounds us in what is true, beautiful, and simple. It takes away stress. It reminds us that we belong here on this beautiful planet. It takes us to a place where heaven is already connected to earth with all its manifested miracles. Take walks or hikes in the midst of trees, plants, and animals. Nature is a healer of the mind, body, and soul.

Exercise: Feet on the Ground

The earth produces an electromagnetic field that encompasses all of life. When your bare feet touch the ground, your body gets grounded—literally—by the earth, and the field shifts around you. Rubber is a great insulator, so if you wear shoes with rubber soles, you're missing out on this important grounding signal. Take off your shoes and socks and stand on bare earth. Take a walk barefoot. Feel the earth with your soles and give grounding to your soul.

Exercise: Plant Your Proposal

In our manifestation workshop, we have students write out their proposal to the gods (page 132) and roll it into a tight ball of paper, which represents the seed of their vision. We then have them plant their "seed" in the ground. Plant your proposal in your garden, in your favorite place in nature, or in the dirt of a houseplant. Miracles are possible when you plant the right seed in the right soil. Manifestation is creating the right conditions for your seeds to grow. The seed is your potential, carrying all the information necessary to become fulfillment of that potential. It just needs earth and water, sunlight and air, the right vibration, and plenty of light to reach back up to the heavens.

> **Manifestation Tip: Complete each piece and then release.**
>
> Your dream is not fully manifested until everything is complete and whole. Don't quit until every step of your dream is completely realized. The old sports metaphor is true: "Winners never quit. Quitters never win."

Completing Every Cycle

Werner Erhard, a philosopher and founder of Landmark Education, identified an important dynamic regarding satisfaction. He said, "If you put 100 percent commitment and energy into your task, you get 100 percent satisfaction from doing it. If you hold back and put out anything less than 100 percent, even 99 percent, you get zero satisfaction." Incomplete tasks, projects, and commitments require a small amount of energy or attention to keep them incomplete. For example, when you leave clothes on the floor or somewhere they don't belong, you can't help but use a small amount of attention to notice them every time you walk in the room. When you see the dishes left unwashed, you feel a bit guilty. Your attention bleeds out, bit by bit. "Oh, that still needs attending to." You try to ignore the drain of energy, but it takes a certain amount of attention energy to keep ignoring it. All that leaking energy takes you away from your intention. As soon as you complete a task, the bit of attention you had focused on that incomplete item gets released, and you get a little jolt of energy from freeing it up. If you then use that extra energy and attention to complete another task, you get more energy. This is why you feel so good when you *finally* clean out the closet or garage, where so much energy has stagnated. You get all of that energy back, and it feels great!

Everything that exists comes into creation for a purpose. In the natural world, when the purpose of a being or thing has been fulfilled, it becomes food for something else in the process of natural recycling. In the human world, we need to put things away or throw them away to make room for something new. Completing incomplete cycles—whether or not they are related to your dream—is a powerful act of magic that will lead you to becoming a master manifestor.

A perfectly legitimate way to complete an unfinished project is to declare it moot. This means letting it go, crossing it off your list, and taking your attention off of it. Declaring it moot means letting go with certainty; it says "I don't need or want this project anymore." When you throw away a half-done project, give away books you'll never finish, or give up on goals that you're not getting any traction on, you free up attention that you can then use to create what's important in your life—making your dream come true.

Exercise: The Completion Exercise

This is one of the most radical and powerful exercises you can do to improve your life. It may take weeks, months, or years to accomplish, but we guarantee it will transform your life.

Step 1: Make a list of everything in your life that is incomplete: tasks you started but aren't now working on, projects you've worked on but didn't complete, things you've wanted but don't have, things you've wanted to do but haven't done, books left unfinished or never started, clothes not mended, repairs not completed, relationships left hanging, classes or degrees not completed, communications not delivered or not responded to, things about which you are dissatisfied, things you wanted to say that you didn't say, things you can't get started, things you wanted to change but never changed, and anything in your life that is incomplete in any way. Keep writing down the incompletes until you are completely exhausted. If you are like most people, you will be writing for hours. Add additional incompletes to the list as you remember them or create them.

Step 2: Review the list carefully. For the most significant ones (the ones that create strong feelings), fill in the blanks:

- I would be _____ if I completed this.
- I am _____ for not being/doing/having that.

Notice whether any self-judgments come up with words such as *right* or *wrong, stupid* or *smart, worse* or *better,* and *bad* or *good.* If they do, notice that they're just beliefs and take them into "The Belief Process" exercise (page 70).

Step 3: After you've completed Step 2, review the list again. Make a commitment to yourself to complete every incomplete item that didn't clear up in the process of writing the list. You don't have to complete them in a day, a week, or a year, but commit to completing them as soon as you can.

If you know you are never going to complete an item, declare it moot and cross it off. By doing so, you let go of ever having to handle it or deal with it again. Make sure there's no leftover regret. (Sadness at letting go of some things is appropriate.) For physical items, such as unfinished art projects, throw them away or give them away (don't just store them elsewhere). For incompletes with people, relationships, and communications, don't just declare them moot and cross them off your list. That would be equivalent to throwing someone away rather than coming to a good resolution. Completion in relationships comes from communicating everything that has to be communicated, finding essential love for the other, and then declaring the relationship complete. In addition, be careful about declaring moot anything that you would benefit from completing, such as finishing a college degree—especially if completing it would really build your self-esteem or grant you esteem from others.

Dedicate yourself to completing at least one incomplete thing each and every day until everything on the list has been crossed off. This could take the rest of your life, but what a life it will have been!

Guarantee: Even though completing every incomplete thing on your list seems like an overwhelming task, remember the reward: You will become freer and lighter, and you will regain an enormous amount of attention that you can then use to create your dreams. You will feel this benefit at each step along the way.

Exercise: Make a Physical Symbol of Your Dream or Goal

Since chakra one represents the physical world, it is helpful to create a physical object that represents each of your big goals. The act of concretizing your objective into something you can see and touch mirrors the process of condensation that is essential to manifestation. For example, buy a new key to represent the house you want to own. Find a newspaper with an article about someone who is doing something similar to what you want to do and paste your own picture onto it. Put a picture of a person who is fit and vital on your refrigerator to remind you of your health goals. Write a check to yourself for a large amount of money and post it on your mirror. Pick an object to represent your dream, such as a special stone that fits your pocket, a charm you can hang from your rearview mirror, or a letter that you write to yourself. Keep your symbol close by as a constant reminder of your dream and connect with it regularly to ground your vision.

The Final Key

If you complete all the steps in this course, clearing your intentions and beliefs (chakra seven), honing your vision (chakra six), rooting out the negative voices and communicating clearly (chakra five), cultivating the right relationships (chakra four), making a plan and doing what is necessary (chakra three), calling in what you need and making it fun (chakra two), and then completing each step in a timely fashion (chakra one), you *will* manifest your dream. It may take weeks, months, years, or a lifetime, but if you keep walking along the path toward your goal, completing each step along the way, you will eventually arrive. And you'll have a great life!

The only step left—and it's an important step—is to celebrate the result and share it with others.

Celebration

The more you praise and celebrate your life,
the more there is in life to celebrate.

—Oprah Winfrey

Congratulations on your completion! Now you know you can do it. You have the map and know the territory. You can apply these navigational steps to any project in the future, *creating on purpose* the world of your dreams and a better world for all. With practice, these steps will become automatic. Your manifestations will occur more easily. As you gain confidence, you may choose to work on bigger and more complex projects.

Take a moment to appreciate how far you've come. In this chapter, we review the steps so you can admire all your hard work and the path you took to get here. In your journal, answer the questions following each chakra below. Write down the lessons you've learned and the steps you've taken as a way of acknowledging what you've already accomplished. All relationships are enhanced through acknowledgment. You'll enhance your relationship with your inner manifestor by acknowledging each skill acquired, each technique practiced, and each action taken. What you appreciate appreciates.

Review of the Steps

Chakra Seven: Consciousness Creates. You began with emptiness in the seventh chakra, opening to grace, receiving, and conceiving. You declared your intentions into existence by clearing crosscurrents, and you learned what it means to create in your own personal universe. You examined your beliefs, changing limiting and negative beliefs into empowering ones that will serve your intentions.

- What was your original idea or dream when you began the book? How did it change over time?
- What was your original intention? What percentage of it has been accomplished?
- What new beliefs have you created to support your intention?

Chakra Six: Vision Vitalizes. As you stepped down into the sixth chakra, you divined your life purpose and brought that purpose into your dreams in several areas of your life, learning to dream *big*. From your dreams, you created a vision—the vehicle through which you could realize your dreams and fulfill your life purpose. You then visualized the fulfillment of your vision, seeing it as a future reality (along with the inevitable obstacles), and clarified the steps along the way.

- How clear are you now about your life purpose?
- What is your primary vision for fulfilling your life purpose?
- What major obstacles have you already overcome, and what remains?
- What techniques were most helpful in overcoming each obstacle?

Chakra Five: Conversation Catalyzes. As you took the step down into the fifth chakra, you refined your vision through communicating with others. You created SMART goals that were specific and measurable. You learned how to speak about your dream in a way that inspires others, talking about it with as many people as possible. You dealt with your internal voices of doubt and shame, creating allies within and without. You wrote a proposal to the gods and made an offering in return.

- How many of your SMART goals have you accomplished thus far?
- How realistic were those goals? Did they need refinement?
- What is the essential message that your dream communicates to others?
- Are you more able to share your dream and vision with others? Does your dream and vision inspire them?

Chakra Four: Love Enlivens. In the fourth chakra, you brought your dream into the realm of relationships. You summoned up the partners you needed and created a dream team for support. You looked at how your dream serves others and focused on what you love about your dream. You spread your ideas through your networks and expanded your web of relationships—and with it, your span of influence.

- What is the essential contribution that your dream makes to others?
- What do you love most about creating your dream?
- What relationships have provided the best support for your manifestation process?
- How have you effectively expanded your network of contacts and relationships?

Chakra Three: Power Produces. Coming down into the third chakra, you made an action plan. You broke down your goals into more manageable projects and an action plan, and you committed to *doing* those actions by putting them on your calendar. You learned to make your energy bigger than your obstacles and to use your will to stay focused.

- What were the most difficult tasks to accomplish?
- What were your most distracting obstacles?
- What did you learn about asserting your will effectively?

- What do you now know about project planning that you can teach others?

Chakra Two: Pleasure Pleases. After all this work, you entered the waters of pleasure in the second chakra. You learned that you could be specific about your wants and needs and ask for what you most desire, exactly as you desire it. You stepped into the stream of creation, which began to carry you downward to the last steps of manifestation. Your passion was stirred as you saw progress along the way.

- What were your most pressing needs as you explored this path of creation?
- Are you now able to ask for what you want specifically?
- When did you feel "in the flow"? When did things seem to happen effortlessly?
- What part of the process most incited your passion?

Chakra One: Matter Matters. At the first chakra, you touched down on earth. You completed each step, one at a time, moving toward the fulfillment of your goals. You condensed your proposal to the gods into a seed that contained your dream, and you planted that seed into the earth, symbolically bringing it down to the ground.

- What do you now have as a result of your efforts?
- How does having that result enhance your life and the lives of others?
- What still needs to be completed?
- What matters most?

If you complete each step along this path (which may take longer than it took to read this book), you will *have* your manifestation. You'll be able to enjoy your creation. If you got hung up along the way, review the steps and see whether you might have skipped one or didn't really engage in the serious work. Are any old beliefs still blocking your success? Are you giving more energy to your crosscurrents than to your dream? Do you still have those nagging internal voices? Is your will being distracted by all your other priorities, desires, or the needs of others?

We've offered you a set of tools for creating on purpose. It's now a matter of choice: Will you use them often and wisely? Or will you set them on a shelf for "someday"? There's no excuse for not living the life of your dreams right now! You have everything you need—the information, the tools, and a lighted path that leads you toward fulfilling your life purpose. The world is filled with people who want to see you succeed, who want your dreams to come alive—including us! The world needs your vision, your dreams, and your contribution.

Celebrate and Enjoy

There's a reason that the ancients called the downward current through the chakras *bhukti,* or enjoyment. It's because creation *is* ecstasy. It's important to enjoy the fruits of your labor and celebrate your success. Let your subconscious mind and your Inner Child know that they did a great job. Take a night off, go out to dinner, and order champagne. Better yet, take a vacation! Even if your parents are no longer alive, imagine them patting you on the back and telling you how proud they are. We all do better when we're appreciated. Recognize and love your co-creators—and your inner parts—for the work they've done to support you and your creation. Love is the universal lubricant that makes everything smoother, and it will open doors for your future projects. Celebration is essential to completing each cycle, because it proves that the result was more than worth the effort. Creation can be hard work. Celebration prevents burnout.

Admire your work. Paste your reviews on a bulletin board. Have a housewarming party for your new home. Create a christening event for your new retreat center. Interview guests on video at your art show, theater opening, or workshop. Get your clients to write testimonials and then display them prominently on your website. Have a book-release party. Take a spa day and get a massage. Go shopping. We don't need to tell you how to celebrate—just follow your heart and feel what would bring you the most joy and satisfaction. You deserve to be pleased with yourself!

It is said that when the goddess Shakti returns to the first chakra after a heavenly night, there is nothing more for her to do, so she rests. If *she* can do it, so can you. Take a breath and rest! Creation requires a huge outpouring of energy. Remember to inhale once in a while in order to keep going. Celebrations usually happen at the end, but they can happen throughout a project, as you accomplish smaller goals, to benchmark your progress. In bigger projects, it's especially important to pace yourself with little rewards along the way.

Include as many of these principles as you can, not only in your formal celebrations but also in your daily life:

- Expressing gratitude
- Sharing
- Savoring
- Celebrating
- Having
- Being
- Not-doing

- Resting
- Relaxing
- Enjoying leisure time
- Having fun
- Feeling peace
- Sleeping
- Restoring harmony

Co-creating Heaven on Earth

We have a confession to make: We had a secret agenda in writing this book. We have our own purpose, vision, and dreams, but we need help—from millions of people like you.

We share a vision of a magnificent world—one in which everyone feels safe and has their basic needs fulfilled. In this world, children can play together, laughing and learning, without being concerned about war, poverty, disease, or starvation. In our world, wars are a distant memory, because people have awakened to what is really important, and they have set out to create a world based on love, harmony, generosity, truth, wisdom, and kindness. It's not a perfect world, but it's a very good world, where people take care of themselves, each other, and their environment. This is the future we want to co-create.

To create that world, which we call *heaven on earth,* we need more people on the team with imagination, passion, drive, and capabilities.

We need people who can communicate their vision, work well with others, ground their dreams in reality, and bring those dreams to fruition. We need *you* to be a master manifestor in order to accomplish this *collective dream.*

Whenever someone learns that they can manifest the reality they want, they make the world a little bit better. Every improvement you make helps move our society in the right direction. Our hope is that after learning these steps, you will join in the larger co-creation of heaven on earth—a creation that's already underway. If your best dream for the future includes others, you'll be helping to create a better world for everyone.

We believe there is a divine plan and that you are part of it. You wouldn't have read this book if you weren't. (Actually, you wouldn't have been born if you weren't.) You need only awaken to your true purpose, your power to manifest, your ability to create on purpose, and your willingness to do the work.

We invite you to imagine the miracles that are possible and to actively recognize them happening around you every day. We also invite you to spark this possibility in others. Doing so will enhance your own spark, fuel your passion, and help turn your dreams into realities.

Take this work out into the world. Keep alive the vision of a world that works for everyone. Teach these methods to your friends. Teach your coworkers by conducting in-service trainings at your workplace. Teach your children. Teach youth in underprivileged communities. Imagine what you might have created if you had grown up knowing what you know now.

Together we can dance in a world of wonder and joy. We can revel in the mysteries of creation and know that we are co-creators. We can create from our highest purpose. We can evolve to the next level of human capacity. We can create heaven on earth.

Thank you for taking this journey with us. Thank you for dreaming up a better world. Thank you for manifesting your dreams. Your grandchildren and your great-great-grandchildren will thank you, as well. The future world thanks you for doing your part.

Now, let's celebrate!

Recipe for the World

Lion Goodman

I

Our world is made of our assumptions.
Create it yourself . . .

Begin with plenty of raw belief,
mixing carefully with old ideas of how and should and must.

Add a sprinkling of supposed-to, a jigger of always-has,
a flight of ought, and a thimble full of never-has-been-before.

Bake slowly at just right for forever and a day.

Remove from oven. Present it on a silver tray for their approval,
cut into tiny consecutive moments of now.

Pass it out to waiting generations.
They'll taste it tastefully, checking to see if and when and how much
was allowed,
if rules were followed, traditions kept,
and limits set for rising made it rise just the right amount.

Atop the cake set rightness itself,
an icing full of righteous indignation
that Pride could be truly proud of.

But can we have our cake and freedom too?

II

Must every morsel be just so?

Where lies creative license? Wild and crazy half-measures?
Imbalanced spontaneity and frivolous additions?

Let's open the hidden vault where love-crazed recipes are kept,
the ones that crazy wisdom loves—
where cakes fall into lovely tumbles,
themes are badly out of tune, composures fracture,
and adjustments made to every here and now.

The cook has our permission to just go nuts—

Improvise new configurations never been thought,
drip wild ideas that splash among the tasters,
whose ravenous eyes crave new sensations—
not satisfied with always-was and never-has-been-before.

Burst former boundaries into flame, set ancient patterns aside, asunder,
bring forth colors never seen. Let frenzied freedom have its way,
and this dish begins to taste even better.

The kitchen's a mess.

But boy, have we had fun!

Addendum

Structure for Success is anything that provides you with support as you pursue your dream. Coaches, mentors, and your dream team all provide external structures to keep you accountable and on track. Setting time on your calendar for self-care—whether going to the gym or getting to bed by a certain hour—is another form of self-imposed structure that supports you in achieving your goals. On the following page is a list of Structures for Success that you can refer to when you're uncertain about what to do or what resource you need in order to solve particular problems that come up along the way or to spur your progress. We are happy to hear your recommendations as well. Send your suggestions through our website, creatingonpurpose.net.

The Powers of Manifestation

Each chakra provides a particular power in the art of manifestation. Remembering to invoke these powers will help you manifest more easily. When you get stuck, you can come back to these powers and see where you got diverted from your path of intention.

Chakra Seven: The Power of the Divine, The Power of Knowledge and Wisdom

There is a great power in the universe that brings order to the flow of everything and calls you to the future. Thank God/Goddess for that, because if it were left up to us mere mortals, we'd probably continue to make a mess of things, just as we have been doing for centuries.

Table 3 Structures for Success

Structure	What It Does for You	Exercises / Resource
Set Clear Intentions	Clarifies your dreams, goals, and projects	Write down your intentions every day
Handle the Inevitable Crosscurrents	Moves interference out of the way, getting you back on track	Declaration, Belief Process, Seven Voices
Project Planning	Identifies what needs to be done and when	Project-planning software and education
Accounting for Your Money	If you measure it, you can manage it. Illuminates your finances and cash flow	Accounting software and a bookkeeper or accountant
Clear Communication	Helps you establish clear agreements and expectations and stay informed	Communication for Action
Accountability	Fosters commitment to doing what you say you'll do	Coaching, buddies, your dream team, and a coach or partner
Prioritizing	Helps get the important things done first	Important-urgent analysis
Completing Cycles	Releases energy back to you each time you complete something	The Completion Exercise
Asking for Help	Prevents overcommitment and burnout, and gives you the support and partnership you need	Make clear requests; build a dream team
An Attitude of Gratitude	Keeps you in a state of grace and confirms your requests to the universe	Be thankful—early and often!
Work-Life Balance and Self-Care	Prevents you from being sucked into the maelstrom of the to-do list	Exercise, diet, take time off for rest and relaxation
Spiritual Practices	Regularly connects you with Source—that which is larger than yourself	Meditation, yoga, chanting, self-inquiry
Strengthening the Will	Strengthens your ability to focus, stay on task, and keep going through the difficulties	Pushing through obstacles and focusing exercises
Enhancing Your Pleasure Principle	No pleasure, no gain. Keeps you moving toward your goals	Make each task fun, engage with others, enjoy
Breathing . . . and Patience	We breathe, and we are breathed by something bigger than us—manifesting takes time	Breathe early and often, stay present, be patient

When in doubt, get out from under the roof over your head and go outside where you can get an expansive view of the heavens—be it day or night. Take time out for meditation and ask a question of Source. Then listen for the answer. Pick up a book that might be relevant and look for information that will inspire you or help you on your path.

The Law of Infinite Knowledge says that there is always something you don't know. Add new information to what you already know; then stir. According to Margaret Wheatley, in *Leadership and the New Science,* whenever a system is faltering—be it a company, small group, or relationship, *add information* and distribute that information to as many people in the system as possible. Information is like food. It nourishes us and gives us vital nutrients. It makes us smarter!

The Law of Infinite Knowledge also says that you know more than you realize. Most of your information is stored in your unconscious mind. Your brain is working on solutions to your problems even while your attention is on other things, but you need to tune in to download the solution. Many people notice that they get improvements in a skill—such as in a sport or playing a musical instrument—when they take a break from it for a few days or weeks. Solutions may pop up in a dream, in an idle moment of enjoyment, or in a chance conversation. When you get confused, simply file the question in the back of your mind; tell your brain and your spirit to work on it and let you know when it's been worked out. Solutions can appear in unexpected ways, so always be on the lookout.

Wisdom is what you get when you put knowledge together with—and apply it to—life; it's the perception of deep order, the larger gestalt. It often comes as an "*a-ha.*" In the manifestation process, we want you to work smarter, not harder. Wisdom doesn't jump to conclusions. Instead, it continuously adds new data and makes new combinations out of older data. If you've drawn a conclusion about something, try to find at least four more conclusions that are also possible before you move forward. Weigh their future possibilities, then choose the best one and move forward with vigor!

Chakra Six: The Power of Vision

There is nothing like the power of a compelling vision. It excites others and draws them toward you. It also attracts what you need. When builders look at a drawing of how the project they are working on will appear when finished, if that vision is creative and beautiful, they will feel inspired to do their best. Your vision for the world draws that reality forward. Keep your attention on your vision. It will pull you inevitably toward your goal through the invisible force of intention.

Infuse your vision with imagination. Allow yourself to think outside the box. Imagine different ways to do each thing, including silly things you might never do. Allow yourself to pretend and imagine—it increases the powers of your sixth chakra. Remember Alice and her "six impossible things before breakfast" (page 95).

Chakra Five: The Power of Truth, The Power of Story

To manifest your vision, communicate it to others as often as possible. Talking to people about facts—even important ones—doesn't usually move or inspire them, even if the facts are important. Telling a good story, on the other hand, grabs people's attention. It moves them and enrolls them in your vision, especially when your story reveals deeper truths with which people resonate. Telling your own story creates intimacy, bonding, and resonance. The more resonant your communication, the more power it has.

Truth is simple, elegant, and powerful. During Gandhi's nonviolent movement in India, he coined the term *satyagraha,* or "the force of truth." His acts of speaking truth to power threw off oppressive British rule, despite all odds. Stay in touch with your truth: the truth of your intention, your vision, your love, your needs, and the positive impact and benefit your goals and dreams will have on the world.

Chakra Four: The Power of Love

None of us can do it alone. There are millions, if not billions, of others on this planet who want a better world, just like you do. You can co-create with others. You can ask for help. You can offer help.

When you contribute to others' visions, they, in turn, want to contribute to yours. Generosity is a virtue by itself, but it also has a positive impact when it returns to you.

There is a great question floating around on bumper stickers: "What would love do?" When you get stuck in your interpersonal relationships, go to the highest principles of the heart and choose the course of action that produces the most love for all concerned. That includes *you* in the category of "all concerned," because sometimes the most loving act is to make a strong boundary or to say "no."

What you appreciate appreciates, so remember to appreciate the little things as well as the big ones. Follow your heart. Doing what you love brings more of it, and if you create more of what you truly love, you can't go wrong.

Chakra Three: The Power of Will

We can think, dream, and talk all we want, but every project involves some kind of willful action. No matter what you dream, you'll meet obstacles and difficulties along the way, as well as detours, delays, frustrations, distractions, and discouragement. Behind every great accomplishment, there was someone with a strong will who could forge circumstances into alignment with their desired goal—and who kept going when the going got tough.

When your will is aligned with your intention and higher purpose, and when it's fueled by your passion and tempered by your heart, nothing can stop you. The only thing left is to collaborate: Unite your will with the will of others. When you get stuck, go back to the co-laboratory!

Chakra Two: The Power of Passion

Nothing supports your will like passion. Passion is the power that keeps the will focused; it is the desire that pulls you toward your goal. Passion ignites the will and tempers it. Your passion for what's possible inspires others to join you in your dream. If you are emotionally aligned with your intention, your arrow will go straight to its target. Your passion will grow as you see your vision manifest. Passion is like a river that flows downward to sea, carrying with it everything needed to reach the goal.

Chakra One: The Power of Commitment, The Power of Completion

Commitment is the anchor of manifestation. It pulls things down toward earth, where they ultimately must go to take form. Committing yourself—to another person, to your action steps on your calendar, to a contract with the bank or the publisher, or to a significant return to your investors—is a powerful act of creation. When molten bronze is poured into a mold, it is committed to that form; it takes the shape designed for it and becomes solid. Your intention does the same.

There's a difference between commitment and involvement. We can be involved in many things but not necessarily committed to them. Commitment means you do whatever it takes to keep your word and get to your goal.

The Law of Completion says that if you complete each step along the way, you will have a complete manifestation. If you don't yet have your manifestation, look for a step or goal that you haven't completed or a place where you haven't been fully committed.

Dancing Down the Chakras

A final step in bringing your dream down through your body is to dance it down through your chakras. We complete our workshops with a chakra dance, using music for each chakra, from top to bottom. This is a lot of fun. It gets people out of their heads and brings their energy down into their bodies, where they can move creatively and express their joy through each step. You can make your own playlist for this activity, but we are often asked for ours. All of the songs in Table 4 can be bought through iTunes. There are many choices for each chakra, though John Lennon's "Imagine" for the sixth chakra just doesn't have a rival. Choose one for each chakra that suits you best and send us your suggestions.

Seven Steps to Effective Prayer

When you communicate with the Divine, there are two parts to the process: speaking and listening. Prayer is the part where you speak, and

Table 4 Dancing Down the Chakras—Discography

Chakra	Song	Artist	Album
7	"Be Still"	Shawna Carol	Goddess Chants
	"Heaven"	Talking Heads	Stop Making Sense
	"God Is My Source"	Karen Drucker	Songs of the Spirit I
6	"Imagine"	John Lennon	Imagine (Remastered)
5	"Making a Noise"	Robbie Robertson	Contact from the Underworld of Redboy
	"Thy Song"	Sophia	Chakra Healing Chants
4	"I Am Loved"	Karen Drucker	Songs of the Spirit III
	"One Love"	Reggae Beat	Reggae
	"Return to Innocence"	Enigma	The Cross of Changes
3	"I've Got the Power"	Karen Drucker	All About Love
2	"Take Me to the River"	Talking Heads	Stop Making Sense
	"Are You Ready to Receive"	Karen Drucker	Songs of the Spirit I
1	"Closer to the Ground"	Joy of Cooking	American Originals
	"Prosperity Chant"	Karen Drucker	Songs of the Spirit II

meditation is the part where you listen. Both are essential. Prayer is a request to connect to God, Goddess, Higher Mind, Source, the Force, or a deity by any name. It is an opening to grace that unifies mind and heart, initiating a conversation with the intelligence of the Universe. It doesn't matter what you call the Source; it is always there, and it's most easily found in the gap between thoughts and in the gap between the way things are and the way we want them to be.

The seven stages to effective prayer can be practiced by anyone, anywhere, within any spiritual framework. They are a template for harvesting the blessings and guidance needed to create a positive future.

Step 1: Humility

Humility begins with what is. It is an admission of the limitations of our personal power, the realization that there are always pathways we cannot see, and that there is a power greater than our own. Humility is a way of emptying our mental and emotional constructs that have previously gotten in the way. In twelve-step programs for healing addictions, it is the first step: "Humbly admitting we are powerless over our addiction and that there is a greater power that can restore us to health."

Humility relates to chakra one, as it typically takes us downward, toward the earth—a realm that some spiritual systems have deemed as lowly or inferior. The classic postures of humility are kneeling, prostration, or child's pose in yoga. It is the first step in making room for a greater power. Humility brings us into simplicity, into the sacred, and empties the vessel so that it can then be filled.

Step 2: Alignment

After humbly emptying yourself, the next step is to align your body, mind, and spirit in such a way that spirit can best move through you. Align your core, the *axis mundi* that runs through your body from crown to ground. Think of the chakras as jewels on the necklace of the soul. When you pull vertically on the two ends of the necklace, the jewels line up, one on top of the other. Align your chakras and open to grace. Become an effective vessel for channeling spiritual energies.

Alignment brings you into chakra two by setting you in a particular direction. Alignment is like putting a vessel under running water so it can fill. Aligning with the Divine allows you to begin channeling your highest purpose. Open your channels to receive the grace you know is always there, awaiting your readiness.

Step 3: Purpose

Now that you have oriented yourself to the force of Source, you are ready to state your purpose. This is the larger context in which your prayer is nested, the call you make from your highest virtues. If you are praying for a friend's recovery from illness, what is the greatest benefit of that healing? If you are praying for peace in war-torn areas of the world, what is the greater vision to which the transformation can be directed? If you are praying for something for yourself, what is the greater benefit to others, should your request be granted?

Purpose is the framework formed by consciousness that congeals possibilities into manifestation. Alignment sets you up to receive, and purpose names the benefit. This is the intention of the prayer, and it relates to the power of the third chakra.

Step 4: Offering

According to tribal peoples around the world, the universe operates on the principle of reciprocity—mutual gift-giving. If you want something from a store, you offer money. If you receive a favor from a friend, you offer them a backrub or a night on the town. The ancient practice of making a sacrifice to the gods came from this principle of giving something away before asking for something in return.

Your offering can be a contribution or a sacrifice. You may offer your loyalty, creativity, steadfastness, openness, or dedication. This willingness to contribute and offer creates an opening in spiritual space. Think of how you react when someone offers to help you in some way.

You can also offer something you are willing to give up, including what stands in the way of your request. If your prayer is to find love, you can offer to give up your perfectionism or your complaining—whatever stands in the way of love. If your prayer is peace, you can release anger or grudges you've been harboring. You can offer up bad habits, such as cigarettes, sugar, television, jealousy, or selfishness. If you truly let go of what stands in your way, you have nothing left but the product of your intentions. The best offerings come from the heart, in chakra four.

Step 5: Gratitude

After making your offer, move toward appreciation of what is and what will be when your vision is fulfilled. In this step, you express gratitude *before* it happens. Gratitude is the currency of the gods. What you appreciate appreciates. You don't have to wait for your vision to be fulfilled; you can be grateful for the vision itself. It's like saying to someone, "I would be so grateful if you were willing to watch my kids for an hour." This is gratitude in advance. It greases the gears. When you offer gratitude for what *will be,* you affirm your belief that your intention will be fulfilled in the best way possible.

It isn't enough to feel gratitude—it must be expressed. Express it as often as you can to those around you. Your co-creators will feel appreciated and be willing to do their best. Your family will feel loved, and you will have even more appreciation for the things you usually take for granted. Communicating your gratitude relates to chakra five.

Step 6: Reception

In this step, you create a space for your prayer to be answered. Focus on the picture of your desired outcome and hold it with the openness of a vessel, ready to receive its fulfillment. Your vessel gives reality its shape, but your vessel must be empty to receive. Create an attitude of openness that allows in whatever is best—whether or not it fits your picture. Feel the beneficence of the Universe, which has your best interest at heart. Prayers are best ended with ". . . or something better that benefits all beings." Allow the energies and gifts from Source to pour into you and fill your cup. Visualize the time and space you'll need to enjoy all the blessings coming your way. Make room for a vision bigger than your own. This step relates to chakra six.

Step 7: Realization and Fulfillment

The realization of your dream is its fulfillment. Can you truly allow it to happen? Can you open yourself wide enough? Can you let yourself have it? Can you truly believe it?

Some people block their manifestation at this point, because they don't let themselves get filled up. Some don't go into quiet and emptiness long enough to receive. You must be receptive, open to change, and open to fulfillment. If all the other steps are done fully, this step should be the easiest, for you've already set up the coordinates. Receive it and feel what it feels like to be fulfilled. Let this feeling radiate out in all directions, as you sing the praise of Source, adding your voice to the chorus of angels.

May this process for prayer be among your tools for fulfilling your purpose and may the Divine respond in the best possible way. May all our prayers for the world be fulfilled where they are most needed.

Manifestation Tips

- You can do anything, but you can't do everything.
- Never let your reality define your reality.
- Begin in emptiness.
- Make your dream come true by seeing it through.
- Talk is cheap. Do lots of it.
- What serves the greater good puts the wind in your sails.
- If you don't plan, it won't withstand.
- Make it fun until it's done.
- Complete each piece and then release.

The Demons of the Chakras (and How to Deal with Them)

Each chakra has what I (Anodea) call a *demon*. By this I don't mean that it's a critter with nasty fangs or slimy skin; rather, it's a psychologically based energy or behavior that interferes with a chakra's best functioning. The demons of the chakras are discussed in detail in my book on chakra psychology, *Eastern Body, Western Mind.*

The demons are important to mention here because they can interfere with your manifestation process. If a demon pops up, consider what chakra it is related to. Then ask yourself what beliefs the demon represents and do a Belief Process (page 70) on it or engage it in Voice Dialogue (page 124). (They love that!)

Just remember that demons are always kinder and more cooperative when you respect them. Realize that they appeared for a good reason once upon a time, and they have had an important role in your psyche. You just need to find out if that reason is still valid and, if so, what you can do about it. You can shift these forces of consciousness by using the solutions that follow.

- **Chakra Seven: Attachment, arrogance, ignorance, confusion**

    Solution: Be humble, open, and willing to learn. Meditate to clear your mind.

- **Chakra Six: Illusion**

  Solution: There's a fine line between imagination and illusion. Visualizing what you want is important, but don't be blind to the reality of obstacles. When in doubt about what you see, ask for a second or third opinion from trusted friends.

- **Chakra Five: Lies**

  Solution: This one's simple. Tell the truth, even if it's difficult. It's much easier in the long run.

- **Chakra Four: Grief**

  Solution: This one's a little tougher. Unexpressed or unacknowledged grief makes the heart chakra heavy, even though its nature is to be light. The paradox is that the more fully you express your feelings of grief and sadness, the sooner the weight lifts off your heart. The real solution? Feel it fully. Have a good cry.

- **Chakra Three: Shame**

  Solution: This wily demon can seep into everything if you're not vigilant. Eliminate negative voices using Step 3 of the "Voice Dialogue" exercise (page 126). Set a *being intention* of courage, confidence, or self-appreciation. Find out what belief your shame is based on using "The Belief Process" exercise (page 70), and change your belief.

- **Chakra Two: Guilt**

  Solution: Examine the source of your guilt. If you made a genuine mistake and caused harm, seek to rectify it by making amends as soon as possible. Otherwise, examine your beliefs about worthiness, morality, sexuality, and any other beliefs, religious or otherwise, that might be hindering your progress. Check whether those beliefs serve you and your vision. Change the ones that don't.

- **Chakra One: Fear**

   Solution: Like all demons, fear must be faced to be transformed. It often comes from not having support (as the first chakra name, *Muladhara,* means "root support"). Get support from your dream team or loved ones. Practice the first chakra "Grounding" exercise (page 227) to combat fear in your body. If you fear genuine obstacles, find ways of clearing them by standing in your power. Use the "Remove Obstacles with Your Will" exercise (page 187).

   FEAR can be recognized in this anagram: False Events Appearing Real. Replace FEAR with FAITH: Finding All In True Harmony.

Remember you are bigger than your demons. Most of them began as a protector, but then got out of hand, limiting your growth. The stronger you are in your spiritual connection, intention, vision, communication, love, will, passion, and grounding, the better chance you have of transforming these demons into trusted advisors.

   Let your light and vision shine!

Notes

1. Tom Atlee, co-intelligence.org/crisis_fatigue.html.

2. Aristotle invented the word *entelechy* by combining *entelēs* ("complete, full-grown") with *echein* (from *hexis,* "to be a certain way by the continuing effort of holding on in that condition"), while at the same time punning on *endelecheia* ("persistence") by inserting *telos* ("completion"). This three-ring circus of a word is at the heart of everything in Aristotle's thinking, including his definition of *motion.*

3. Ken Wilber, *A Brief History of Everything* (Boston: Shambhala, 1996), 11. For more on how this kind of thinking evolved and its effect on our culture, see Anodea Judith's book on social evolution, *Waking the Global Heart: Humanity's Rite of Passage from the Love of Power to the Power of Love* (Fulton, CA: Elite Books, 2006; Revised edition: Shift Books, 2013).

4. Ibid., p 134.

5. John Friend, *Weaving a Life of Beauty*, audio CD (The Woodlands, TX: Anusara Yoga, 2010).

6. The cosmos is the entire physical universe. The term *kosmos* has come to mean not only the physical universe but also the nonphysical universe, including such aspects as consciousness, mind, and archetypes. *Kosmos* is thus considered to mean "everything, leaving nothing out."

7. Peter Guber, *Tell to Win: Connect, Persuade, and Triumph with the Hidden Power of Story* (New York: Crown Business, 2011).

8. Developed by Chilean engineer, entrepreneur, and philosopher Fernando Flores and popularized by Werner Edward, creator of *est* and Landmark Education.

9. For more information on Voice Dialogue, read *Embracing Our Selves,* by Hal and Sidra Stone (Novatom CA: New World Library, 1998), or visit VoiceDialogue.org for access to a wide range of articles, books, and audio programs.

10. Jeffery Gitomer, *Little Black Book of Connections* (Austin, TX: Bard Press Austin, 2006).

11. James Hillman, *Kinds of Power: A Guide to Its Intelligent Uses,* (New York: Currency Doubleday, 1995), p 2.

12. Ibid., p 10.

13. Interview with Amy Goodman on *Democracy Now,* December 26, 2010. alternet.org/world/149325/trauma:_how_ we've_created_a_nation_addicted_to_shopping,_work,_ drugs_and_sex.

14. Hillman, p 76.

15. Wesley, "More Sad Stories of Lottery Winners Ending Up Broke, Depressed, and Lonely," *Life Two: Midlife Improvement,* April 26, 2007, lifetwo.com/production/ node/20070425-more-sad-stories-of-lottery-winners- ending-up-broke-depressed-and-lonely.

Resources

Creatingonpurpose.net: Our website is designed to provide you with additional information, resources, and support. Email us at info@ creatingonpurpose.net to let us know what you manifested while using the steps and instructions in this book. Send your comments and questions as well. We'll post the best comments and questions on the website, along with answers to help you on your journey.

Sacredcenters.com: Anodea's website contains information about her chakra books, classes, seminars, articles, and certification program. Register for her newsletter and get access to her complete library of resources, including workshops, books, videos, audio products, free teleseminars, blogs, and the Sacred Centers community.

Transformyourbeliefs.com: Lion's website about beliefs and the BeliefCloset Process. When you register, you'll get his multimedia ebook *Transform Your Beliefs* as a gift. Lion offers training in the BeliefCloset Process, which shifts beliefs permanently at the core of the psyche. "The Belief Process" exercise (page 70) used in this book is a small taste of this important inner-change technology. He offers private sessions, as well as referrals to BeliefCloset Practitioners—coaches and therapists who have been trained in the methodology.

Luminaryleadership.net: Lion's executive coaching and leadership training website provides information about his consulting program for high-level executives, owners and leaders of businesses, corporations, and organizations.

We also highly recommend the following additional resources for your manifestation journey:

Truepurpose.net: Tim Kelley helps change agents find their specific life purpose and offers them tools for manifesting their purpose. Lion is a trained True Purpose coach, and together Lion and Tim developed a program called Massive Belief Relief.

Theshiftnetwork.com: Both Lion and Anodea have presented programs through The Shift Network, an educational organization that offers teleseminars, trainings, and programs in the areas of spiritual awakening, sustainability, health, peace, and men's and women's issues.

Dreamuniversity.com: Marcia Weider is an inspiring friend and colleague who has trained thousands of coaches to help people fulfill their dreams. She offers trainings, coaching, and products to help you on your manifestation journey.

Kripalu.org: This is a school for yoga, health, and awakening in the Berkshires of western Massachusetts. Anodea and Lion offer courses at Kripalu on the manifestation process and other topics each year.

Voicedialogue.org: Hal and Sidra Stone are the founders of Voice Dialogue, one of our favorite processes for internal change. They offer an abundance of books, audio programs, and trainings, all of which come with our recommendation.

Promisegame.com: A new model of accountability in the form of a no-lose game that can help you achieve consistent results.

Moonwish: A lovely guided meditation by Nini Gridley on chakra manifestation that can be done during the new moon. Available through ninigridley.com.

SoundsTrue.com: Our publisher, and the publisher of myriad outstanding resources for your journey to greater consciousness.

Acknowledgments

Lion Goodman: I am deeply grateful—for everything. Gratitude is surely the best cure for whatever ails you. When I remember all of the help, support, and gifts I've received throughout my life, it feels like I'm in a state of constant grace (regardless of how I feel at the moment). Rob Brezsny, author of *Pronoia,* points out that "the whole world is conspiring to shower you with blessings." A list of everything and everyone I'm grateful for would be as long as this book. Our editor at Sounds True, Amy Rost, would never let me get away with it. I'm grateful for her guidance—otherwise I'd still be writing.

I am deeply grateful for you, Dear Reader. A book is a creation in the social universe, and it requires both a writer and a reader to be a real manifestation. Without you, this book would be a waste of trees. When you read it, you give it meaning. Thank you for receiving the information and the teaching we have to offer.

Deep gratitude goes to Anodea, my co-writer, co-creator, and life partner for eight years. Our relationship brought uncountable gifts into my life, including a platform for my teaching, great leaps of growth, and tremendous love. She is an amazing and awesome woman who lives her vision of creating heaven on earth every day. It has been a privilege to be her co-heart in manifesting this vision together.

I have had the good fortune to learn from many great teachers throughout my life. I can only acknowledge a small number of them here. Thank you to T. D. Lingo, my first true teacher and mentor; Peter Ossorio, founder of Descriptive Psychology; Samuel Avital, teacher of mime and Kabbalah; Werner Erhard, creator of the *est* Training; Tai Sheridan, my Zen therapist; Hal and Sidra Stone, creators of Voice Dialogue; Seataka Franzen, who introduced me to the Avatar Course, and Harry Palmer, author of the Avatar materials; Marcia Wieder, of Dream University, who first encouraged me to become a coach (the best career advice I ever received); Ida Rolf, whose healing hands opened my kundalini; Tom Pinkson, my friend and urban shaman; Ron Tilden, who taught me to be a masterful consultant; Buckminster Fuller, who inspired me to think outside all boxes; my loyal employees and corporate clients through twenty-five years of headhunting; the great men in my men's groups (especially those in the Tribe of Men); Stephen Dinan of The Shift Network, who provided a platform on which to shine; and Ray, the young man who pulled out a gun and shot me four times, intending to kill me, and who became the subject of my most famous true story, *A Shot in the Light*. Even the most notorious characters in our lives are our teachers. It's important to recognize their role and express our gratitude so we can sweep clean our field of emotions and awareness.

I could not have accomplished everything set before me without the gracious support of my assistants. This past year, Katherine Wethington, Joshua Gribschaw-Beck, and Tim Emert enabled me to get everything done. Thanks also to our book muse, Geralyn Gendreau, for her excellent recommendations on our first version.

I have loved and been loved by amazing women and great men throughout my life. That love has carried me through difficulties, challenges, and struggles. I am grateful to each of you (you know who you are) for the love and support you offered during our time together. I am grateful to my father, Jerry Goodman, who passed into the Mystery, and my mother, Joanne Goodman, who raised me to be the good man that I am (the last name helped—thanks, Dad). My brothers, Archer and Bret, have been good friends to me throughout my life. My first wife, Janet, was a stellar presence and influence, and together we gave our daughter, Sara Rose, her launching platform. Sara, you have always made me proud of you, and I'm honored to be your Dad.

I am especially grateful to my divine partner, Carista Luminare, with whom I learn, play, and co-create, and from whom I receive unparalleled support and love. May our future bring even more wonder and joy as we give our greatest gifts to the world.

And a final acknowledgment to Spirit, Creator, God, Goddess, Great Mystery, Source—without whom we would not have glorious life. Thank you for giving us the power to be your co-creators. I offer gratitude, praise, and great love for your divine and worldly gifts of this creation.

Anodea Judith: Gratitude is one of my basic attitudes of life. Expressing it frequently helps create abundance and eases the way for others to help you.

Nothing is ever accomplished alone, and we all stand on the shoulders of giants who came before us. I echo Lion's expression of gratitude to teachers we have shared and to all of our readers—especially for your efforts in learning this process and helping to co-create heaven on earth. I would also like to thank all the students who have taken our manifestation course over the past ten years, as we honed this material. You were brave adventurers!

My parents taught me that anything is possible, while my brother, Martin Mull, lifted the bar through his own accomplishments as an artist, musician, comedian, and actor. My son, Alex Wayne, manifested the art for my DVD, *The Illuminated Chakras,* and continues to inspire me. My granddaughter, Seraphine, continually opens my heart and delights me.

We have gleaned wisdom from many teachers along the way. In the realm of lifting to the Divine, I would like to thank my yoga teacher and long-time colleague, John Friend, and all others I have studied with in the past forty years—too numerous to name. In the manifestation department, I also would again like to thank Marcia Wieder, for her inspiration, as well as Dave Ellis, Alan Seale, Harville Hendrix, and the countless others who have written books from which I gained insight that shaped these ideas.

I would, of course, like to thank my co-author, Lion Goodman, for the eight good years we have had together as partners and for his contribution in shaping this material during that time. This book is far fuller and more grounded for his influence. He is an awesome coach and co-creator. I am grateful for the many adventures we had teaching our workshops around the globe.

Amy Rost, our editor, is an author's dream. She was fastidious and fun, patient and wise, through all the stages of editing and shaping this manuscript. In advance, I want to thank all the folks at Sounds True, who will also touch this manuscript as it goes through production, as well as to Tami Simon, chief executive officer of Sounds True, for manifesting her bright vision back in the days of cassette-tape recorders.

I wouldn't have any time at all for writing or teaching if it were not for my very capable staff at Sacred Centers: Shanon Dean-Milon, who masterminds the office; Gianna Perada, who fills in the details; Nini Gridley, who handles the Sacred Centers Certification Program; and Ramone Yaciuk, director of programs and partner extraordinaire.

Ramone gets extra special thanks for bringing such love and laughter into my life, for his wonderful support, for his Rolfing hands, and for keeping my vision constantly refreshed. He is a blessing in my life.

To the wondrous mystery of Spirit itself, to the evolutionary impulse that is constantly unfolding, and to all the miracles we experience every day—my gratitude is infinite. What an amazing time we live in and how grateful I am to witness the co-creative process of bringing heaven down to earth. May I see its manifestation in my lifetime!

About the Authors

Anodea Judith, PhD, is a groundbreaking thinker, writer, and spiritual teacher. She is the founder and director of Sacred Centers, a teaching organization dedicated to personal and global transformation. She is considered a foremost expert on the combination of chakras and therapeutic issues and on the interpretation of the chakra system for the Western lifestyle. She holds masters and doctoral degrees in psychology and human health; is a five-hundred-hour registered yoga teacher; and is a lifelong student of healing, mythology, history, sociology, systems theory, and mystic spirituality. She lives in California and teaches workshops and trainings worldwide. For more details about Anodea and her work, please visit SacredCenters.com.

Lion Goodman is an *evocateur,* one who evokes the best in others. He is cofounder of Luminary Leadership Institute, an evolutionary initiatory program for leaders of businesses and organizations. With his partner, Carista Luminare, PhD, he provides transformational coaching to high-achieving executives and business owners. He offers workshops on discovering your true purpose, virtues-based living, soulful leadership, and creating extraordinary relationships. He was the first director of men's programs for The Shift Network, an Internet-based educational organization, and is cofounder and council member of the Tribe of Men, an initiatory program for men in Northern California. For more information on Lion and his work, please visit his websites: transformyourbeliefs.com, luminaryleadership.net, and tribeofmen.com.

Visit the authors' website, creatingonpurpose.net, for free access to recordings of the exercises in this book and complimentary membership in the Creating On Purpose community.

About Sounds True

Sounds True is a multimedia publisher whose mission is to inspire and support personal transformation and spiritual awakening. Founded in 1985 and located in Boulder, Colorado, we work with many of the leading spiritual teachers, thinkers, healers, and visionary artists of our time. We strive with every title to preserve the essential "living wisdom" of the author or artist. It is our goal to create products that not only provide information to a reader or listener, but that also embody the quality of a wisdom transmission.

For those seeking genuine transformation, Sounds True is your trusted partner. At SoundsTrue.com you will find a wealth of free resources to support your journey, including exclusive weekly audio interviews, free downloads, interactive learning tools, and other special savings on all our titles.

To listen to a podcast interview with Sounds True publisher Tami Simon and authors Anodea Judith and Lion Goodman, please visit SoundsTrue.com/bonus/CreatingOnPurpose.